The New Campaign Finance Sourcebook

The New Campaign Finance Sourcebook

Anthony Corrado

Thomas E. Mann

Daniel R. Ortiz

Trevor Potter

BROOKINGS INSTITUTION PRESS
Washington, D.C.

Library of Congress Cataloging-in-Publication data

The new campaign finance sourcebook / Anthony Corrado . . . [et al.].
   p.   cm.
   Summary: "Comprehensive exposition of federal campaign finance law and administration
following the enactment, constitutional defense, and implementation of the 2002 Bipartisan
Campaign Finance Reform Act (McCain-Feingold)"—Provided by publisher.
   Includes bibliographical references and index.
   ISBN-13: 978-0-8157-0005-0 (pbk. : alk. paper)
   ISBN-10: 0-8157-0005-9 (pbk. : alk. paper)
   1. Campaign funds—United States. 2. Campaign funds—Law and legislation—United States.
I. Corrado, Anthony, 1957–
   JK1991.N48   2005
   324.7'8'0973—dc22   2005022910

9 8 7 6 5 4 3 2 1

Typeset in Adobe Garamond

Composition by Cynthia Stock
Silver Spring, Maryland

Printed by R. R. Donnelley
Harrisonburg, Virginia

Contents

Foreword

The health of American democracy is one of the signature subjects of research here at Brookings, one that often leads our scholars straight to the issue of money in politics. This book is the latest example—and it could hardly be more timely. Recent years have witnessed extraordinary changes in federal campaign finance regulations and practices. In 2002, six years after the explosion of election-related issue advertising financed with unregulated soft money, Congress enacted the Bipartisan Campaign Reform Act (BCRA). In 2003, the Supreme Court upheld the major pillars of BCRA in a landmark ruling, *McConnell* v. *FEC.* The new law, in force for the 2004 election cycle, led to further administrative and judicial actions and substantial changes in the financing of federal election campaigns. It also was followed by continuing controversy about the efficacy of regulating the flow of money in federal elections and calls for further changes in the law.

This volume provides a comprehensive, up-to-date review of the statutory, judicial, and administrative dimensions of campaign finance regulation, one designed to guide readers over an exceedingly complex legal terrain. The *New Campaign Finance Sourcebook* replaces a book first published by Brookings in 1997. The original volume, *Campaign Finance Reform: A Sourcebook,* was built around a set of key documents, including the text of the Federal Election Campaign Act and of major campaign finance court cases, which are now available together with subsequent documents on the Brookings campaign finance website. Consequently, this new volume consists entirely of original essays by its four coauthors: Anthony Corrado of Colby College, Thomas Mann of Brookings, Daniel Ortiz of the University of Virginia, and Trevor Potter of Caplin & Drysdale and the Campaign Legal Center. Tony and Trevor also are nonresident senior fellows at Brookings. I join them in thanking the Joyce Foundation and the Stuart Family Foundation for their support for the project.

Strobe Talbott
President

July 2005
Washington, D.C.

The New
Campaign
Finance
Sourcebook

Introduction

THOMAS E. MANN AND ANTHONY CORRADO

The first edition of this book, *Campaign Finance Reform: A Sourcebook*, was published in the wake of the well-documented fundraising abuses in the 1996 presidential election. At that time there was a good deal of confusion over whether the scandal involved primarily violations of existing laws (and thus indicated a problem of enforcement) or exploitation of legal loopholes (which could be closed only by new legislation). Few observers had a firm grasp of campaign finance law and how it was being interpreted by the courts and enforced by the Federal Election Commission (FEC) and other agencies. The book was designed to bring all interested parties up to speed— by providing a repository of key documents (statutes, court decisions, FEC advisory opinions, and reports) and a series of original expositions on the state of the art in critical areas of campaign finance regulation. It focused not on the impact of money on elections and policymaking but instead on the statutory, judicial, and administrative dimensions of the regulatory regime for financing federal elections, what might have contributed to its apparent collapse in 1996, and what strategies were available for rehabilitating or replacing it.

The intervening years have constituted one of the most eventful periods of change in campaign finance law and practice in the nation's history. In 2000,

Congress adopted an amendment to the Internal Revenue Code establishing disclosure requirements for nonparty political groups known as section 527 organizations, which were not required to register with the FEC because their principal purpose purportedly was something other than influencing federal elections. Two years later Congress enacted the Bipartisan Campaign Reform Act (BCRA), the first major revision of federal campaign finance law in more than two decades. In 2003, in its landmark ruling in *McConnell* v. *FEC*, the Supreme Court upheld the major pillars of BCRA—the elimination of party soft money and the regulation of candidate-specific issue advertising—and charted new jurisprudential ground on corruption, circumvention, and express advocacy.

The new law was in effect during the 2004 federal election cycle, shaping the sources and flow of money in the campaign.[1] Candidates, parties, and nonparty organizations adapted their campaign finance strategies to the new legal regime and to the special circumstances of the 2004 election. Record amounts were raised and spent by all of the major players in federal elections—most notably presidential candidates George Bush and John Kerry and the national party committees—and the number of small donors skyrocketed. Controversies erupted over regulations implementing BCRA, the interpretation of federal rules as applied to the activities of section 527 groups, and the political activities of nonprofit groups. Federal and state courts began to recalibrate their opinions in campaign finance cases in light of *McConnell*, especially its dismissal of the "express advocacy" standard as constitutionally required or functionally useful. Reformers rushed to respond to new developments with appeals to administrative agencies and the courts and with fresh legislative proposals.

This successor volume to the original *Sourcebook* incorporates the many and diverse changes in campaign finance law and practice over the past decade. While it retains the the first volume's focus on the statutory, judicial, and administrative dimensions of campaign finance, this book excludes the text of key documents (which are now readily available on the Brookings campaign finance website) and relies entirely on original essays written by its four coauthors.[2]

Chapter 1 recounts how concerns about the influence of money in politics stretch as far back as the 1830s, when political parties began to finance their campaign activities with assessments on those who enjoyed the "spoils" of office. Later in the nineteenth century, civil service reform largely dried up that source of party money and shifted the fundraising focus to corporations, which were beginning to have increasing stakes in the direction of national policy. Anthony Corrado traces how early twentieth-century attempts to reduce the influence of corporations and wealthy individuals, limit spending, and disclose sources of campaign funds, though enacted into law, were frustrated by legal loopholes and woefully inadequate mechanisms for enforcement. It was only after the Watergate scandal and reports of fundraising abuses in the 1972 Nixon campaign that Congress embraced a comprehensive approach to campaign finance regulation. Yet the system envisioned in the Federal Election Campaign Act (FECA) Amendments of 1974 was never fully realized, as court decisions, subsequent amendments, and the combination of resourceful actions of entrepreneurial politicians and a weak Federal Election Commission reshaped it almost beyond recognition. Another set of fundraising abuses—this time in the 1996 presidential election—set the stage for the eventual passage of the Bipartisan Campaign Reform Act of 2002. BCRA is the end point of this chapter, but surely not of the history of campaign finance reform.

Chapter 2 gives an overview of the current state of campaign finance law. Trevor Potter describes the regulated portion of the federal election finance system, as well as those entities, funds, and activities that might influence federal elections but are not defined as federal political committees. He specifies the legal standing of individuals, political parties, political action committees, section 527 organizations, corporations, unions, and nonprofit groups and discusses the restrictions (if any) that govern their contributions, expenditures, and advocacy activities. The chapter also describes the civil and criminal mechanisms for enforcing campaign finance law.

The First Amendment looms large in the path of campaign finance regulation, and no single action had a greater impact in narrowing the reach of federal election law and in limiting the ambitions of reformers than the Supreme Court's decision in *Buckley* v. *Valeo*. In chapter 3, Dan Ortiz describes how *Buckley*, which dealt with a challenge to the 1974 FECA amendments, created a framework that continues to define constitutional limitations on campaign finance law. *Buckley* gave Congress broad scope to regulate contributions in order to prevent corruption. However, it found no compelling state interest in limiting independent expenditures, which the Court took to be a form of political expression protected by the First Amendment. Subsequent decisions by the Court introduced some inconsistency and confusion into the jurisprudence, but the basic structure of *Buckley* remained intact. To the dismay of its critics, the Supreme Court in *McConnell* v. *FEC* argued that BCRA's regulation of party soft money and so-called "sham issue advocacy" also fit squarely within the framework of *Buckley*.

Ortiz also provides a brief guide to the lively constitutional debate that *Buckley* and its progeny have precipitated outside the confines of the U.S. Supreme Court. His review illustrates how differences of opinion between those supporting and opposing reform are rooted in different normative and descriptive assumptions about democratic politics.

Public disclosure has long been considered the cornerstone of campaign finance law. In chapter 4, Trevor Potter explains how and why disclosure nonetheless remains a contested area of election law. He outlines the disclosure regime currently in place in federal and selected state elections, describes the constitutional framework that the Supreme Court has put in place for disclosure cases, reviews important cases in federal and state courts implementing the Supreme Court's rulings, and highlights new disclosure issues arising in legislative, administrative, and judicial settings.

Party fundraising strategies and successes changed dramatically in the 2004 election, partly as a result of BCRA's ban on soft money, partly because of special circumstances that led to a flood of new small donors. In chapter 5, Anthony Corrado traces the legislative, administrative, and judicial actions that have determined the legal boundaries within which the political parties raise and spend money on behalf of their candidates. He reconstructs the sequence of events, including crucial FEC advisory opinions and rules, that enabled the parties to operate outside the limits of federal election law and fueled the soft money explosion during the 1996 election. He also plumbs the BCRA statute and the *McConnell* decision to clarify the legal regime under which national and state party committees operate today. The chapter includes a discussion of the legal basis for various types of party expenditures: contributions, coordinated spending, independent spending, "hybrid" spending (shared by a presidential candidate and his or her party based on a supposedly generic party message), and Levin fund activity.

The 1974 FECA amendments created a voluntary system of public funding of presidential campaigns. The system includes matching funds for candidates during the nominating process, grants to parties for national nominating conventions, and full public financing of candidates in the general election campaign. Funding comes from a voluntary individual tax return check-off program, and acceptance of public funds is tied to limits on spending. In chapter 6, Corrado explains how this public financing system, after playing a major role in every presidential election since 1976, has fallen into disrepair. In the 2004 election both major party candidates opted out of the matching fund program, freeing them from prenomination spending limits. And what was designed as full public funding for the national party conventions and general election campaigns became but a modest share of their budgets as candidates and parties continued to find new ways of circumventing the spending limits.

A central issue in campaign finance law concerns the scope of political communications that are properly subject to regulation under the First Amendment. In chapter 7, Potter and Kirk Jowers describe the genesis of the legal distinction between issue advocacy and express advocacy and why that distinction shaped political communications prior to BCRA. The initial boundary between the two forms of advocacy was drawn by the *Buckley* Court as an exercise in statutory interpretation designed to salvage the 1974 FECA. The Court believed that the law's language regulating independent spending "in connection with" or "for the purpose of influencing" a federal election was unconstitutionally vague and overly broad. Issue advocacy was effectively defined as all independent communications that did not expressly advocate the election or defeat of a candidate. Years later that expansive conception of protected speech became the basis of a major loophole in election law that allowed candidates, parties, and groups to raise and spend campaign funds that violated restrictions on the source and size of contributions. Potter and Jowers explain BCRA's response to that development, the *McConnell* Court's constitutional reasoning in upholding the new law's treatment of "electioneering communications," and subsequent decisions by lower courts applying this broader definition of campaign speech.

Weak enforcement has long plagued campaign finance law. Congress sought to address the problem in 1974 by establishing the Federal Election Commission. But the shortcomings of the commission became increasingly apparent, especially in the development of party soft money, the explosion of sham issue advocacy, and the failure to restrain new 527 groups active in the 2004 presidential elections. In chapter 8, Thomas Mann discusses how and why Congress structured the FEC to ensure that it would not develop into an aggressively independent enforcement agency; outlines the agency's responsibilities, activities, and resources; and reviews various proposals for improving disclosure and strengthening enforcement.

The Internet became a critically important campaign tool for candidates, parties, groups, and citizens in the 2004 election. The great fundraising potential of this medium is only the tip of the iceberg. Major questions arise regarding the suitability of the current campaign finance regulatory structure in a world of digital communications. In chapter 9, Potter and Jowers explain the FEC's legal and regulatory approach to governing political activity over the Internet. While the Internet remains largely unregulated under

BCRA and subsequent FEC decisions, important policy issues lie on the horizon.

In the final chapter, Mann canvasses the campaign finance reform agenda after BCRA and *McConnell*. Some proposals—repairing the presidential public funding system, strengthening enforcement, regulating 527 organizations, and reducing restrictions on party expenditures—are adjustments to the present system. Others, including tax credits for small donors, public subsidies, and free air time, are designed to enhance competition and participation. Still others are much more ambitious in scope, designed to replace rather than repair or supplement current law. These include full public funding, deregulation, and a wholesale rejection of the *Buckley* framework.

Campaign finance reform will always be a work in progress—an ongoing effort to satisfactorily manage rather than definitively solve the inherent problems of money in politics.

Notes

1. For an assessment of the impact of BCRA in the 2004 election, see Michael J. Malbin, ed., *The Election after Reform: Money, Politics, and the Bipartisan Campaign Reform Act* (Rowman & Littlefield, 2005).

2. See www.brookings.edu/campaignfinance.

1

Money and Politics: A History of Federal Campaign Finance Law

Anthony Corrado

C ontroversy over the role of money in politics did not begin with Water-gate. Nor did it start with the clamor over the high costs of campaigning that accompanied the growth of radio and television broadcasting in post–World War II America. Money's influence on the political process has long been a concern, an outgrowth of the nation's continuing struggle to reconcile basic notions of political equality, such as the principle of "one person, one vote," with fundamental political liberties, such as the freedoms of speech and political association. The unequal distribution of economic resources and the participation of a relatively small minority of the citizenry in the financing of campaigns have, throughout U.S. history, spurred concerns about the influence of wealth in the political process and the corruptive effects of campaign donations. Though public criticism of the campaign finance system has been particularly acute in recent decades, the issues raised, and the consequent demand for campaign finance reform, can be traced to before the Civil War.

Early Legislation and Progressive Era Reforms

In the early days of the republic, campaign funding was rarely a source of public controversy. There were few "campaigns" in the modern sense of the term, since candidates usually "stood" for election without engaging in the types of personal politicking or direct solicitation of votes that have come to characterize modern elections.[1] Candidates typically paid any expenses incurred in a political contest out of their own pockets or with the assistance of friends and relatives. Those expenses usually entailed the costs of printing and distributing pamphlets or "treating" constituents to food and drink on election day. The nascent party organizations also provided some assistance, most commonly in the form of favorable coverage provided by newspapers owned or financed by party supporters.

As the nation grew and the political system matured, the issue of campaign funding became more contentious. The rise of party politics and the expansion of the franchise that accompanied the rise of Jacksonian democracy opened the political system to those who lacked the personal resources needed to seek elective office. Party organizations therefore began to develop more systematic means of raising funds to support their candidates.

The development of the "spoils system," wherein the victor in an election awarded government positions to party supporters, led to the formation of an "assessment" system for raising money from government workers and party supporters. By the 1830s, party organizations were raising money from those they had placed in government jobs or other political positions by requiring them to contribute a percentage of their salaries to the party (the "assessment"). The assessment system became a principal means of party support, and it was soon attacked by critics who claimed that it posed a threat to the "freedom of elections." Such charges encouraged some members of Congress to attempt to end the practice, producing what are generally regarded as the first proposals to regulate campaign funding. In 1837, Representative John Bell of Tennessee, a member of the Whig Party, introduced the first bill to prohibit assessments.[2] Two years later, a House investigating committee found that the Democratic Party had imposed levies on U.S. customs employees in New York City. Bell's bill, which would have made it illegal for a federal officer to "pay or advance" any money toward the "election of any public functionary, whether of the General or State Government,"[3] was submitted again. In 1840 it even reached the House floor, but no action was taken on the proposal. Party leaders thus continued to require political contributions from individuals who had been given a place on the government payroll.

Congress did decide to take a small step against the assessment of government workers after the Civil War. An act of March 2, 1867, concerning naval appropriations for fiscal year 1868, included a final section that prohibited the solicitation of political contributions from government workers employed at navy yards. It read as follows:[4]

> And be it further enacted, That no officer or employee of the govern-ment shall require or request any workingman in any navy yard to con-tribute or pay any money for political purposes, nor shall any working-man be removed or discharged for political opinion; and any officer or employee of the government who shall offend against the provisions of this section shall be dismissed from the service of the United States.

This restriction, which is considered to be the first provision of federal law relating to campaign finance, had little effect on party funding. In the years following its adoption, the Republicans controlled the White House and continued to fill their campaign coffers with funds from officeholders and appointees.[5]

During the Reconstruction era, attacks on the use of patronage and the assessment of government workers increased. By 1872, liberal Republicans were expressing outrage over the corruption within President Ulysses S. Grant's administration and began to argue for an end to assessments and for civil service reform.[6] Grant created a civil service commission, but it was not enough to appease his fellow Republicans. In 1876, Congress included a pro-vision in the appropriations legislation for the coming fiscal year that barred government workers not appointed by the president from imposing assess-ments on other government workers. The law declared "that all executive officers or employees of the United States not appointed by the President, with the advice and consent of the Senate, are prohibited from requesting, giving to, or receiving from, any other officer or employee of the Govern-ment, any money or property or other thing of value for political purposes."[7] When President Rutherford B. Hayes took office, he strengthened and extended the ban on assessments by issuing an executive order that prohib-ited electioneering by government officials. In addition to barring assess-ments on officers or subordinates for political purposes, the order stated that "no officer should be required or permitted to take part in the management of political organizations, caucuses, conventions or election campaigns." The president, however, noted that "their right to vote and to express their views on public questions, either orally or through the press, is not denied, pro-vided it does not interfere with the discharge of their official duties."[8]

The ban on assessments and the end of patronage became a permanent feature of federal employment with the passage of the Pendleton Civil Service Act of 1883.[9] The law restrained the influence of the spoils system in the selection of government workers by creating a class of federal employees who had to qualify for office through competitive examinations. It also prohibited the solicitation of political contributions from those employees, thus protecting them from forced campaign assessments. The act reduced the reliance of party organizations on government employee contributions and shifted the burden of party fundraising to corporate interests, especially the industrial giants in oil, railroads, steel, and finance, which held major stakes in the direction of government policy.

Business leaders and the corporations they headed were a source of campaign funding before the 1880s, but after the adoption of the civil service reforms they became the principal source. Money from corporations, banks, railroads, and other businesses filled party coffers, and numerous corporations reportedly were making donations to national party committees in amounts of $50,000 or more. By the turn of the century, Mark Hanna, the Republican Party boss who organized the presidential campaigns of William McKinley in 1896 and 1900, had established a formal system for soliciting contributions from large Wall Street corporations, asking each company to "pay according to its stake in the general prosperity of the country and according to its special interest in a region in which a large amount of expensive canvassing had to be done."[10] Hanna's emphasis on corporate fundraising produced the monies needed for rising campaign expenditures, which totaled at least $3 million in each of the McKinley campaigns, or more than twice the amount spent by Republican Benjamin Harrison when he won in 1888.[11]

Such lavish contributions from corporate sources alarmed progressive reformers and spurred a demand for campaign finance legislation at the national level. Progressive politicians and muckraking journalists contended that wealthy donors were gaining special favors and privileges as a result of their campaign gifts, thereby corrupting the democratic process. They demanded regulation to prevent such abuses. By the late 1890s, four states had passed laws to prohibit corporate contributions.[12] But in Congress the clarion call for reform went unheeded until a controversy regarding the financing of the 1904 presidential race led to the first organized movement for campaign finance reform.

In 1904, Judge Alton B. Parker, the Democratic presidential nominee, alleged that corporations were providing President Theodore Roosevelt with campaign gifts to buy influence with the administration. Parker also claimed that Roosevelt was "blackmailing monopolies" to raise money for his campaign.[13] Further, Roosevelt supposedly summoned two of the country's richest men, E. H. Harriman and Harry C. Frick, to the White House and solicited their financial help with the understanding that "before I write my message (to Congress) I shall get you to come down to discuss certain governmental matters not connected with the campaign."[14]

Roosevelt denied the charges. But in investigations conducted after the election, several major companies admitted making large contributions to the Republican campaign. The most damaging evidence emerged from investigations conducted by a joint committee of the New York state legislature, under the guidance of state senator William Armstrong and committee general counsel Charles Evans Hughes, into the business practices of major New York insurance companies.[15] The investigation revealed that New York Life had made a $48,000 contribution from a "non-ledger" account to the Republican National Committee for the 1904 campaign. That revelation attracted a substantial amount of attention from national newspapers and led to increased demand for legislative action to address the role of corporate contributions in national elections.

Roosevelt responded to the controversy by including a call for campaign finance reform in his annual message to Congress in 1905 and in 1906. In the 1905 message, written only a month after the election, Roosevelt supported the adoption of measures to guard against corruption in federal elections and to require public disclosure of campaign contributions and expenditures. In doing so, he stated:[16]

> There is no enemy of free government more dangerous and none so insidious as the corruption of the electorate. . . . I recommend the enactment of a law directed against bribery and corruption in Federal elections. The details of such a law may be safely left to the wise direction of the Congress, but it should go as far as under the Constitution it is possible to go, and should include severe penalties against him who gives or receives a bribe intended to influence his act or opinion as an elector; and provisions for the publication not only of the expenditures for nominations and elections of all candidates but also of all contributions received and expenditures made by political committees.

The next year, Roosevelt repeated those ideas before offering an even stronger remedy—a ban on corporate political contributions. He declared to Congress:[17]

> All contributions by corporations to any political committee or for any political purpose should be forbidden by law. . . . Not only should both the National and the several State Legislatures forbid any office of a

corporation from using the money of the corporation in or about any election, but they should also forbid such use of money in connection with any legislation save by the employment of counsel in public manner for distinctly legal services.

He continued to give verbal support to that proposal in 1907, highlighting the importance of such a law by repeating the call for a ban on corporate giving at the very start of his annual message that year.[18] But his efforts on behalf of reform did not extend much further. He did not follow up his use of the bully pulpit with a specific legislative proposal or a lobbying effort to force Congress to act.

Roosevelt, however, was not the only advocate urging congressional action. By that time, progressive reformers and journalists had been joined by a growing group of politicians who sought to reduce the influence of money in politics. A number of civic organizations also were working for reform. The most important of them was the National Publicity Law Organization (NPLO), a citizens' group formed as a result of the 1904 controversy that dedicated itself to lobbying for the regulation and public disclosure of political spending.

In 1907, faced with increasing public sentiment in favor of reform, Congress finally acted. At the urging of Senator Benjamin "Pitchfork Ben" Tillman of South Carolina, who had been calling for an investigation into corporate donations since 1905, the legislature considered a bill that had been introduced in an earlier Congress by Senator William Chandler, a New Hampshire Republican, to restrict corporate giving in federal elections.[19] Eager to appease advocates of reform, the Republican Senate and House passed the proposal with little debate, but not before changing the bill so that it did not apply to state-chartered corporations active in state and local elections. The law, known as the Tillman Act, made it "unlawful for any national bank, or any corporation organized by authority of any laws of Congress, to make a money contribution in connection with any election to any political office." It also made it illegal "for any corporation whatever to make a money contribution in connection with any election at which Presidential and Vice-Presidential electors or a Representative in Congress is to be voted for or any election by any State legislature of a United States Senator."[20] This ban on corporate gifts to federal candidates became a cornerstone of federal campaign finance law and was reaffirmed in many subsequent statutes.

Though the Tillman Act constituted a landmark in federal law, its adoption did not quell the cries for reform. Eliminating corporate influence was only one of the ideas being advanced at the time to clean up political finance. Reducing the influence of wealthy donors also was a concern, and some reformers pushed for limits on individual donations. Still others advocated even bolder ideas. The NPLO continued to press for disclosure of party campaign receipts and expenditures so that voters would know which interests were financing which campaigns. William Bourke Cockran, a Democratic representative from New York associated with Tammany Hall, had an even more radical idea. In 1904 he suggested that the problems caused by campaign funding might be relieved if the government paid for some or all of the expenses of a presidential election.[21] His proposal for public funding was never considered by Congress. However, President Roosevelt adopted the idea, noting in his December 1907 message to Congress that "the need for collecting large campaign funds would vanish if Congress provided an appropriation for the proper and legitimate expenses of each of the great national parties, an appropriation ample enough to meet the necessity for thorough organization and machinery, which requires a large expenditure of money."[22] Yet even Roosevelt's embrace could not persuade many legislators to pursue the notion. Instead, reformers concentrated on other alternatives.

The continuing pressure for reform led to additional legislation a few years later. On the eve of the 1910 elections, the Republican majority in Congress passed a bill initiated by the NPLO that established the first requirements for the disclosure of campaign receipts and expenditures. As adopted, the Federal Corrupt Practices Act, more commonly known as the Publicity Act of 1910, required party committees "operating in two or more states" to report any contributions or expenditures made in connection with campaigns for the House of Representatives.[23] While an important step, the law required nothing more than postelection reports of the receipts and expenditures of national party committees or committees operating in two or more states. Consequently, the act affected only the national party committees and their congressional campaign committees, and it did not require any disclosure prior to an election. Such a modest measure failed to appease the more vocal advocates of reform.

In the 1910 elections the Democrats took control of the House and picked up seats in the Senate. When the new Congress convened, the Democrats sought to revise the Publicity Act to include preelection reporting. House Republicans hoped to defeat the bill by adding provisions that would be unacceptable to Southern Democrats. Since Southerners favored states' rights and considered primaries the most important elections, House Republicans called for the regulation of committees operating in a single congressional district and the disclosure of primary campaign finances. Senate Republicans went even further, adopting a bill that included limits on campaign spending. But their tactics backfired; the Republican game of one-upmanship failed to defeat the bill. Instead, Congress approved a package of reforms that were far more extensive than those originally proposed.

The 1911 Amendments to the Publicity Act improved disclosure and established the first spending limits for federal campaigns.[24] The amendments extended disclosure in two ways: they required Senate as well as House campaigns to report receipts and expenditures, and they required campaign committees to report their finances both before and after an election, in primary contests as well as general elections. The law also limited House campaign expenditures to a total of $5,000 and Senate campaign expenditures to $10,000 or the amount established by state law, whichever was less.

The spending limits quickly became controversial, and they were contested in court. Truman H. Newberry, a Michigan Republican who defeated Henry Ford in a fiercely contested Senate primary in 1918, was convicted of violating the spending limit in that race. His campaign committee reported spending close to $180,000 in its effort to secure the nomination, an amount almost 100 times the limit established by Michigan law. Newberry challenged the conviction, arguing that Congress had no authority to regulate primaries. Besides, the argument went, he and his codefendants had not violated the law, which applied to campaign committees, not to the candidate or to individual supporters.[25]

In 1921, the Supreme Court ruled in *Newberry* v. *United States* that the congressional authority to regulate elections did not extend to party primaries and nomination activities, thus striking down the spending limits.[26] That narrow interpretation of congressional authority stood until 1941, when in *United States* v. *Classic*, the Court ruled that Congress did have the authority to regulate primaries wherever state law made them part of the election process and wherever they effectively determined the outcome of the general election.[27] Congress fully reasserted its authority to regulate the financing of primary campaigns in 1971, when it adopted the Federal Election Campaign Act.

The Court's decision in *Newberry* was not the only event that highlighted the inadequacy of federal regulations. Shortly afterward, the Teapot Dome scandal drew attention once again to the corruptive influence of large contributions—in this case, gifts made by oil developers in a nonelection year to federal officials responsible for granting oil leases. The scandal led Congress to act once more, this time passing the Federal Corrupt Practices Act of

1925, which stood as the basic legislation governing campaign finance until the 1970s.

The Federal Corrupt Practices Act of 1925 essentially followed the regulatory approach outlined by earlier legislation with little substantive change, except for the deletion of regulations governing primaries.[28] The act revised the disclosure rules to account for the type of financial activity that led to the Teapot Dome scandal by requiring all multistate political committees (as well as House and Senate candidates) to file quarterly reports that included all contributions of $100 or more, even in nonelection years. The law also revised the spending limits. Senate campaigns would be allowed to spend up to $25,000 and House campaigns up to $5,000, unless state law called for a lower limit.

Despite the changes, an effective regulatory regime was never established. Though the law imposed clear reporting requirements, it provided for none of the publicity or enforcement mechanisms needed to ensure meaningful disclosure. The law did not specify who would have access to the reports; it did not require that the reports be published; it did not even stipulate the penalties if committees failed to comply. As a result, many candidates did not file regular reports. When they did, the information was provided in various forms. Gaining access to the information through the clerk of the House or secretary of the Senate was difficult, and the reports were usually maintained for only two years and then destroyed.

The spending ceilings were even less effective, and they were almost universally ignored. Because the limits applied to party committees, they were easily skirted by creating multiple committees for the same candidate or race. Each of the committees could then technically comply with the spending limit established for a particular race, while the total monies funneled into the race greatly exceeded the amount intended by the law. Establishing multiple committees also facilitated evasion of disclosure requirements. Donors could make gifts of less than $100 to each committee without incurring any reporting obligation or give larger amounts to a variety of committees, thus obscuring the total given to any single candidate.[29]

Wealthy donors also contributed monies through family members, and there were widespread reports of corporations providing "bonuses" to employees who passed them on to candidates. Yet in the history of the 1925 act, no one was prosecuted for failing to comply with the law. Only two people—Republicans William S. Vare of Pennsylvania and Frank L. Smith of Illinois—were excluded from office for violating spending limits, and they were excluded in 1927 as a result of violations that occurred in the first election in which the law was in effect.[30] Over the next forty-five years, no other candidates were punished under the act.

The New Deal Era

Even though it was well known that candidates and party committees were not complying with the dictates of federal law, Congress did not return to the issue of campaign financing until the success of Franklin Roosevelt's New Deal coalition led conservative Democrats and staunch Republicans to seek additional reforms. With the approach of the 1940 election, these opponents of Roosevelt's liberal politics became increasingly concerned that the rapidly expanding federal workforce that arose under the New Deal would become a permanent political force in the Democratic Party. Although the "classified" offices covered under the provisions of the 1883 Pendleton Act had been expanded over time, many of the thousands of workers added to public payrolls during the New Deal were not subject to the act's restrictions. New Deal opponents were especially concerned about the tens of thousands of relief workers hired under the Works Progress Administration, some of whom had allegedly been mobilized to assist Democratic Speaker of the House Alben Barkley of Kentucky in his hard-won reelection campaign in 1938.[31] In an attempt to minimize the political role of these and other public employees, Congress passed the Hatch Act of 1939, named after its sponsor, Senator Carl Hatch, a Democrat from New Mexico.[32]

The 1939 Hatch Act, which was also called the Clean Politics Act, prohibited political activity by those federal workers who were not constrained by the Pendleton Act. It also specifically prohibited the solicitation of political contributions from workers on federal public works program payrolls. The law thus removed a major source of revenue for state and local party organizations, but it did not eliminate all of the monies raised from government workers. Because it did not protect state and local government employees, they remained an important source of congressional campaign revenues.[33]

In 1940, Congress passed amendments to the Hatch Act to restrict the amount of money donated to political campaigns in another way.[34] The revisions imposed an annual limit of $5,000 each on individual contributions to federal candidates and to national party committees and of $3 million per calendar year on the total amount that could be received or spent by a party committee operating in two or more states. The law also prohibited political contributions to candidates and to party committees by federal contractors. Like earlier regulations, the new restrictions had little effect on political giving.

Donors could still contribute large sums by giving to multiple committees or by making contributions through state and local party organizations, which were not subject to the $5,000 limit. Furthermore, the party committees interpreted the $3 million spending limit to apply only to party committees, not to nonparty organizations operating independently.[35] That interpretation of the law spurred the proliferation of independent nonparty political committees, each of which claimed the right to raise and spend money in support of federal candidates. By the time of the 1940 election, both parties had exceeded the new law's limit.[36]

Another change in political finance during the New Deal era was the rise of labor unions as a major source of campaign money. Roosevelt's policies, many of which were regarded as pro-labor, encouraged union membership and led to the growth of organized labor as a political force in national politics. Unions supported Roosevelt in part by beginning the practice of making direct contributions to his campaigns; union funds therefore became an important source of Democratic Party campaign money. In 1936, for example, unions contributed an estimated $770,000 to help Roosevelt's bid for reelection, including $469,000 from the United Mine Workers.[37]

In 1943, Republicans and Southern Democrats responded to mounting concerns over labor's political activities and wartime strikes by adopting the Smith-Connally Act, or War Labor Disputes Act of 1943.[38] The law, which was passed over the president's veto, was designed to reduce labor's political influence by extending to labor union contributions the restrictions on corporate political giving adopted under the Tillman Act. It prohibited labor unions from using their treasury funds to make political contributions to federal candidates. But the act was adopted as a war measure, and it was scheduled to expire automatically six months after the end of the war.

When the Republicans recaptured Congress in 1946, they reinstated the ban on labor union contributions and made it permanent by including it among the provisions of the Taft-Hartley Act, or the Labor Management Relations Act, which was adopted on an override of President Truman's veto.[39] The prohibition of the use of labor union treasury funds as a source of candidate contributions has been a component of federal campaign finance law ever since. The act sought to strengthen the prohibition on *contributions* by also prohibiting any *expenditures* by labor unions or corporations in connection with federal elections. In that regard, section 304 of the act amended the ban on corporate contributions that had been established under the Tillman Act and included in the 1925 Federal Corrupt Practices Act by making it unlawful "for any corporation whatever, or any labor organization to make a contribution or expenditure in connection with any [federal] election," including primary elections and political conventions or caucuses, as well as general elections. Section 304 was designed to ensure that labor unions or corporations could not circumvent the ban on contributions by simply spending money directly to support or defeat a candidate.[40]

Unions responded to the prohibition on the use of treasury funds by organizing auxiliary committees to support federal candidates. Those committees, which came to be known as "political action committees" (PACs)— the name given to the original group formed for that purpose—collected monies from members apart from dues and used the funds to make contributions to candidates and to finance other types of political activity, such as political education programs and voter turnout drives.[41] The first committee of this type was formed in 1943 by the Congress of Industrial Organizations Political Action Committee (CIO-PAC). In 1944, the first year in which it was active, it raised more than $1.4 million for use in federal elections. The committee was considered so influential that Republicans charged that anything done by the Roosevelt administration had to be "cleared with Sidney," in reference to Sidney Hillman, the leader of the CIO.[42]

In the years after 1944, other labor unions followed the CIO model and formed PACs of their own, while the CIO-PAC became part of the powerful AFL-CIO Committee on Political Education (COPE). In the 1956 elections, seventeen national labor PACs were active in federal elections, contributing a total of $2.1 million. By 1968, the number had doubled, with thirty-seven labor PACs spending at least $7.1 million.[43] Business organizations did not immediately adopt labor's tactics; for the most part, business PACs did not begin to emerge until the early 1960s. Among the earliest such committees were the American Medical Political Action Committee (AMPAC), which was affiliated with the American Medical Association, and the Business-Industry Political Action Committee (BIPAC), which was formed by affiliates of the National Association of Manufacturers.[44] In 1964, AMPAC spent an estimated $400,000 on federal candidates, while BIPAC spent more than $200,000.[45] But major growth in the number of PACs and in their role in the financing of federal candidates did not occur until the mid-1970s, after the adoption of the Federal Election Campaign Act.

A change in campaign funding during the postwar era that was even more important than PACs was a result not of adaptation to the law but of a change in the style of campaigning. While party organizations remained an important source of revenue, campaigns became increasingly candidate-based. Candidates for federal office established their own committees and raised their own funds. At the same time, television was becoming an essential means of political communication, significantly increasing the cost of seeking federal office. The rising cost of campaigns renewed concerns about the campaign finance system and the role of wealth in national elections. Yet despite the concerns, Congress took no action. The only serious gesture made toward reform between World War II and the Vietnam War era was President John F. Kennedy's decision to form a Commission on Campaign Costs to explore problems in the system and develop legislative proposals. The commission's 1962 report offered a comprehensive program of reform, including such innovative ideas as a system of public matching funds for presidential candidates.[46] However, Congress was not receptive to the president's proposals, and no effort was made to resurrect those ideas after his assassination.

In 1966, under the leadership of Senator Russell Long (D-La.), the powerful chair of the Senate Finance Committee, Congress did pass a related bill, the first major reform bill since 1925. However, it never took effect. Campaign finance issues were once again in the news following criticism of the Democratic "President's Club"—a group of donors, including some government contractors, who each gave $1,000 or more—and the censure of Senator Thomas Dodd (D-Conn.) for using his political funds for personal purposes.

Long hoped to reduce the potential influence of wealthy donors and ease the fundraising demands generated by the rising cost of campaigning in presidential elections by providing public subsidies to political parties to help pay these costs. The subsidies would be appropriated from a Presidential Election Campaign Fund, which would be financed by allowing taxpayers to use a federal tax check-off to allocate $1 for that purpose. The proposal met with widespread criticism, but Long forced the Senate to approve the unusual measure by attaching it as a rider to the Foreign Investors Tax Act.[47]

Long's victory was short-lived. In the spring of 1967, Senator Albert Gore, a Democrat from Tennessee, and Senator John Williams, a Republican from Delaware, sponsored an amendment to repeal the Long Act. Gore favored public financing, but he claimed that the Long plan discriminated against third parties and that it would do little to control campaign costs, since it simply added public money to the private funds already raised. Others simply opposed the idea of using government funds to finance campaigns or argued that a system of party subsidies would place too much power into the hands of the national party leaders.[48] Eventually, after much legislative maneuvering, Congress decided to make the Long Act inoperative by voting to postpone the check-off until guidelines could be developed governing disbursement of any funds collected thereby.

Even if the Long Act had been implemented, it would not have addressed the major problems that had emerged in the campaign finance system. By this time, it was obvious to most observers that the reporting requirements and spending limits set forth in the Federal Corrupt Practices Act had proven wholly ineffective and needed a complete overhaul. There was also increasing concern about the rising cost of campaigns. In the 1956 elections, total campaign spending was approximately $155 million, $9.8 million of which was used for radio and television advertising. By 1968, overall spending had nearly doubled, to $300 million, while media expenditures had increased by almost 500 percent, to $58.9 million.[49]

Such dramatic growth worried many members of Congress, who feared that they might be unable to raise the sums needed in future campaigns if costs kept escalating. Legislators also worried about competing against wealthy challengers who could use their own resources to finance expensive media-based campaigns. Democrats were particularly concerned about the rising costs, since Republicans had demonstrated greater success in raising large sums and had spent more than twice as much as the Democrats in the 1968 presidential contest.[50] Changing patterns of political finance thus sparked interest in further reform, and Congress responded by passing the Federal Election Campaign Act (FECA) of 1971.

The FECA and Its Development

The adoption of the FECA signaled the beginning of the modern era of campaign finance reform. The act and its subsequent amendments were the products of a wave of reform that swept through Congress during the 1970s. The statute altered most of the major provisions of federal campaign law. The effects of the law determined the patterns of campaign funding for three decades and led to marked improvements in the regulation of political money. But it also generated new issues and problems and thus spurred continuing debate about the need for reform.

Federal Election Campaign Act of 1971

The Federal Election Campaign Act of 1971 was signed into law by President Richard M. Nixon on February 7, 1972, and it went into effect sixty days later.[51] The legislation sought to address problems stemming from the inadequacies of the Federal Corrupt Practices Act and to cut rising campaign costs. It therefore combined two different approaches to reform. The first part of the law established limits on the amount that a candidate could contribute to his or her own campaign and set ceilings on the amount that a candidate could spend on the media. The second part imposed strict public disclosure procedures on federal candidates and political committees in an effort to remedy the lack of effective disclosure under the Corrupt Practices Act.

The FECA's major provisions limited personal contributions, established specific ceilings for media expenditures, and required full public disclosure of campaign receipts and disbursements. The act limited personal contributions by candidates and their immediate families to a combined total of $50,000 for presidential and vice presidential candidates, $35,000 for Senate candidates, and $25,000 for House candidates. It limited the amounts that federal candidates could spend on radio, television, cable television, newspapers, magazines, and automated telephone systems in any primary, run-off, special, or general election to $50,000 or to $0.10 multiplied by the voting-age population of the jurisdiction covered by the election, with the limit set at the greater sum. In addition, the law declared that no more than 60 percent of a candidate's overall media spending could be devoted to radio and television advertising. The limits were to apply separately to primary and general elections and were indexed to reflect increases in the consumer price index.

In the area of disclosure, the act required every candidate or political committee active in a federal campaign to file a quarterly report of receipts and expenditures. The reports were to list any contribution or expenditure of $100 or more and include the name, address, occupation, and principal place of business of the donor or recipient. During election years, additional reports had to be filed before an election, and any contribution of $5,000 or more had to be reported within forty-eight hours of receipt. The reports were to be filed with the secretary of state of the state in which the campaign activities took place and with the appropriate federal officer, as established under the act. For the latter purpose, House candidates filed with the clerk of the House, Senate candidates with the secretary of the Senate, and presidential candidates with the General Accounting Office. All reports had to be made available for public inspection within forty-eight hours of being received.

The 1971 FECA was based on the premise that media costs were the primary cause of rising campaign expenditures. The law may have helped to limit outlays on the media in the 1972 elections, but it did little to slow the surge in total campaign spending. According to the best available estimate, total campaign spending continued to grow, rising from $300 million in 1968 to $425 million in 1972, with the sharpest increase in the presidential race—general election spending alone rose from $44.2 million in 1968 to almost $104 million four years later.[52] President Nixon spent more than twice as much in 1972 as he did in 1968. His Democratic opponent, George McGovern, spent more than four times the amount that Democrat Hubert Humphrey expended in 1968—and was still outspent by a substantial margin. This pattern of spending suggested that more extensive expenditure limits would be needed if costs were to be brought under control. But before the new law could be tested in another election, the Watergate scandal broke and Congress decided to adopt a more comprehensive approach to regulation.

Federal Election Campaign Act Amendments of 1974

In 1974 Congress thoroughly revised federal campaign finance law in response to the pressure for reform generated by the Watergate scandal and other reports of financial abuse in the 1972 presidential campaign. Detailed investigations into the Nixon campaign revealed a substantial number of large contributions and an alarming number of improprieties, including the acceptance of illegal corporate gifts and the existence of at least three undisclosed slush funds containing millions of dollars from which monies were drawn to help finance the Watergate break-in.[53] The investigations also raised questions about money's influence in the political process. For example, the inquiries led to allegations that contributors had "bought" ambassadorial appointments, gained special legislative favors, and enjoyed other special privileges. The scandal created a national uproar, and Congress responded by completely overhauling the rules governing political finance.

The FECA amendments of 1974 represent the most comprehensive campaign finance reform package ever adopted by Congress.[54] Although technically a set of amendments to the 1971 statute, the 1974 law left few of the original provisions intact. It strengthened the disclosure provisions of the 1971 law, established stringent limits on contributions, replaced the media spending ceilings with aggregate spending limits for all federal campaigns, and restricted party expenditures made on behalf of candidates. Moreover, it created an innovative public funding program for presidential elections and a new agency, the Federal Election Commission, to administer and enforce the law. In short, it erected a new regulatory regime.

The 1974 FECA imposed a set of strict limits on political contributions in order to equalize financial participation among donors and reduce the risk of corruption posed by large donations. The legislation retained the 1971 caps on the amounts that candidates and their immediate families could spend on candidates' own campaigns, as well as the prohibitions contained in earlier legislation on corporate and labor union donations. It added restrictions on other sources of funding. An individual was allowed to contribute no more than $1,000 per candidate in any primary, run-off, or general election. An individual also was barred from giving more than $25,000 in annual aggregate contributions to all federal candidates or political committees. Donations by political committees—in particular the political action committees that the law sanctioned for use by labor unions and other groups—were limited to $5,000 per election for each candidate, with no aggregate limit on a PAC's total contributions to all candidates. Independent expenditures made by individuals or groups on behalf of a federal candidate were limited to $1,000 a year, and cash donations in excess of $100 were prohibited.

The media spending ceilings established by the 1971 act were replaced with stringent limits on total campaign expenditures that applied to all federal candidates. Under the new provisions, Senate candidates could spend no more than $100,000 or $0.08 multiplied by the voting-age population of the state in a primary election and no more than $150,000 or $0.12 multiplied by the state's voting-age population in a general election, whichever amount was greater. House candidates in multidistrict states were limited to total expenditures of $70,000 in each primary and general election. Those in states with a single representative were subject to the ceilings established for Senate candidates.

Presidential candidates were restricted to a total of $10 million in a nomination campaign and a total of $20 million in a general election. The amount that they could spend in a state primary election also was limited, to no more than twice the sum that a Senate candidate in that state could spend. All of the ceilings were indexed to reflect increases in the consumer price index, and candidates were allowed to spend up to an additional 20 percent of the spending limit for fundraising. The latter provision recognized the added fundraising burden placed on candidates by the contribution limits imposed by the act, which required that they finance their campaigns through small contributions.

The amendments also set limits on the amounts that national party committees could expend on behalf of candidates. These organizations were allowed to spend no more than $10,000 per candidate in House general elections; $20,000 or $0.02 multiplied by the voting-age population for each candidate in Senate general elections, whichever was greater; and $0.02 times the voting-age population (approximately $2.9 million) for their presidential candidate. The amount that a party committee could spend on its national nominating convention also was restricted. Each of the major parties (defined as a party whose candidates received more than 25 percent of the popular vote in the previous election) was limited to $2 million in convention expenditures, while minor parties (defined as parties whose candidates received between 5 and 25 percent of the popular vote in the previous election) were limited to lesser amounts.

The reforms included a number of amendments designed to strengthen the disclosure and enforcement procedures of the 1971 act. The most important of them was a provision creating the Federal Election Commission (FEC), a six-member, full-time, bipartisan agency responsible for administering election laws and implementing the public financing program. This agency was empowered to receive all campaign reports, promulgate rules and regulations, make special and regular reports to Congress and the president, conduct audits and investigations, subpoena witnesses and information, and seek civil injunctions to ensure compliance with the law.

To assist the commission in its task, the amendments tightened the FECA's disclosure and reporting requirements. All candidates were required to establish one central campaign committee through which all contributions and expenditures had to be reported. They also were required to disclose the bank depositories authorized to receive campaign funds. In election years, each committee had to file a financial report with the FEC every quarter, with additional reports ten days before and thirty days after every election, unless the committee received or spent less than $1,000 in the quarter. In non-election years, each committee had to file a year-end report of its receipts and expenditures. Furthermore, contributions of $1,000 or more received within fifteen days of an election had to be reported to the commission within forty-eight hours.

The most innovative aspect of the 1974 law was its creation of the options of full public financing for presidential general election campaigns and public matching subsidies for presidential primary campaigns. It thus brought into being the first program of public campaign finance at the national level, putting into place an idea that had been offered from time to time since the turn of the century. The subsidy was adopted to reduce fundraising pressures in national contests and to encourage candidates to solicit small donations from large numbers of donors, thereby broadening citizen financial participation in presidential campaigns and reducing the potential influence of any particular donor.

Under the terms of the public funding program, presidential general election candidates of the major parties could receive the full amount authorized by the spending limit ($20 million) if they agreed to refrain from raising any additional private money. Qualified minor party or independent candidates could receive a share of the subsidy based on the proportion of the vote that they received in the prior election. New parties and minor parties also could qualify for postelection funds on the same proportional basis if their percentage of the vote in the current election entitled them to a larger subsidy than that generated by their share of the vote in the previous election.

In primary elections, presidential candidates were eligible for public matching funds if they fulfilled certain fundraising requirements. To qualify, a candidate had to raise at least $5,000 in contributions of $250 or less in at least twenty states. Eligible candidates would then receive public monies on a dollar-for-dollar basis for the first $250 contributed by an individual, provided that the contribution was received after January 1 of the year before the election year. The maximum amount that a candidate could receive in such payments was half of the spending limit, or $5 million under the original terms of the act. In addition, national party committees were given the option of financing their nominating conventions with public funds. Major parties could receive the entire amount authorized by the spending limit ($2 million), while minor parties were eligible for lesser amounts based on their proportion of the vote in the previous election.

Funding for the program came from a voluntary tax check-off established before the 1974 FECA, by the Revenue Act of 1971.[55] The act revived a tax check-off and public funding plan that had been adopted in 1966 but never implemented. The provision allowed individuals to designate on their federal income tax form $1 of their tax payment ($2 for married couples filing jointly) for the Presidential Election Campaign Fund, a separate account maintained by the U.S. Treasury. Under the original terms of the act, the monies deposited in the account could be earmarked for a candidate of a designated party or placed in a nonpartisan general account. Major party candidates were to receive a subsidy at the rate of $0.15 per eligible voter, with minor party contenders receiving a proportionate share. To avoid a threatened veto by President Nixon, implementation of the check-off was delayed until 1973, with the subsidies to begin in the 1976 presidential campaign. The FECA changed the terms of the subsidy payments but retained the check-off as the funding mechanism.

The Revenue Act also provided a federal income tax credit or tax deduction for small contributions to political candidates at all levels of government and to some political committees, including those associated with national party organizations. Like the matching funds program, it was designed to promote broad-based participation in campaign financing. Initially, individuals making an eligible contribution could claim a federal income tax credit for 50 percent of their contribution, up to a maximum of $12.50 on a single return or $25 on a joint return. Alternatively, a political contributor could claim a tax deduction for the full amount of any contributions, up to a maximum of $50 on an individual return and $100 on a joint return.

Those tax provisions were amended a number of times. In a 1973 amendment to legislation continuing a temporary debt ceiling, Congress made two changes in the check-off provision to simplify its implementation and promote public participation: the option of earmarking a contribution for a specific party was repealed, and the Internal Revenue Service was directed to place the check-off box in a visible location on tax forms. The allowable tax credit for political contributions was increased to $25 on an individual return and to $50 on a joint return by the Tariff Schedules Amendments of 1975,[56] and it was doubled again by the Revenue Act of 1978.[57] The credit was later repealed as part of the Tax Reform Act of 1986.[58] The tax deductions allowed under the law were doubled under the FECA of 1974, but they were repealed under the Revenue Act of 1978.

Like its 1971 predecessor, the 1974 FECA was substantially revised before it took full effect. Implementation of the act was complicated initially by President Gerald Ford's delay in appointing members to the Federal Election Commission, which stalled the administration of the law. But the Supreme Court's decision in *Buckley* v. *Valeo* (see chapter 3) forced Congress to revisit some of the basic provisions of the law and to adopt further changes. In particular, the Court struck down the spending limits established for House and Senate candidates and the contribution limit for independent expenditures, which substantially weakened the potential efficacy of the act. The Court ruled that spending limits were allowable only if they were accepted voluntarily as a condition for receiving public funding. It further held that limits on contributions by candidates and members of their immediate families were unconstitutional under the First Amendment, unless a candidate had accepted public funding. Finally, the decision also struck down the original method of appointing members of the FEC. Under the 1974 legislation, the president, the Speaker of the House, and the president pro tempore of the Senate each appointed two of the six commissioners. The Court ruled that method unconstitutional because four of the six members were appointed by Congress but exercised executive powers. As a result, the FEC was prohibited from enforcing the law or certifying public matching fund payments until it was reconstituted under a constitutional appointment process. The law therefore had to be changed to accommodate the Court's ruling before it could be applied in the 1976 election. Congress quickly responded by adopting a set of additional amendments in 1976, in the midst of the first elections conducted under the 1974 regulations.

Federal Election Campaign Act Amendments of 1976

The *Buckley* decision was handed down in January 1976. Congress had to act quickly if the campaign finance regulations adopted less than two years earlier were to have any effect on the 1976 elections. Because the 1976 campaign was already under way, President Gerald R. Ford asked for a bill that simply reconstituted the FEC. But Congress, still operating in a climate of reform, decided to draft a more extensive bill that included revisions to the public financing program, contribution limits, and disclosure procedures. As a result, the bill that President Ford signed into law in May 1976, known as the FECA Amendments of 1976, did more than revise the regulations to conform to the Court's ruling.[59]

The 1976 bill changed the method of appointing FEC commissioners. Instead of giving the president, Speaker of the House, and president pro tempore of the Senate two appointments apiece, with a requirement that appointees belong to different parties and be approved by the Senate, the new rules called for the appointment of all six members by the president, subject to Senate confirmation. This process avoided the separation of powers issue raised by the Court in *Buckley*.

The amendments improved the FEC's enforcement powers by granting the agency exclusive authority to prosecute civil violations of the law and jurisdiction over violations previously covered only in the criminal code. But at the same time, Congress restricted the commission's ability to act by requiring an affirmative vote of four members before regulations could be issued or civil actions initiated. Congress also limited the commission's advisory decisions to the specific factual situation presented in an individual advisory opinion request. Opinions could not be issued in response to hypothetical situations or to questions about issues that might arise in implementing the law.

In response to the Court's ruling on contribution limits, Congress restored the $50,000 limit on contributions by presidential or vice presidential candidates and their families to their own campaigns, but applied it only to publicly funded candidates. Congress also established new contribution limits. In addition to the limits on individual gifts to candidates, ceilings were placed on the amount that an individual could give to a PAC ($5,000 per year) and to a national party committee ($20,000 per year) under federal law, and those amounts were included in the aggregate ceiling of $25,000 a year that was imposed on individual donors under the 1974 reforms. The amount that a PAC could donate to a national party committee was set at $15,000 a year, and the Democratic and Republican senatorial campaign committees each were allowed to give no more than $17,500 to a Senate candidate. The law thus folded party contributions into the scheme of contribution limits so that individuals could not circumvent the law by giving money to the parties. It also sought to reduce loopholes in the law by stipulating that all PACs created by a company or international union would be treated as a single committee for the purpose of determining compliance with contribution limits.

Since the Court had struck down the ceiling on independent expenditures in the 1974 law, the 1976 amendments contained a number of disclosure provisions designed to ensure reporting of independent spending. Other important changes affected the candidate spending limits and public financing program. Congress created a minor loophole in the spending limits applied to publicly funded presidential campaigns by exempting legal and accounting expenses incurred to comply with the law. Those payments, however, had to be disclosed to the FEC. Lawmakers also modified the provisions of the matching funds program to ensure that the availability of public money did not encourage a losing candidate to remain in the race. Under the new rules, a presidential candidate who received less than 10 percent of the vote in two consecutive primaries in which he or she was on the ballot would be ineligible for additional matching payments. Candidates who withdrew from the race were required to return any remaining public monies to the U.S. Treasury.

Federal Election Campaign Act Amendments of 1979

Despite its shaky start, the FECA's regulatory approach was a great improvement over the patchwork of largely ineffective regulations that it replaced. The disclosure and reporting requirements enhanced public access to financial information and regulators' ability to enforce the law. The contribution ceilings eliminated the large gifts that had tainted the process in 1972. Public financing quickly gained widespread acceptance among the candidates, and small contributions became a staple of presidential campaign financing.

But the new regime was not without its critics. Candidates and political committees complained that the law's detailed reporting requirements forced unnecessary and burdensome paperwork on them, increasing their administrative costs. State and local party leaders contended that the law reduced the level of spending on traditional party-building activities (such as voter registration and mobilization drives) and discouraged grassroots volunteer efforts, because parties were limited in the amount that they could spend on behalf of candidates.

The initial experience with the FECA in 1976 therefore led party leaders to call for further adjustments, and Congress responded by modifying the law once again. To ensure quick passage, Congress focused on "noncontroversial" changes, many of which eased requirements or restrictions in the law. Some provisions of the FECA Amendments of 1979 sought to streamline disclosure procedures and make reporting requirements less burdensome.[60] The amendments reduced the maximum number of reports committees had to file during an election cycle and exempted from the disclosure requirements candidates who raised or spent less than $5,000, as well as party committees that raised less than $5,000 or spent less than $1,000 a year in federal elections or less than $5,000 on certain volunteer activities. For candidates and committees not exempt from disclosure, the threshold amount for reportable contributions or expenditures was increased from $100 to $200. The threshold for disclosing independent expenditures was raised from $100 to $250. The changes substantially reduced the amount of information candidates and committees had to file with the FEC, making reporting less onerous without significantly diminishing the information available on larger donations or expenditures.

To enhance the role of political parties and foster political participation, the law changed some of the rules on party spending. The revisions exempted certain types of party-related activity, such as grassroots volunteer activities and voter registration and turnout drives, from the expenditure ceilings imposed on party spending in federal elections. The new rules allowed party committees to spend unlimited amounts on voter registration and get-out-the-vote activities, provided that they were conducted primarily on behalf of the party's presidential nominee. The committees also were allowed to spend unlimited amounts on materials related to grassroots or volunteer activities (such as buttons, bumper stickers, posters, and brochures), provided that the funds used were not drawn from contributions designated for a particular candidate. The statute noted, however, that the exemption did not apply to any monies spent on public political advertising.

Contrary to some understandings, the 1979 law did not create "soft money," the unregulated "nonfederal" funding that became a major source of controversy in the late 1980s and 1990s (see chapter 5). The amendments simply allowed party committees to use regulated or "hard" dollar contributions to fund certain narrowly defined activities without having the expenditures count against the limits on a party's contribution to its candidates or against coordinated spending ceilings. The parties still had to abide by the law's contribution restrictions. But the eased spending provisions gave state and local party committees an opportunity to play a much larger role in federal campaigns.

Finally, the 1979 amendments included three other noteworthy changes. First, Congress clarified some of the compliance and enforcement procedures. As part of the revision, Congress stripped the FEC of its authority to conduct random audits, which it had been given to ensure effective enforcement of the law. Following the 1976 election the agency had undertaken random audits of 10 percent of House and Senate candidates, and while the audits exposed minor inaccuracies in the reports filed by a number of incumbents, they led to no major enforcement actions.[61] The findings, however, were a source of embarrassment to some officeholders, and that, combined with more general concerns about the uncertainties associated with random audits, was enough to convince Congress to eliminate the FEC's ability to conduct such investigations.

Second, the amount of the public subsidy for a presidential nominating convention was increased. Under the 1974 law, the base amount from the public funding program available to a party to pay for convention expenses was set at $2 million, plus a cost-of-living adjustment. The base amount was raised to $3 million in 1979, but it did not remain at that level for long. Congress changed it again in 1984, when it passed a bill that raised the convention subsidy to $4 million.[62]

Third, the new regulations prohibited candidates or officeholders from using excess campaign funds for personal expenses, except for those members already serving in Congress on January 8, 1980. Personal use of leftover campaign funds already was prohibited by Senate rules, for both sitting and retired members. House rules applied the prohibition only to retired members. The FECA thus ensured that the same rules would be applied to all members in the future. The exemption or "grandfather clause" for those serving prior to 1980 was revised in 1989, when Congress adopted the Ethics Reform Act, which contained provisions that repealed the exemption by 1993.[63]

The Reform Debate after the FECA

The 1979 FECA was the last major campaign finance bill to be passed at the federal level until the adoption of the Bipartisan Campaign Reform Act of 2002. In the two intervening decades, Congress made minor changes or modifications in the law but did not revise statutory provisions to account for the substantial changes in political financing that occurred during that period. Candidates, parties, and political practitioners adapted to FECA regulations in ways both intended and unintended. Many of the innovations undermined the efficacy of the law and raised questions about the FECA's ability to control the flow of political money. The response to the FECA therefore kept campaign finance reform on the legislative agenda, and almost every Congress between 1986 and 2002 debated major reform plans. Yet the legislative struggle produced little more than a lengthy stalemate on campaign finance issues, characterized by deep partisan disagreement over the best approach to strengthen the efficacy of the law.

While candidates and political organizations quickly adjusted their practices to meet the requirements of the law in federal elections in the decade after the initial passage of the FECA, the improved disclosure of campaign monies revealed a number of patterns that gave reformers cause for concern. Congressional campaign spending continued to rise, which renewed the debate about the role of money in federal elections. Incumbents amassed funds from their broad sources of support and outspent their challengers by substantial margins, which led some observers to question whether challengers could compete financially under FECA restrictions and whether the rules were serving to protect incumbents. Much of the financial advantage enjoyed by incumbents was due to the contributions and expenditures of PACs, which became an increasingly important source of campaign money. By the mid-1980s PAC funding had become so significant that some reformers, including Common Cause, began to describe the need for more stringent regulation of PACs as the most pressing issue in the campaign finance debate.

The proliferation of PACs was one of the most notable direct consequences of the FECA. From 1974 to 1986, the number of committees registered with the FEC increased from 1,146 to 4,157, while the amounts that they contributed to candidates rose from about $12.5 million to $105 million.[64] While there were many causes of that growth, the campaign finance regulations were a major factor.[65] The FECA sanctioned PACs, and because the law established a higher contribution limit for PACs than for individual donors, groups and organizations had an incentive to form PACs. The FEC also encouraged PAC formation in the advisory ruling it issued to Sun Oil Company in 1975.[66] Sun Oil had asked the FEC whether the PAC it planned to establish and other political activities it proposed would be allowable under the FECA; it also had asked whether it would be legal to use corporate funds to establish, administer, and raise money for the PAC. The FEC confirmed that the company could establish a PAC and ruled that it would be legal to finance the administrative and overhead costs with corporate funds. That decision resolved the most significant ambiguities regarding corporate

PACs, and hundreds of corporations, trade associations, and other groups took the guidance as an authoritative guideline for forming and administering PACs of their own.

The most notable indirect consequence of the FECA regulations was the rise of a new form of party finance, which came to be known as *soft money.* Soon after the FECA took effect, party organizations and presidential campaign organizers in particular began to seek out methods of circumventing the expenditure and contribution limits that accompanied public funding. Among the tactics they pursued was the aggressive exploitation of the exemption for party-related grassroots and party-building activities. As a result of a number of FEC advisory opinions issued in the late 1970s, party committees were allowed to accept and spend monies not raised under federal contribution limits to pay administrative costs and to finance other nonfederal election–related activities.[67] Soon thereafter, similar rules were applied to national party committees, allowing them to receive and spend funds not regulated by federal law to finance the nonfederal share of their administrative costs and other activities.[68] So two separate streams of regulatory decisionmaking began to merge: Congress was loosening the restrictions on party spending, while the FEC was loosening the restrictions on party fundraising. The party committees took advantage of the opportunity to raise unrestricted funds and use them to supplement the hard dollars that they were spending to support federal candidates. Within a couple of election cycles, the FEC decisions and innovative party practices had led to a new approach to campaign funding and a fundamental change in the regulatory structure. That transformation occurred without congressional deliberation, public comment, or much apparent thought to the enormous consequences it would have on the effectiveness of federal campaign finance laws.

By the end of the 1980s, soft money funding had become a major component of national election financing, with both national parties spending tens of millions of soft dollars on staff salaries, overhead, voter turnout programs and other political efforts designed to affect the outcome of federal contests, especially the presidential race. Most of the money was raised through unlimited contributions from sources such as corporations and labor unions, which had long been banned from participating in federal elections. Critics argued that soft money funding violated the provisions of the FECA and charged the FEC with failing to fulfill its responsibility to enforce the law (see chapter 8). But the FEC took no action to prohibit party committees from raising soft money, so this type of funding became a staple of federal campaigns.

In the 1990s, the national parties raised increasingly large sums of soft money. Receipts rose from $86 million in 1992 to about $260 million in 1996 to more than $495 million in 2000. That steep jump was spurred in part by the parties' discovery of "issue advocacy" advertising, which offered another method of circumventing FECA restrictions. Beginning with the 1996 election cycle, the national party committees sponsored candidate-specific issue advertisements that were designed to promote their presidential nominees and, in subsequent elections, their House and Senate candidates. Because the ads did not "expressly advocate" the election or defeat of a federal candidate, they were not regulated under the FECA and therefore could be financed in part with soft money. Accordingly, the ads provided party committees with an effective means of supporting candidates without worrying about contribution ceilings or coordinated spending limits. Parties capitalized on this option by raising as much soft money as possible for that purpose.

These financial trends led to a consensus among policymakers that the FECA was no longer working and that fundamental reform was necessary. But there was wide disagreement on how the problems should be fixed. Debates regarding the desirability and potential effects of various proposals—including spending limits in House and Senate races, public subsidies at the congressional level, restrictions on PAC contributions, the elimination of soft money, regulation of issue advocacy, and even the deregulation of campaign funding—often produced more heat than light. While Congress considered different proposals and at times achieved majorities in both houses in favor of a particular bill, partisan gridlock and irreconcilable differences between the House and Senate stymied major reform.

From time to time Congress did adopt some modifications of the campaign finance rules, but they were mostly minor adjustments included in bills devoted to other subjects. In addition to the 1984 increase in the amount of the public convention subsidy, the legislature repealed the tax credit as part of a 1986 tax package[69] and tripled the amount of the income tax check-off for the presidential election fund in 1993, raising it from $1 to $3 on single returns and from $2 to $6 on joint returns, as part of the Omnibus Budget Reconciliation Act.[70]

Congress also amended the reporting and disclosure provisions of the FECA in 1995 and 1999 to facilitate electronic filing of disclosure reports. In December 1995, President William J. Clinton signed a law that required the FEC to establish the technical and regulatory framework to enable committees to file reports on computer disks or by other electronic means.[71] The law sought to promote online access to FEC reports and reduce the amount of paper filing and manual processing required by the disclosure system by offering more efficient and cost-effective procedures for filing. In 1996, the FEC set forth rules to make electronic filing a reality, establishing the protocol for accepting reports, amending reports, and verifying the authenticity of reports.[72] Later, a provision of the Treasury and General Government Appropriations Act of 2000 made electronic reporting, which been voluntary at first, a requirement for most of the candidates and committees registered with the FEC.[73] Adopted in 1999, the act required the FEC to have electronic filing requirements in effect as of January 1, 2000. Under the rules adopted by the FEC to comply with the new statute, any political committee or person, with the exception of Senate candidates, is required to file disclosure reports electronically if total contributions or expenditures within a calendar year exceed, or are expected to exceed, $50,000. Committees or persons raising or spending less than the threshold sum have the option to file electronically, but they are not required to do so.[74] As of the 2004 election cycle, the Senate had yet to take action to apply the electronic reporting requirement to its own campaigns.

The most significant change in political finance regulations adopted before 2002 was an amendment to the tax code adopted in 2000 that required committees organized under section 527 of the Internal Revenue Code to disclose their political activities. That amendment was a response to a new tactic in political finance that emerged in advance of the 2000 elections.

Section 527 of the tax code exempts "political organizations" from income taxes. The exemption originally was intended to cover political party committees, candidate committees, and state and federal political committees that are registered with and report to the FEC. But recent changes in Internal Revenue Service (IRS) advice and court rulings in the area of issue advocacy made it possible for section 527 groups to engage in political activity without having to register with either the FEC or state campaign finance authorities. The IRS determined that an organization may engage in activities that seek "to influence the outcome of federal elections" without being subject to FECA restrictions or disclosure requirements provided that it does not "expressly advocate" the election or defeat of federal candidates. Moreover, because the organizations are exempt from federal taxation, they can receive gifts of more than $10,000 without being subject to the federal gift tax.[75]

Section 527 was established before issue advocacy advertising became a popular campaign strategy. It did not require the disclosure of an organization's contributors or expenditures, since Congress at the time assumed that they already would be disclosed to the FEC or the appropriate state agency. The gap between the Internal Revenue Code and the FECA, a gap created largely by the gray area of issue advocacy, provided groups with a loophole in the disclosure requirements that they rapidly began to exploit in anticipation of the 2000 election. Groups or individuals, including members of Congress, began to sponsor or establish committees under section 527 for the express purpose of raising and spending unlimited sums on candidate-specific issue advocacy advertising or other political efforts designed to support federal candidates. In the first few months of 2000, more than a dozen such committees formed and announced their intention to raise tens of millions of dollars in connection with federal elections. One such group, Republicans for Clean Air, gained national attention for the advertisements it broadcast against Senator John McCain in a number of presidential primaries.[76]

In an uncharacteristic move given the recent history of campaign finance reform, Congress reacted swiftly to this development, passing legislation to place disclosure requirements on section 527 committees.[77] The law, which was signed by President Clinton on July 1, 2000, imposed reporting obligations on section 527 political organizations that are not required to report to the FEC and have annual gross receipts in excess of $25,000. All section 527 organizations meeting that revenue threshold must file annual income tax returns similar to Form 990, which is filed with the IRS by unions and other organizations that are exempt under section 501 of the tax code. In addition, the organizations must report all contributors of $200 or more during a calendar year and expenditures of more than $500 in a calendar year on any one source of goods and services.

Congress did not address many of the issues raised by the advent of issue advocacy in its section 527 reform legislation, but it did make a start by placing minimal reporting requirements on section 527 organizations. Congress was not able to agree on other proposed changes, including the imposition of limits on contributions, the extension of disclosure to other committees organized under the tax code, or the establishment of restrictions on issue advocacy advertising. So even that regulatory change did not obviate the pressing need for more comprehensive campaign finance reform.

The Bipartisan Campaign Reform Act of 2002

History suggests that the prospects for reform are best when a new Congress faces some major financial controversy or scandal that began in a previous election. For that reason, many advocates of reform hoped that the 1996 election would prove to be a catalyst for fundamental changes in the system. Following national controversy over the Democrats' fundraising practices and alleged "selling" of access to the White House, campaign finance reform became a major issue in a presidential election for the first time in decades. The unprecedented financial activities of 1996, especially the jump in soft money contributions and the advent of candidate-specific issue advertising, clearly demonstrated that the FECA's regulatory structure had essentially become meaningless and that a wholesale change in the system was sorely needed.

By the spring of 1997, Congress, the Department of Justice, and the FEC had initiated separate investigations into party fundraising practices during the 1996 election. As a result, the Democratic National Committee (DNC) was forced to admit that it had received at least $3 million in contributions from illegal or questionable sources, which the party returned to the donors.[78] The White House also released documents that indicated that President Clinton had attended 103 "coffee klatches" with political supporters and donors who contributed a total of more than $25 million to the Democrats in 1996. The documents further revealed that Vice President Al Gore had made a number of fundraising telephone calls from his office, seeking contributions for the DNC in amounts of $50,000 or more.[79]

Congress reacted by placing reform high on the legislative agenda and deliberating on a number of major reform proposals. The leading plan, known as the McCain-Feingold bill for its two principal sponsors in the Senate, Republican John McCain of Arizona and Democrat Russell Feingold of Wisconsin, focused on eliminating soft money and restricting the funding of candidate-specific issue advertising. A companion bill was sponsored in the House by Republican Christopher Shays of Connecticut and Democrat Martin Meehan of Massachusetts. McCain and Feingold had sponsored a bipartisan reform proposal in 1996, but the plan was defeated by a Republican-led filibuster. At the start of the 105th Congress, the outlook for reform was promising, particularly since McCain and Feingold had trimmed down the broader legislative package that they had presented in the previous Congress to focus on soft money and issue advocacy advertising. But in both the 105th and 106th Congresses, their bill achieved majority support in both houses only to be defeated by a filibuster in the Senate led by Republican Mitch McConnell of Kentucky, the legislation's leading opponent.[80]

When the new Congress convened in 2001, advocates of reform pressed their cause with renewed conviction and strength. A spike in soft money fundraising, which nearly doubled from the $262 million raised in 1996 to

$495 million in 2000, and a surge in issue advocacy advertising in federal races—combined with McCain's unexpectedly strong bid for the 2000 Republican presidential nomination—strengthened the resolve of congressional reformers to pass the McCain-Feingold proposal.[81] The prospects of passage were improved by the results of the congressional elections, which produced a few additional supporters of the bill, thus narrowing by possibly three or four votes the seven- or eight-vote margin that had upheld filibusters in previous sessions of Congress.[82]

Under the leadership of McCain and Feingold, the Senate took action on reform legislation early in the new session, holding a wide-ranging, open debate on the bill in the spring of 2001 that produced a number of amendments to the original proposal. The modified proposal passed easily, by a margin of 59 to 41, which represented a gain of six votes over the cloture vote that failed in the previous Congress.

However, the bill continued to face determined opposition in the House. The Republican leadership continued to advocate its alternatives and refused to bring the Shays-Meehan bill to the floor. The deadlock was not broken until January 2002, when House advocates of the bill garnered the support needed for a successful discharge petition to force a rule for debate onto the floor of the House.[83]

The legislative effort in the House took place in a favorable political climate created by the bankruptcy of Enron Corporation, a giant energy company, and subsequent questions about the influence of the corporation's political contributions on legislative and administrative actions that benefited the company. Enron's chief officer, Kenneth Lay, was prominently identified as a supporter of President Bush, but both Democrats and Republicans had accepted contributions from the company, which gave all members an additional incentive to embrace the cause of reform. Once the bill reached the floor, it easily passed the House, but not before a number of changes were made, including additional restrictions on the financial activities of state and local parties in federal elections.[84]

The Senate responded quickly to the House action. Democrats held majority control in the Senate, and with the prospects of a successful filibuster now unlikely, the major issue was whether the Senate would accept and adopt the House version of the bill or go to conference committee to iron out differences. Since a conference committee was viewed by reformers as a vehicle for killing the bill, McCain and Feingold pressed for adoption of the House bill as a substitute for the version of the bill approved by the Senate in its previous session. After a few weeks of procedural wrangling, a motion to end debate on a consent agreement to move the House bill to the floor was adopted by a 68-32 vote, and the Senate adopted the bill, now known as the Bipartisan Campaign Reform Act (BCRA), by a 60-40 vote.[85] On March 27, 2002, President George W. Bush signed the bill into law with little fanfare.[86]

As soon as BCRA was adopted, its constitutionality was challenged in court. By that time, a legal challenge was widely anticipated, since Senator McConnell had announced weeks before final passage in the Senate that he was preparing a legal complaint against the proposed legislation. In all, eleven separate complaints were filed against the act in the U.S. District Court for the District of Columbia, involving more than eighty plaintiffs, ranging from the Republican National Committee and California Democratic Party to the National Rifle Association, American Civil Liberties Union, and AFL-CIO. The actions challenged the constitutionality of virtually every aspect of the law.

BCRA's congressional sponsors, expecting a court challenge, had included in the law a provision invoking procedural rules for federal courts that expedite court review of statutes that Congress deems to be in need of prompt resolution. Accordingly, the district court seated a special three-judge panel, consisting of two district court judges and a presiding circuit court judge, to conduct a trial on an expedited basis, with appeal directly to the U.S. Supreme Court.[87] To expedite review, the three-judge panel consolidated the eleven complaints into one case, *McConnell* v. *Federal Election Commission*, and set strict timetables for gathering evidence and filing briefs. In early December 2002, the panel heard oral arguments in the case, and in May 2003 issued a 1,638-page opinion that upheld some provisions of the law but found others to be unconstitutional or nonjusticiable.[88] The ruling, however, had no effect on the implementation of the law, which went into effect on November 6, 2002, the day after the midterm federal elections, because the district court had issued a stay of the ruling soon after it was released, pending review of its decision by the Supreme Court.

The Supreme Court quickly began its review in order to determine the law in advance of the 2004 elections. By the end of the summer of 2003, briefs had been submitted to the Court, and in early September, the Court scheduled an unusually long four hours of oral argument to consider the array of issues raised in the complicated case. Three months later, the Court issued its opinion. In a ruling that surprised many observers, particularly given the divisions in the lower court's ruling, the Court upheld all of the major provisions of the law, albeit in some instances by the narrow margin of

5-4.[89] The Court struck down only the law's prohibition on contributions by minors and a provision that would have required party committees to decide whether to make independent or coordinated expenditures in support of a candidate at the time of a candidate's nomination.

BCRA was designed to restore the regulatory structure established by the FECA by addressing the problems raised by soft money and issue advocacy advertising. But the legislative maneuvering required to pass the bill and the focus of advocates on possible methods of evading the law led to a number of other major provisions, including restrictions on fundraising by federal politicians for organized groups, increases in some contribution limits, and special provisos for candidates facing self-financed opponents. As a result, BCRA is a complex and technical statute that moves the regulation of political finance beyond the original borders established by the FECA.[90]

One of the central pillars of BCRA is a ban on soft money at the national level. The law prohibits a national party committee—including any entities directly or indirectly established, financed, maintained, or controlled by such a committee or any agent acting on a committee's behalf—from soliciting, receiving, spending, transferring, or directing to another person any funds that are not subject to federal source prohibitions, contribution limits, and reporting requirements. It also restricts fundraising and expenditures by federal officeholders or candidates and by agents acting on behalf of an officeholder or candidate. Such individuals may not solicit, receive, direct, transfer, or spend funds in connection with an election for federal office, including funds for any activity defined as a federal election activity, unless the monies used for the activities conform to the limitations, prohibitions, and reporting requirements of the act.

To discourage attempts to circumvent the restrictions, the law also regulates fundraising by federal officeholders or candidates and national party committees for other organizations that conduct activities related to federal elections. For example, national party committees and their agents, as well as state and local party committees and their agents, are specifically barred from soliciting funds for or otherwise financially supporting tax-exempt organizations that are engaged in activities, such as voter registration and mobilization drives, that are carried out "in connection with" federal elections. Similarly, national and state party committees and their agents are banned from raising soft money for certain organizations that operate under section 527 of the Internal Revenue Code. In short, the law attempts to prevent party committees from circumventing the soft money ban and disclosure requirements by raising unregulated funds for interest groups or section 527 committees.

In recognition of the multiple and varied roles that federal elected officials and candidates often fulfill, the law does make some allowances for certain types of fundraising that might occur outside the federal limits. It exempts from the soft money prohibition candidates for state or local office who are raising money under state law for activities that refer only to a state or local candidate. So a member of the House who is running for governor can solicit contributions for the gubernatorial campaign in excess of the amounts allowed by federal law, as long as the monies are raised in accordance with state law and used only for the gubernatorial race, not a federal contest. Federal officeholders and candidates and national party committee officials can participate in state and local party fundraising events as a speaker or featured guest, but they may not solicit funds for the event that are not subject to federal contribution limits. Finally, federal elected officials and candidates may raise money from individuals (not corporations or labor unions) of up to $20,000 for certain tax-exempt charitable organizations provided that the principal purpose of the organizations is not to conduct voter registration and turnout drives.

BCRA also sets forth more explicit rules regarding the types of state and local party activity that must be financed with federally regulated funds. Most important, the statute closed the issue advocacy loophole by requiring that any state or local party–financed public communication that features a federal candidate and promotes, supports, attacks, or opposes a candidate for federal office must be funded with hard money. Furthermore, any voter registration drives conducted in the last 120 days of a federal election are defined as federal election activity that must be funded with hard money. As for voter identification and turnout programs, the provisions generally limit state and local parties to hard money only if they occur in an election in which a federal candidate is on the ballot. BCRA thus places greater restrictions on state and local party campaign spending than did previous FEC rules.

The congressional sponsors of BCRA recognized that a ban on soft money would reduce the revenues available to national party committees. To provide some partial compensation for the anticipated loss, the statute increased some contribution limits and indexed them for inflation. The law increased the aggregate amount of hard money that an individual donor may contribute to candidates, parties, and PACs to $95,000 (now $101,400) per election cycle, nearly double the FECA's aggregate ceiling of $25,000 per calendar year (the equivalent of $50,000 per election cycle). Within the aggregate limit, the statute sets a sublimit of $57,500 (now $61,400) every two years in aggregate contributions to parties and PACs (though no more than

$37,500 of that amount may be given to entities other than national party committees, a figure not indexed for inflation). Thus a donor who chooses to do so may contribute up to $61,400 every two years to party committees. With respect to contributions by individuals to specific party committees, BCRA raised the annual limit on contributions to a national party committee from $20,000 to $25,000 (now $26,700) and to a state party committee from $5,000 to $10,000 (under federal law), although that limit is not indexed for inflation. The law also raised the amount that an individual may contribute to a federal candidate from $1,000 per election to $2,000 (now $2,100) per election, and it increased the combined amount that a national party committee and a senatorial committee may give to a Senate candidate to $35,000 (now $37,300), double the $17,500 allowed by the FECA. But the changes are limited to individual donations. The law made no changes in the amounts that an individual may contribute to a PAC or in the sum that a PAC may contribute to a party committee or another PAC.

In a marked departure from the approach under the FECA, the new rules eased contribution limits and party coordinated spending ceilings in certain circumstances. Because the Supreme Court has ruled that candidates can spend unlimited amounts of their own money (unless they accept public funds), Congress adopted an approach that would make it easier for candidates to raise money when running against a wealthy opponent. That aspect of the law is known as "the millionaire's provision," since it was designed to address the concerns of incumbent legislators who feared the possibility of facing a wealthy, free-spending opponent. The statute sets forth a complicated set of formulas that trigger higher contribution limits and higher levels of party support for candidates opposed by a self-funded challenger who is spending substantial amounts of personal money on his or her own campaign. In both the Senate and House, once a self-funded candidate exceeds a designated threshold of personal spending on a campaign (called the "opposition personal funds amount," which is a measure of the personal spending of such a candidate minus the amount spent by an opponent), higher contribution limits are applied to the candidate who is not self-funded. The law establishes a threshold in Senate elections of $150,000 plus a sum equal to $0.04 multiplied by the state's eligible voting population; in House races, the threshold is $350,000. Once a self-funded candidate has reached 110 percent of the total "opposition personal funds amount," higher contribution limits are allowed for his or her challenger. Depending on the amount spent by the self-funded candidate, contributions can be increased by up to sixfold in Senate races ($12,000 per donor) or up to threefold ($6,000) in House races. In both Senate and House contests, when the highest trigger amounts of personal spending are reached, the ceilings on party coordinated expenditures are lifted for the candidate who is not self-funded.

Given the recent flood of issue advocacy advertising in federal elections, congressional reformers were especially cognizant of the need to strengthen the regulations governing this form of campaign spending. They knew that a ban on soft money and greater regulation of party spending would provide a strong incentive for donors to shift their contributions to PACs or other organized political groups, which would be able to use unregulated funds for issue advocacy advertising campaigns. The other central pillar of BCRA, complementing the soft money ban, was regulation of the funding of issue advocacy communications, particularly advertisements that featured federal candidates.

To address the problem of issue advocacy, BCRA expanded the realm of regulated political communications beyond the "magic words" doctrine that the Supreme Court suggested in *Buckley* (where the inclusion of words such as "vote for" or "elect" in communications was viewed as the trigger for regulation) to encompass advertisements that targeted federal candidates but did not use the magic words to express advocacy. Accordingly, the law establishes a new regulatory standard for express advocacy by defining "electioneering communications" as any broadcast, cable, or satellite communications referring to a clearly identified federal candidate that are made within sixty days of a general election or thirty days of a primary election and that target the electorate of the candidate. The law also contains an alternative standard that includes any broadcast, cable, or satellite communication that promotes or supports—or attacks or opposes—a federal candidate (regardless of whether it expressly advocates a vote for or against a candidate) and suggests no plausible interpretation other than as an exhortation to vote for or against a candidate.

BCRA seeks to redefine the concept of express advocacy to include the types of issue ads targeting federal candidates that have proliferated in recent elections. It does so by stating criteria that principally seek to eliminate corporate and union funding for such advertisements and by limiting regulation to television and radio advertisements. Communications that qualify as electioneering communications can still be broadcast or otherwise distributed, but they cannot be financed with corporate or labor union funds. To give further effect to this aspect of the law, BCRA calls on the FEC to develop new regulations for determining what constitutes "coordinated activity" to ensure that organized groups and political committees do not coordinate their efforts with federal officeholders and candidates or with party committees.

BCRA also requires the disclosure of the costs of electioneering communications by any spender (including individuals and unincorporated associations) who exceeds $10,000 in aggregate expenditures and the disclosure of any contributions of more than $1,000. If an organization establishes a separate fund to finance electioneering communications consisting exclusively of donations from individuals, only donors to the fund need to be disclosed; if no separate fund is created, then donors to the organization generally have to be disclosed.

Even with these new provisions, BCRA leaves a number of areas of interest group electioneering unregulated. No new restrictions are placed on any interest group communications that occur outside of the sixty- or thirty-day windows; independent, non–express advocacy advertising done during the pre-window period, even if it features a federal candidate, can be financed with unregulated monies, just as it could before BCRA was adopted. Furthermore, this expanded sphere of regulation does not include other communications, including voter guides, direct mail, Internet communications, or telephone calls. The new law places no new restrictions on the financing of such communications.

Conclusion

The adoption of BCRA represents the most recent step in the nation's long history of regulating the role of money in federal elections. It will not be the last. Even before the fate of BCRA was decided, advocates of reform noted that BCRA was an incremental step that failed to address the need for comprehensive reform of the system. In the wake of its adoption, reform groups renewed their calls for further legislation to reform the presidential public funding system, provide some sort of reduced-cost or free broadcast time to federal candidates, and restructure the FEC. The calls became more urgent in response to the initial experience under BCRA and the financing of the 2004 campaign. As soon as the FEC issued regulations to implement the new law, advocates of reform filed complaints against the agency charging that the commission had created new loopholes that violated BCRA's provisions, and they pressed the case for the creation of a new enforcement agency. In the presidential race, both major party nominees rejected public funding during the primaries, which raised fundamental questions about the future of public funding of presidential election campaigns. The growing role of section 527 organizations in the financing of electioneering activities and a major controversy concerning the application of federal campaign finance restrictions to the groups renewed the debate on the regulation of 527s. A new era of reform has thus begun, but like those that preceded it, it has not resolved the enduring debate concerning the role of money in American politics.

Notes

1. Robert E. Mutch, *Campaigns, Congress, and Courts: The Making of Federal Campaign Finance Law* (New York: Praeger, 1988), p. xv.

2. Robert E. Mutch, "The First Federal Campaign Finance Bills," in *Money and Politic$*, edited by Paula Baker (Pennsylvania State University Press, 2002), p. 35. Here Mutch identifies the 1837 House bill submitted by Bell as the "first federal campaign finance bill," revising his earlier identification of an 1839 Senate bill to prohibit assessments as "the first bill to regulate campaign financing" in *Campaigns, Congress, and Courts*, p. xvi.

3. Cited in Mutch, *Campaigns, Congress, and Courts*, p. xvi.

4. Cited in *Congressional Campaign Finances: History, Facts, and Controversy* (Washington: Congressional Quarterly, 1992), pp. 29–30.

5 Mutch, *Campaigns, Congress, and Courts*, p. xvi; *Congressional Campaign Finances*, p. 30; Louise Overacker, *Money in Elections* (New York: Macmillan, 1932), pp. 102–05.

6. Paula Baker, "Campaigns and Potato Chips; or Some Causes and Consequences of Political Spending," in Baker, ed., *Money and Politic$*, p. 18.

7. This appropriations act was adopted by the 44th Congress on August 15, 1876. See 19 Stat. 169 (1877).

8. Executive order, June 22, 1877. See Charles Richard Williams, ed., *The Diary and Letters of Rutherford B. Hayes, Nineteenth President of the United States,* vol. 3 (Columbus: Ohio State Archeological and Historical Society, 1922), p. 438 (www.ohiohistory.org/onlinedoc/hayes/Volume03/Chapter35/EXECUTIVEJune221877.txt [August 2, 2004]).

9. 22 Stat. 403 (1883).

10. Herbert Croly, *Marcus Alonzo Hanna: His Life and Work* (New York: Macmillan, 1912), p. 325.

11. Based on the data reported in Herbert E. Alexander, *Financing Politics* (Washington: Congressional Quarterly, 1980), p. 4.

12. In 1897, Nebraska, Missouri, Tennessee, and Florida passed bans on corporate contributions in reaction to the corporate fundraising efforts of McKinley's 1896 presidential campaign. All four states had cast their electoral votes for William Jennings Bryan. See Mutch, *Campaigns, Congress, and Courts*, p. xvii.

13. Quoted in Jasper B. Shannon, *Money and Politics* (New York: Random House, 1959), p. 36.

14. Ibid., pp. 35–36. The quotation is from a 1904 letter from Roosevelt to Harriman.

15. New York State Legislature, *Testimony Taken before the Joint Committee of the Senate and Assembly of the State of New York to Investigate and Examine into the Business Affairs of Life Insurance Companies Doing Business in the State of New York* (Albany: State of New York, 1905). See, in particular, vol. 1, pp. 689–753.

16. Theodore Roosevelt, "Fourth Annual Message," in *The State of the Union Messages of the Presidents 1790–1966,* vol. 2, edited by Fred L. Israel (New York: Chelsea House, 1966), p. 2128.

17. Theodore Roosevelt, "Fifth Annual Message," in Israel, ed., *The State of the Union Messages,* vol. 3, p. 2161.

18. Theodore Roosevelt, "Sixth Annual Message," in Israel, ed., *The State of the Union Messages,* vol. 3, p. 2194.

19. Mutch, *Campaigns, Congress, and Courts,* pp. 5–6.

20. 34 Stat. 864 (January 26, 1907).

21. Mutch, *Campaigns, Congress, and Courts,* p. 35.

22. Theodore Roosevelt, "Seventh Annual Message," in Israel, ed., *The State of the Union Messages,* vol. 3, p. 2276.

23. 36 Stat. 822 (1910).

24. 37 Stat. 25 (1911).

25. For background on this case, see Spencer Ervin, *Henry Ford* v. *Truman H. Newberry: The Famous Senate Election Contest* (New York: Richard A. Smith, 1935).

26. *Newberry* v. *United States,* 256 U.S. 232 (1921).

27. *United States* v. *Classic,* 313 U.S. 299 (1941).

28. 43 Stat. 1070 (1925).

29. Overacker, *Money in Elections,* pp. 249–71; *Congressional Campaign Finances,* p. 32; Mutch, *Campaigns, Congress, and Courts,* pp. 27–28.

30. *Congressional Campaign Finances,* p. 32, and Shannon, *Money and Politics,* pp. 50–51.

31. Shannon, *Money and Politics,* p. 55.

32. 53 Stat. 1147 (1939).

33. Mutch, *Campaigns, Congress, and Courts,* p. 34.

34. 54 Stat. 767 (1940).

35. Mutch, *Campaigns, Congress, and Courts,* p. 35.

36. Louise Overacker, *Presidential Campaign Funds* (Boston University Press, 1946), p. 34.

37. Ibid., p. 50.

38. 57 Stat. 167 (1943).

39. 61 Stat. 136 (1947). In overriding Truman's veto, House members cast 331 votes in favor of the bill, with a majority of both parties supporting it. At the time, the 331 votes was the largest vote ever recorded in the House to override a veto. See Fred A. Hartley Jr., *Our New National Labor Policy* (New York: Funk and Wagnalls, 1948), p. 91.

40. Mutch, *Campaigns, Congress, and Courts,* pp. 154–59.

41. Frank J. Sorauf, "Political Action Committees," in *Campaign Finance Reform: A Sourcebook,* Anthony Corrado and others, p. 123 (Brookings, 1997).

42. Alexander, *Financing Politics,* p. 71

43. Joseph E. Cantor, *Political Spending by Organized Labor: Background and Current Issues,* Report for Congress 96-484 GOV (Congressional Research Service, May 29, 1996), pp. 1–2.

44. Bernadette A. Budde, "Business Political Action Committees," in *Parties, Interest Groups, and Campaign Finance Laws,* edited by Michael J. Malbin (Washington: American Enterprise Institute, 1980), p. 10.

45. George Thayer, *Who Shakes the Money Tree?* (New York: Simon and Schuster, 1973), p. 88.

46. President's Commission on Campaign Costs, *Financing Presidential Campaigns* (Washington, 1962).

47. Foreign Investors Tax Act, Pub. L. 89-809. Mutch, *Campaigns, Congress, and Courts,* pp. 37–39.

48. Alexander, *Financing Politics,* p. 28.

49. Congressional Quarterly, *Dollar Politics* (Washington: Congressional Quarterly Press, 1982), p. 8, and Alexander, *Financing Politics,* p. 11.

50. Alexander, *Financing Politics,* p. 5. See also Herbert E. Alexander, *Financing the 1968 Election* (Lexington, Mass.: Lexington Books, 1971), pp. 79–86.

51. Pub. L. 92-255.

52. Herbert E. Alexander, *Financing the 1972 Election* (Lexington, Mass.: Lexington Books, 1976), pp. 78, 80.

53. For a review of the Watergate scandal and the financial improprieties of the 1972 Nixon presidential campaign, see Alexander, *Financing the 1972 Election,* pp. 39–76.

54. Pub. L. 93-443.

55. Pub. L. 92-178.

56. Pub. L. 93-625.

57. Pub. L. 95-600.

58. Pub. L. 99-514.

59. Pub. L. 94-283.

60. Pub. L. 96-187.

61. Association of the Bar of the City of New York Commission on Campaign Finance Reform, *Dollars and Democracy: A Blueprint for Campaign Finance Reform* (Fordham University Press, 2000), p. 155.

62. Pub. L. 98-355.

63. Pub. L. 101-194.

64. Frank J. Sorauf, *Money in American Elections* (Glenview, Ill.: Scott, Foresman, 1988), pp. 78–79.

65. Ibid., pp. 73–77.

66. FEC Advisory Opinion 1975-23.

67. See FEC Advisory Opinions 1978-10 and 1978-50.

68. See, among others, FEC Advisory Opinions 1979-17 and 1982-5.

69. Pub. L. 99-514.

70. Pub. L. 103-66.

71. Pub. L. 104-79.

72. See FEC, *Record* 22 (November 1996): 2; and 61 *Federal Register* 42371.

73. Pub. L. 106-58.

74. FEC, "Mandatory Electronic Filing Rules Published," press release, June 23, 2000, p. 1. Instead of placing themselves under the same requirements as presidential and House candidates, senators decided to continue the practice of having Senate candidates file official reports with the Secretary of the Senate, who then sends the reports to the FEC. Senate candidates, however, are invited to file "unofficial" copies of their reports electronically with the FEC.

75. For a discussion of section 527 as it applies to political committees, see Milton Cerny and Frances R. Hill, "Political Organizations," *Tax Notes,* April 29, 1996, p. 651, and Frances R. Hill, "Probing the Limits of Section 527 to Design a New Campaign Finance Vehicle," *Exempt Organization Tax Review,* November 1999, p. 205.

76. Common Cause, *Under the Radar: The Attack of "Stealth PACs" on Our Nation's Elections* (Washington: 2000), and "McCain Camp Files FEC Complaint Charging 'Clean Air' Ads Violate Law," *BNA Money and Politics Report,* March 7, 2000, p. 1.

77. Pub. L. 106-230, 114 Stat. 477.

78. Stephen Labaton, "Democrats Say They'll Return about $1.5 Million More in Questionable Gifts," *New York Times* (New England edition), March 1, 1997, p. 8.

79. David E. Rosenbaum, "White House Guests Differ over Solicitation of Money," *New York Times,* September 17, 1997, p. A26, and Tom Squitieri, "Campaign Fund-Raising Probe Turns Focus on Gore," *USA Today,* August 28, 1997, p. 7A.

80. For background on the legislative debate, see Diana Dwyre and Victoria A. Farrar-Myers, *Legislative Labyrinth: Congress and Campaign Finance Reform* (Washington: Congressional Quarterly Press, 2001); and Robert E. Mutch, "The Reinvigorated Reform Debate," in *Financing the 1996 Election,* edited by John C. Green (Armonk, N.Y.: M. E. Sharpe, 1999).

81. FEC, "FEC Reports Increase in Party Fundraising for 2000," press release, May 15, 2001.

82. Kenneth P. Doyle, "McCain-Feingold Supporters Need Only One or Two More Votes to Break Filibuster," *BNA Money and Politics Report,* November 21, 2000, p. 1.

83. Cheryl Bolen, "Petition Gains 218 Signatures, but Reform Bill Still Face Hurdles," *BNA Money and Politics Report,* January 25, 2002, p. 1. A discharge petition is a rarely successful legislative action used to force a committee to report a bill to the House floor. To be successful, a discharge petition requires the signatures of 218 members. Prior to this petition, only eleven discharge petitions had been successful since 1967.

84. Cheryl Bolen, Nancy Ognanovich, and Kenneth P. Doyle, "Daschle Seeks to Move Quickly on House-Passed Campaign Reform Bill," *BNA Money and Politics Report,* February 15, 2002, p. 2. The bill passed by a margin of 240-189, with 198 (of 211) Democrats, 41 Republicans, and one independent voting in favor of the proposal.

85. Karen Foerstel, "Campaign Finance Passage Ends a Political Odyssey," *Congressional Quarterly Weekly Report,* March 23, 2002, p. 799.

86. Pub. L. 107-155.

87. Anthony Corrado, Thomas E. Mann, and Trevor Potter, eds., *Inside the Campaign Finance Battle* (Brookings, 2003), pp. 4–8.

88. *McConnell* v. *FEC,* 251 F. Supp. 2d 176 (D.D.C. 2003).

89. *McConnell* v. *FEC,* 124 S. Ct. 619 (2003).

90. For a summary and background on the provisions of the BCRA, see Joseph E. Cantor and L. Paige Whitaker, *Bipartisan Campaign Reform Act of 2002: Summary and Comparison with Existing Law* (Library of Congress, Congressional Research Service, 2002), and Robert F. Bauer, *Soft Money, Hard Law: A Guide to the New Campaign Finance Law* (Washington: Perkins Coie, 2002). For adjustments based on inflation to federal contribution limits, see FEC, "New Federal Contribution Limits Announced," press release, February 3, 2005.

2

The Current State of
Campaign Finance Law

Trevor Potter

The Federal Election Campaign Act (FECA) was adopted by Congress in 1971. The act was amended substantially in 1974 and again, more recently, by the Bipartisan Campaign Reform Act of 2002 (BCRA, commonly known as the McCain-Feingold law).[1] Congress has written federal campaign finance law broadly, to cover all money spent "in connection with" or "for the purpose of influencing" federal elections. The intent of Congress has always been to regulate all funds raised or spent for federal election purposes. However, in *Buckley* v. *Valeo* and subsequent cases, the Supreme Court defined those statutory phrases to have a more limited reach.[2] The Court held that federal election laws must narrowly and clearly define the activity covered so as not to "chill" speech protected by the First Amendment and that they must give speakers notice that the activity is regulated. In the Supreme Court's latest campaign finance case, *McConnell* v. *FEC,* the Court accepted a clearly delineated but congressional approach to defining the reach of federal regulation of political spending, deferring to Congress's ability to identify and regulate the appearance of corruption or undue influence as a reasonable balance on certain First Amendment rights.[3] This chapter describes the nature and extent of federal campaign finance regulation, particularly limits on campaign contributions and expenditures in connection with federal elections. It also describes the many entities engaged in political speech and spending, from party committees to labor unions to tax-exempt organizations.

Direct Contributions to Federal Candidates and National Committees of Political Parties

Federal law defines "contribution" to include "anything of value" given to a federal candidate or committee, a definition that encompasses not only direct financial contributions, loans, loan guarantees, and the like, but also in-kind contributions of office space and equipment, fundraising expenses, salaries paid to persons who assist a candidate, and the like.[4]

Individuals

Federal law permits individuals to contribute up to $2,100 to a candidate per election.[5] The term "election" under the act includes "a general, special, primary, or run-off election; an individual therefore may contribute up to $2,100 to a candidate's primary campaign and another $2,100 to the general election campaign."[6] Each individual has his or her own limit, so that a couple may give $8,400 in total per election cycle to each federal candidate. In addition, minor children may give if the money given is their own, under their own control and voluntarily contributed—requirements that politically active parents of infants and schoolchildren sometimes ignore.

Individuals also are limited in the amounts that they can contribute to other political entities. BCRA established higher limits for most federal contributions (as a partial response to the elimination of "soft money") and separated the limits for candidate campaign and party committees. Individuals are limited to $26,700 a year in contributions to the federal accounts of a national party committee, such as the Republican National Committee (RNC) or Democratic National Committee (DNC).[7] In addition, individual contributions are limited to $5,000 a year to any other political committee, including a political action committee (PAC).[8] Contributions to state party committees are likewise limited to $5,000 a year. Local party committees are considered part of state party committees, so the $5,000 limit is a combined limit on the two.[9]

In addition to the specific limits on contributions to various candidates and committees, individuals have an aggregate annual federal contribution limit of $101,400 per election cycle.[10] Smaller aggregate limits also apply to categories of contributions: individuals are limited to $61,400 in contributions during an election cycle to federal noncandidate committees, including no more than $37,500 to PACs and state and local parties' federal accounts, and there is a separate $40,000 limit on federal candidate contributions. All of the limits are inflation adjusted, and they will increase modestly for the 2006 election cycle.

Campaign finance laws and Federal Election Commission (FEC) regulations contain a host of exceptions to the definition of "contribution" that apply to individuals. Among the principal exceptions are the donation of personal time to a candidate (unless it is time paid for by someone else, such as an employer), home hospitality of up to $1,000 per candidate per election, and costs of personal travel of up to $1,000 per candidate per election and up to $2,000 a year for party committees.

Political Committees

Whether an organization is a "political committee" required to register with the FEC and subject to the federal limitations on amounts and sources of contributions is a crucial question for any entity engaged in political activity. Federal statutory law defines a "political committee" as

(A) any committee, club, association, or other group of persons which receives contributions aggregating in excess of $1,000 during a calendar year or which makes expenditures aggregating in excess of $1,000 during a calendar year; or

(B) any separate segregated fund established under [the Federal Election Campaign Act]; or

(C) any local committee of a political party which receives contributions aggregating in excess of $5,000 during a calendar year, or makes payments exempted from the definitions of contribution or expenditure as defined [by the act] aggregating in excess of $5,000 during a calendar year, or makes contributions aggregating in excess of $1,000 during a calendar year or makes expenditures aggregating in excess of $1,000 during a calendar year.[11]

In *Buckley* v. *Valeo,* however, the Supreme Court construed the term "political committee" more narrowly than the statute, to "only encompass organizations that are under the control of a candidate or the major purpose of which is the nomination or election of a candidate."[12] In other words, regardless of a noncandidate organization's campaign finance activities, the organization is a political committee under federal law only if its "major purpose" is to nominate or elect a candidate.

Whether an organization is a political committee and thus subject to all the federal election laws or is instead an entity completely unregulated by the FECA and BCRA—though perhaps reporting to the Internal Revenue Service (IRS) as a section 527 political organization—has been the subject of much legal controversy. This is a crucial issue, and the debate will likely continue to be hard fought, because groups that can successfully avoid being categorized as a federal political committee may continue to raise funds—without restriction and with only minimal disclosure requirements—for activities designed to influence federal elections. The debate has centered on whether organizations "organized and operated primarily" for the purpose of influencing the selection of candidates to elected or appointed office (the definition of a section 527 organization) are subject to federal regulation as political committees.

Different forms of federal political committees face differing candidate contribution limits. Political action committees are political committees that may qualify for *multicandidate committee* status. To so qualify, a PAC must demonstrate that it has been registered with the FEC for six months, must receive contributions from at least fifty-one persons, and must contribute to at least five federal candidates.[13] A multicandidate committee may contribute up to $5,000 to a candidate per election and up to $5,000 to other separate PACs each year. In addition, multicandidate committees can contribute up to $15,000 per year to a national party committee, and they have a combined limit of up to $10,000 per year to local and state party committees.

A PAC that does not qualify for multicandidate committee status is limited to contributions of $2,000 per candidate per election, but it may still contribute up to $5,000 to another PAC each year. Such PACs may contribute up to $25,000 a year to national party committees (more than multicandidate committees can), and they have a combined limit of up to $10,000 a year for local and state party committees.

There are two types of noncandidate political committees: nonconnected (or independent) committees and corporate or labor PACs, formally called separate segregated funds (SSFs). Corporations and labor unions may pay all the administrative and solicitation costs of their SSFs, while nonconnected PACs must pay such costs out of the funds that they raise. Corporate and labor PACs, however, face strict rules on whom they may solicit, while nonconnected committees may solicit the general public.

Leadership PACs and Joint Fundraising Committees

Beginning in the 1980s, a number of political committees were established that had an "association" with a member of the congressional leadership. These "leadership PACs" usually use the name of a member of Congress in an honorific capacity such as "honorary chair," and the committee treasurer often is a close associate of the congressional member (and sometimes an employee of the congressional office). Leadership PACs traditionally have been used by legislative leaders to contribute to the campaigns of other members of Congress as a way of gaining a party majority and earning the gratitude of their colleagues or as a way of financing nationwide political activity by party leaders. Leadership PACs may not expend more than $5,000 to elect or defeat a federal candidate, including their "honorary chair."

Members of Congress often personally solicit contributions to "their" leadership PACs, and the news media report contributions and expenditures by the committees as if they were a component of the member's campaign apparatus. Under FEC regulations, all committees "established, financed, maintained or controlled" by the same person or group of persons are "affiliated" and treated as a single committee for the purpose of determining contribution limits.[14] Nevertheless, the FEC has long held that leadership PACs are not "affiliated" with the associated Congress member's campaign committee, a result made explicit by the FEC in 2003.[15] Consequently, leadership PACs do not share a single contribution limit with the candidate's campaign committee.

A leadership PAC may be used to support the campaigns of other candidates and to pay for the associated Congress member's officeholder expenses, because such expenditures are not considered by the FEC to be furthering the associated Congress member's personal campaign for federal office. Leadership PACs may accept contributions of up to $5,000 per person per calendar year (a candidate's campaign committee may accept only contributions of up to $2,000 per person per election). Furthermore, since leadership PACs are not considered an affiliate of the candidate's campaign committee, members of Congress may obtain contributions from the same sources for both committees (a single multicandidate PAC could give $20,000 in an election cycle: $5,000 each for the primary and general elections to the campaign committee and $5,000 per year to the leadership PAC).

However, leadership PACs must take care not to make excessive (more than $5,000) cash or in-kind contributions to the campaign committees of their Congressional sponsors.

Party Committees

FEC regulations define a party committee as "a political committee which represents a political party and is part of the official party structure at the national, state, or local level."[16] A party committee's contribution limits are the same as those for a multicandidate political committee, with three major exceptions:

—For purposes of federal election law (but not necessarily state law), party committees can transfer unlimited federal funds to other party committees without such transfers being treated as contributions.

—A national party committee and the national party senatorial committee may together contribute up to $37,300 to a candidate for the U.S. Senate. The $37,300 limit is for the entire election cycle, rather than for each separate election within the cycle.[17]

—National and state party committees may spend an inflation-adjusted amount for coordinated spending supporting the party's House and Senate candidates; the amount differs by state, depending on the voting age population.

In 1979, Congress amended the FECA to exempt party spending on certain state party-building or volunteer activities from the definition of "contribution" and "expenditure," provided that they were paid for with funds raised under the act ("hard" or "federal" money) by state and local parties and not with funds transferred from the national party committees. The exempted activities include yard signs, pins and bumper stickers, get-out-the-vote programs, and volunteer mailings, but not broadcast advertising or certain activities by paid staff. The exemption has generated years of FEC enforcement investigations and litigation (What is "volunteer" activity? What is a "mass mailing?" When is it paid for by a transfer of funds from a national party committee, using which accounting principles?) because such activity provides an important avenue for state parties to support their federal candidates in priority races outside of federal contribution limits for political parties.

The law now requires state and local parties to finance voter registration activity closely proximate to federal elections, get-out-the-vote activity undertaken in connection with an election in which a federal candidate appears on the ballot, and general public political advertising promoting or attacking clearly identified federal candidates either exclusively with hard money contributions or with a mix of such hard money contributions and so-called "Levin funds."[18]

Expenditures

Campaign finance law defines an *expenditure* to include "(i) any purchase, payment, distribution, loan, advance, deposit, or gift of money or anything of value, made by any person for the purpose of influencing any election for Federal office; and (ii) a written contract, promise, or agreement to make an expenditure."[19] "Expenditure" thus encompasses virtually every payment made in connection with the federal election, including contributions.

Party Committee Expenditures

National and state party committees may expend additional limited amounts for "coordinated" expenditures on behalf of their federal candidates. The amount is based on the voting-age population of the state (or, in the case of House candidates for states with more than one representative, a fixed dollar amount). Such expenditures may be made at any time, but only for the benefit of general election candidates.[20]

Expenditures can pay for goods and services for a candidate, but payments cannot be made directly to the candidate's campaign—that is, party committees may not simply give a candidate money. However, it is important to understand that the expenditures are coordinated with the candidate: they are payments that candidates can specifically request and direct. When a committee makes expenditures independent of a candidate, they are not subject to limits, as explained below.

Independent Expenditures

Independent expenditures are just that—expenditures by individuals and political committees that pertain to elections for federal office but are not coordinated with the candidates seeking office. There are no dollar limits on independent expenditures; *Buckley* v. *Valeo* established that the First Amendment protects the right of individuals and political committees to spend unlimited amounts of their own money on an independent basis to participate in the election process. Independent expenditures, however, must be publicly disclosed through the FEC.

At one time, the FEC presumed that party committees were incapable of making independent expenditures, reasoning that parties and their candidates were so intertwined that there could be no truly uncoordinated expenditures. However, in the first *Colorado Republican Federal Campaign Committee* v. *Federal Election Commission* (*Colorado I*), the Supreme Court ruled that party committees had the same right to make independent expenditures as other committees, if the factual record demonstrates the actual independence of the activity.[21] In the second *Colorado Republican* decision (*Colorado II*), the Court considered the remaining issue in that case: whether party committees may constitutionally be restricted in the amount that they may spend on a coordinated basis to elect their candidates.[22] The Court proceeded to uphold those restrictions, on the grounds that they help prevent circumvention of limits on contributions by individuals to candidates (who, in the absence of party coordinated spending limitations, could arrange for the parties to serve as conduits for contributions in excess of the amounts that individuals may give directly to candidates).

The definition of what constitutes a coordinated expenditure has been clarified over time. The FEC has looked at several criteria in determining the definition. For instance, inside knowledge of a candidate's strategy, plans, or needs; consultation with a candidate or his or her agents about the expenditure; distribution of candidate-prepared material; or use of vendors also used by a candidate were considered by the FEC to be evidence of coordination.[23] Based on the decision of the U.S. District Court for the District of Columbia in *FEC* v. *Christian Coalition,* the FEC issued regulations in December 2000 defining when general public political communications made by outside groups would be considered coordinated with candidates or parties.[24] Those regulations would have found coordination only when the party or candidate controlled the communication or when there was "substantial discussion" between the communication's sponsors and a party or candidate resulting in "collaboration or agreement."[25]

Congress considered the FEC's coordination definition insufficiently comprehensive and, in BCRA, explicitly vacated it. Congress mandated that the FEC promulgate a new regulation defining coordination between outside groups and parties or candidates that addresses a number of factors and, most important, does not require "agreement" or "formal collaboration" to establish coordination.[26]

The FEC responded to Congress by adopting a new coordination rule in 2003. Representatives Christopher Shays and Martin Meehan, sponsors of BCRA in the House, then sued the FEC, alleging that the FEC's new coordination regulation (among other BCRA-related regulations) undermined the language and congressional purposes of BCRA and excluded important forms of coordination. In September 2004, a federal district court ruled in favor of Shays and Meehan and ordered the FEC to rewrite fifteen of its BCRA-related rules, including the 2003 coordination rule.[27] The FEC is currently engaged in a rewriting of the regulations invalidated in *Shays* v. *FEC,* and it also has appealed the district court decision to the D.C. Circuit Court of Appeals.

Electioneering Communications

Perhaps the most significant change in federal campaign finance law resulting from Congress's adoption of BCRA was the new prohibition on the use of corporate or union funds for "electioneering communications." Electioneering communications are defined as broadcast, cable, or satellite communications referring to a clearly identified candidate for federal office, airing within sixty days of the candidate's general election or thirty days of the candidate's primary election, and targeting the candidate's electorate. The definition was crafted to encompass what have been referred to as "sham issue ads" paid for with corporate or labor union funds—ads that clearly intend to influence an election but avoid the use of *Buckley*'s "magic words" (for example, "vote for," "vote against," "support," "oppose") and so escape federal regulation as political express advocacy expenditures (see the discussion of issue advocacy in chapter 7).

Federal law requires disclosure of payments made for electioneering communications and also prohibits the use of corporate or union treasury funds for electioneering communication payments. The Supreme Court in *McConnell* upheld BCRA's electioneering communication provisions against constitutional challenge, holding that the record in the case showed that such communications often are intended to influence federal elections—and achieve that effect—and that therefore they may be regulated by Congress.[28]

Prohibited Contributions, Expenditures, and Payments for Electioneering Communications

While individuals (except candidates using their own funds) and organizations are limited in their ability to make contributions in connection with federal elections, others are entirely prohibited by law from making contributions, expenditures, and payments for electioneering communications.

National Bank, Corporation, and Labor Organization Prohibitions

It is unlawful for any national bank or any corporation organized by authority of any law of Congress, any other corporation, or any labor organization to make contributions, expenditures, or payments for electioneering communications in connection with a federal election or for anyone to accept such contributions. Thus corporations and unions cannot contribute their general treasury funds to a federal candidate (PAC funds, contributed voluntarily by individuals for such purposes, are not covered by the provision). This broad prohibition is subject to three significant exceptions.

—*Nonprofit issue advocacy groups exemption.* The Supreme Court ruled in *FEC* v. *Massachusetts Citizens for Life* (*MCFL*) and *McConnell* that certain small, ideologically based nonprofit corporations must be exempt from the prohibition on independent expenditures and electioneering communications by corporations in connection with federal elections.[29] FEC regulations contain the criteria that a corporation must meet to be exempt under these rulings. According to the FEC, such a corporation:

(1) must have as its only express purpose the promotion of political ideas;[30]

(2) cannot engage in business activities other than fundraising expressly describing the intended political use of donations;

(3) can have:

(i) No shareholders or other persons, other than employees and creditors with no ownership interest, affiliated in any way that could allow them to make a claim on the corporation's assets or earnings; and

(ii) No persons who are offered or who receive any benefit that is a disincentive for them to disassociate themselves with the corporation on the basis of the corporation's position on a political issue;[31]

(4) . . . cannot be established by a business corporation or labor organization or accept anything of value from business corporations or labor organizations.[32]

If those criteria are satisfied, the corporation may make unlimited *independent expenditures* in connection with a federal election.[33]

If a qualified *MCFL* corporation has aggregate independent expenditures of more than $250 in a single year, it must report the expenditures to the FEC, as with any other independent expenditure. *MCFL* corporations also must certify to the FEC that the corporation meets the qualifying criteria for the *MCFL* exemption.

—*The press exemption.* The second major exception to the corporate prohibition exempts certain press activities from the definitions of "expenditure" and "electioneering communication."[34] The definitions specifically exclude any news story, commentary, or editorial distributed through the facilities of any broadcasting station, newspaper, magazine, or other periodical publication, unless such facilities are owned or controlled by any political party, political committee, or candidate. According to the legislative history of the press exemption from the definition of "expenditure," Congress included the provision to indicate that it did not intend "to limit or burden in any way the first amendment freedoms of the press" and to ensure "the unfettered right of the newspapers, TV networks, and other media to cover and comment on political campaigns."[35]

Thus any qualifying media organization can make expenditures and electioneering communications in connection with federal elections provided that the organization falls within the bounds of the exemption. The FEC historically has employed a three-part test to determine the applicability of the press exemption to a particular corporation. In order to qualify for the press exemption, the corporation must

—be a press entity as described by the federal statute (that is, a broadcasting station, newspaper, magazine, or other periodical publication)

—not be owned or controlled by a political party, political committee, or candidate

—must be acting as a press entity in conducting the activity at issue (for example, a TV broadcasting station may not claim the media exemption for expenditures related to sending candidate endorsement literature to voters by mail).[36]

Despite the seemingly clear three-part test, challenges to the application of the press exemption arose during the 2004 presidential election. The greatest difficulty involves determining whether a corporation is a legitimate press entity. Given BCRA's prohibition of direct soft money contributions to political parties and restrictions on electioneering communications, an increasing number of corporations will likely seek through the press exemption an alternative way to support parties and candidates in federal elections.

For example, the National Rifle Association (NRA) is a corporation generally prohibited from using treasury funds to make contributions, expenditures, or payments for electioneering communications. In June 2004, however, the NRA launched a satellite radio news program to discuss the 2004 federal elections. Reasonable minds could disagree as to whether the NRA is an actual news entity or simply a corporation seeking to influence federal elections through its expenditure of treasury funds.

—*Internal communications exemption.* All corporations are permitted to communicate with their *restricted class* whenever they so choose, and labor unions may likewise communicate with their members. A corporation's restricted class is defined as its stockholders and its executive or administrative personnel and their families.[37] Thus a corporation can send mailings endorsing a particular candidate to its restricted class. Similarly, a corporation could invite a candidate to appear before its restricted class and endorse the candidate in connection with the event. However, the corporation must take steps to ensure that only its restricted class receives such communications. Communications with the restricted class generally are not regulated by the FEC, but internal communications costing more than $2,000 per election that expressly advocate the election or defeat of a candidate must be reported.[38]

The exemption for communications with members has been used by labor unions for voter registration drives, telephone banks to turn out the vote on election day, and candidate endorsements. Such communications may be expressly partisan in nature, but they can be directed only to a union's members or to a corporation's restricted class, *not* to the general public (see the discussion of general issue advocacy below and in chapter 7).

Foreign National Prohibitions

For many years there was no ban on foreign contributions, but in 1938, in the face of evidence that Nazi Germany was spending money to influence the U.S. political debate, Congress passed the Foreign Agents Registration Act. The act required agents of foreign entities engaged in publishing political "propaganda" to register and disclose their activities, but it did not regulate political contributions. After congressional hearings in 1962–63 revealed campaign contributions to federal candidates by Philippine sugar producers and agents of Nicaraguan president Luis Somoza, Congress moved in 1966 to prohibit political contributions in *any* U.S. election by any foreign government, political party, corporation, or individual, except foreign nationals who are permanent residents of the United States.[39]

In 1976, the Federal Election Campaign Act incorporated and enhanced the 1966 prohibition.[40] The FECA now directly prohibits foreign nationals from making a "contribution *or donation of money or other thing of value*" in connection with a federal, state, or local election; a "contribution *or donation to a committee of a political party*"; or an expenditure, independent expenditure, or disbursement for an electioneering communication.[41] Federal law prohibits a presidential inaugural committee from accepting donations from foreign nationals—the only restriction on inaugural committee funding. The law also prohibits any person from soliciting, accepting, or receiving such a contribution or donation from a foreign national.[42] It defines "foreign national" as

(1) a foreign principal, as such term is defined by section 611(b) of title 22, except that the term "foreign national" shall not include any individual who is a citizen of the United States;[43] or

(2) an individual who is not a citizen of the United States and who is not lawfully admitted for permanent residence, as defined by section 1101(a)(20) of title 8.[44]

The prohibition also operates to prevent domestic subsidiaries of foreign corporations from establishing PACs if the foreign parent finances the PAC's establishment, administration, or solicitation costs or if individual foreign nationals within the corporation make decisions for the PAC, participate in its operation, or serve as its officers.[45] Similarly, foreign nationals may not participate in the selection of the individuals who run the PAC.

The foreign national ban was strengthened in BCRA to counter arguments that foreign soft money was not prohibited in the 1996 election because it did not meet the definition of a contribution. The FEC then adopted broad regulations implementing the prohibition on foreign spending "in connection with" any election in the United States.[46]

Federal Contractor Prohibition

Federal campaign finance law prohibits anyone who contracts with the United States or any of its departments or agencies to make any contribution to any political party, committee, or candidate for public office, and no such contribution may be solicited from any person between the time of negotiations and completion of the contract. However, federal contractors that are corporations can establish federal PACs.[47]

"In the Name of Another" Prohibition

The law also provides that "no person shall make a contribution in the name of another person or knowingly permit his name to be used to effect such a contribution, and no person shall knowingly accept a contribution made by one person in the name of another person."[48] This section is often enforced in connection with other prohibitions. For example, when a foreign national gives money to a U.S. citizen to be contributed to a federal candidate, two provisions are violated: the one governing foreign contributions and the one governing contributions in the name of another. The same is true if a corporation reimburses an executive for a political contribution.[49]

The Presidential System

Since 1976, the United States has had a system of voluntary public funding for presidential candidates. The system has two components: partial matching funding for presidential primary candidates and full public funding for major party presidential nominees in a general election. The law provides for some public funding for minor party candidates in proportion to their percentage of the votes cast.

Major Parties (Democrats and Republicans)

The contribution and expenditure limits described above apply to all federal elections other than presidential campaigns. Presidential elections are partially publicly funded. Once a major party presidential candidate meets certain requirements, his or her primary or general election campaign or both may choose to receive U.S. government funding from the Treasury accounts funded by the $3 voluntary income tax form check-off.

Presidential Primaries

If candidates choose to participate in the primary funding system, their campaigns are funded through a combination of public and private funding. The partial public funding is provided in matching funds, with public funds matching up to $250 of a single individual's contributions. To qualify for funding, a candidate must demonstrate nationwide support by raising at least $5,000 in individual contributions of up to $250 each in at least twenty separate states. Participating candidates must also agree, among other things, to

—limit primary spending to an inflation-adjusted amount—approximately $37 million in 1996, $45 million in 2000, and $50 million in 2004

—limit spending in each primary state to a specific amount that increases with population

—limit spending of personal funds to $50,000.

Once the requirements are met or agreed to, the candidate can receive matching payments.[50]

Private contributions for presidential candidates are limited as in other federal elections. Individuals may contribute up to $2,100 to a presidential primary campaign committee, and qualified multicandidate PACs can contribute up to $5,000.

The General Election

Once a candidate becomes the nominee of a major party, he or she becomes eligible for a public grant ($67.56 million in 2000 and $74.62 million in 2004). To receive the funds, however, the candidate must agree to spend no more than the grant received and not to accept private contributions.[51] In addition, the two major party national committees may each spend an amount adjusted for the voting-age population ($13.7 million in 2000 and $16.2 million in 2004) in coordination with their presidential candidates.[52] That amount is separate from any get-out-the-vote or generic party-building activities the parties conduct. During the 2004 election cycle, both parties made independent expenditures on behalf of their presidential candidate and collaborated with their candidate in financing "hybrid" communications, which included both generic party messages as well as candidate-related messages.

Candidates Not Accepting Public Funds

Candidates are not required to accept public funds in either the primary or general elections, and those who refuse public funds are permitted to spend as much of their own money as they wish to support their campaigns and as much money as they can raise in contributions from others within the federal contribution limits. As a result, a candidate who refused public funding would have no per-state spending limit or overall spending limit in the primary campaign (Steve Forbes in 1996; George W. Bush in 2000; and Howard Dean, John Kerry, and President Bush in 2004) and no spending limit in the general election campaign (Ross Perot in 1992). Candidates who do not opt into the system for a primary election may opt into it for the general election.

Convention Funding

Each of the major parties' nominating conventions may also be paid for, in part, by public funding.[53] Each major party received a grant of $13.51 million in 2000 and $14.9 million in 2004 to finance its nominating convention. Minor parties may qualify for convention funding based on their presidential candidate's share of the popular vote in the preceding election. The Reform Party received $2.5 million in convention funding in 2000.

Political parties that accept convention funding may spend in connection with the convention only the amount of public funds that they receive. However, the host city and other sponsors support conventions in a variety of ways. The city, through its host committee (a federally registered committee created to support convention activities) may spend money promoting itself as a convention location, pay for the convention hall, and provide local transportation and related services to the convention.[54] In addition, the host city itself may directly accept unlimited cash and in-kind contributions, which often are received by a tax-deductible entity.[55] In some circumstances, corporations also can provide goods (such as automobiles) free to a convention as part of a promotional program. Such exemptions, as interpreted by the FEC, have in practice resulted in extensive convention-related fundraising by the host city and the political parties, usually raising individual, corporate, and labor funds for the convention that are far greater in total than the federal grant. Conventions now have "official" airlines, computer companies, car rental agencies, and the like, all in addition to the federal grants to the political parties.

Third and Minor Party Presidential Candidates

Minor parties (those that received at least 5 percent but no more than 25 percent of the popular vote in the preceding presidential election) and new parties (a party that is not a major or minor party) may also receive partial public funding for the general election, in some instances. New and minor party candidates may accept private contributions, but only within the general limits on such contributions.

A candidate who agrees to abide by the restrictions on publicly funded presidential candidates (including an FEC audit and a $50,000 limit on the use of personal funds) and who then meets a threshold of 5 percent of the general election vote will receive public funding based on his or her share of the vote, but not until *after* the election.[56] (Days after the 1980 general election, independent John Anderson became the first candidate to receive "retroactive" funding, based on unofficial vote totals showing that he had received nearly 7 percent of the popular vote.) In subsequent elections, an individual who has received 5 percent or more of the vote in a previous general election—or the nominee of a minor party whose candidate received 5 percent or more of the vote in a previous general election—may be eligible to receive general election funding *before* the election.[57] The most prominent example is Ross Perot, who ran as an independent in 1992, then appeared on most state ballots as the nominee of the Reform Party in 1996. Even though Perot had not run under the Reform Party banner in 1992, he received general election public funding in 1996 based on his 1992 general election vote total. Likewise, Pat Buchanan—judged to be the Reform Party nominee in 2000 in the wake of party infighting—received $12.6 million in general election public funding based on Perot's 8 percent general election showing in 1996.

In addition, minor party candidates may be eligible for primary funding as well. Examples include Lyndon H. LaRouche, who appeared on the ballot in several states as the candidate of the U.S. Labor Party in 1976 but failed to qualify for public funding in that year's general election. Beginning in 1980, however, LaRouche sought the Democratic Party's nomination for president several times. He secured matching funds for most of those primary campaigns by receiving the necessary individual contributions to meet the statutory criteria for "nationwide support." Similarly, Lenora Fulani received matching funds when she sought the New Alliance Party nomination in 1988 and 1992. However, because of the 5 percent threshold, she failed to qualify for general election funding in both years. In the 2000 presidential elections, Green Party, Reform Party, and Natural Law party candidates received primary funding. No minor party candidates qualified for primary funding in 2004, but Ralph Nader qualified for matching funds as an independent and received slightly more than $865,000 for the 2004 election cycle.

The End of Party Soft Money

In a series of advisory opinions issued in the 1980s, the FEC allowed state and national party committees to accept funds from sources and in amounts otherwise prohibited by federal election law, provided that the funds were placed in separate, "nonfederal" accounts and not used for federal election purposes.

Over time, the FEC created a complex system of allocation formulas regulating the proportions of hard and soft money that party committees could use for "generic" party activity (administration, overhead, get-out-the-vote drives that do not mention specific candidates, issue ads, and so forth), fundraising, and "exempt activities" mentioning federal and nonfederal candidates (sample ballots, slate cards, bumper stickers, and so forth). National—but not state and local—party committees also were required to disclose soft money donations to the FEC.

By the end of the 1996 election, the claim that nonfederal or soft monies were not used for federal election purposes had become farcical. President Clinton personally raised soft money, telling donors that it would assist his reelection, and then selected the states in which it would be spent—on such items as broadcast advertisements praising him and attacking his general election opponent, Senator Bob Dole. The RNC and Senator Dole largely followed suit, with Senator Dole famously saying of the soft money ads, "I hope it's obvious they're about me—I'm the only person in them." The funds for those party advertisements came from very large contributions from corporations and unions not permitted to spend money in federal elections and from individuals who clearly had an interest in the outcome of the election.

In 2002, BCRA outlawed many of the soft money practices sanctioned over the years by the FEC. The new campaign finance law prohibits federal candidates and national party committees from receiving, soliciting, or spending funds not subject to the law's limits, prohibitions, and reporting requirements. That provision serves to ban corporate and labor treasury contributions to national party committees and limit individual and PAC contributions to $25,000 and $15,000 per national party committee per year respectively. BCRA's national party soft money ban extends also to entities "directly or indirectly established, financed, maintained or controlled" by a national party committee, as well as to officers and agents acting on behalf of a national party committee.[58]

BCRA also prevents state, local, and district party committees from spending nonfederal funds on voter registration activity within 120 days of a regularly scheduled federal election; get-out-the-vote, voter identification, and generic campaign activity in connection with an election in which a federal candidate appears on the ballot; and general public political advertising promoting or attacking clearly identified federal candidates (not only advertisements containing express advocacy). A narrow exception permits party committees to spend $10,000 of each donor's permissible nonfederal contribution per year in combination with hard money on voter drive activities that do not mention federal candidates, subject to a number of strict conditions relating to the solicitation and receipt of these federal and nonfederal funds.

Restrictions on Political Fundraising by Members of Congress and Executive Branch Officials

Several statutes regulate the location and form of political fundraising. Most are designed to protect federal employees from pressure to contribute to federal candidates and parties, but one simply prohibits any solicitation or receipt of a federal contribution in a federal workplace. The statutes carry criminal or civil penalties, and their intricacies have been the focus of much attention following reported fundraising activities at the White House during the 1996 election.

A series of criminal provisions makes it unlawful for anyone to attempt to obtain a political contribution from a government employee by means of threat of firing; for a candidate for Congress or federal employee or officer to solicit a campaign contribution from any other federal employee or officer; for a federal officer or employee to contribute to his or her employer's campaign; for any person to solicit a political contribution from someone known to be entitled to funds for federal "work relief"; or for anyone to demote or threaten to demote a federal employee for giving or withholding a political contribution.[59]

In addition, it is a criminal offense (subject to a fine of up to $5,000 or three years in jail or both) for any person to "solicit or receive a donation of money or other thing of value in connection with a Federal, State or local election from a person who is located in a room or building occupied in the discharge of official duties by an officer or employee of the United States."[60] Congress is specifically exempted from the receipt portion of the provision, provided that any funds received are transferred within seven days to a federal political committee and that the contributors were not told to send or deliver the money to the federal office building. During the 1996 investigations of fundraising by President Clinton and Vice President Gore, the attorney general indicated that the Justice Department would pursue prosecutions under this law only if "aggravating factors"—such as coercion or knowing disregard for the law—were present.[61]

Soft Money Fundraising

BCRA amended the provision on fundraising on federal property to cover "a donation of money or other thing of value in connection with a Federal, state or local election," clarifying that the prohibition covers solicitations for soft money.[62] The act also more generally restrains soft money fundraising by federal officeholders and candidates, entities that they establish or control, and their agents—wherever they or a prospective donor may be located. Such individuals and entities may not solicit, direct, receive, transfer, or spend soft money in connection with a federal election, including for general public political advertisements promoting or attacking federal candidates or for get-out-the-vote drives (they would be limited to soliciting hard money in those instances). Along the same lines, they may not solicit soft money for state and local parties to spend on "Federal election activities," though they may attend and speak at state or local party fundraisers. In soliciting funds solely for state and local elections, federal officeholders and candidates may seek donations only from permissible hard money donors in amounts that correspond to the hard money contribution limits (for example, a federal officeholder could suggest that an individual contribute $2,100 to the general election campaign of a gubernatorial candidate but could not ask for corporate or labor treasury contributions to that candidate).[63] In addition to these general rules, BCRA provides more specific guidance regarding permissible solicitations by federal officeholders and candidates on behalf of section 501(c) tax-exempt organizations.

Congress

As noted above, the prohibition on receiving contributions in a federal building does not apply to Congress, as long as certain conditions are met. However, the ban on solicitations from a federal workplace does apply to Congress.

The Committee on Standards of Official Conduct has reminded House members that, entirely aside from the criminal statute, the rules of the House also regulate political fundraising and "are quite specific, and quite restrictive."[64] Under House rules, *"Members and staff may not solicit political contributions in their office or elsewhere in the House buildings, whether in person, over the telephone, or otherwise"* [emphasis in original]. Added the committee, "The rule bars *all* political solicitations in these House buildings. Thus, a telephone solicitation would not be permissible merely because, for example, the call is billed to the credit card of a political organization or to an outside telephone number, or it is made using a cell phone in the hallway." Nor may House telephone numbers be left for a return call if the purpose is solicitation of a political contribution, according to the committee. The memo responds to claims that members of Congress were using cellular telephones in their offices or raising funds in the Capitol instead of using cubicles set aside for fundraising telephone calls in office buildings near the Capitol owned by the Democratic and Republican campaign committees.

The Senate also has rules that regulate campaign activity in Senate buildings and the Capitol and restrict the number of members of a Senator's staff who may handle campaign contributions.[65]

The Hatch Act

The Hatch Act, first passed by Congress in 1939, during President Franklin Roosevelt's second administration, to protect federal employees from political pressure, bans all executive branch federal employees from knowingly soliciting, accepting, or receiving a political contribution from any person (see chapter 1 of this volume).[66] Although "political contribution" is broadly defined as "any gift . . . made for any political purpose," the penalty for violation of the Hatch Act (with discretion not to prosecute) is either thirty days' suspension without pay or removal of the employee from his or her position. The Hatch Act has no criminal penalties.

Political Advertising

Congress and the courts have long debated the extent to which political advertising should and could be constitutionally regulated. For many years, the distinction between "express advocacy" and "issue advocacy" was seen to be the dividing line. The Supreme Court first distinguished between advertising that advocated the election or defeat of political candidates (express advocacy) and advertising related to political issues (issue advocacy) in its 1976 *Buckley* decision. Amendments to the FECA in 1974 contained two expenditure-related provisions that led to that distinction by the Court. One provision restricted independent expenditures "relative to a clearly identified candidate." The other required disclosure of expenditures used "for the purpose of . . . influencing" a federal election.[67]

When the constitutionality of those provisions was before the Supreme Court in *Buckley*, the Court found the phrases "relative to" and "for the purpose of . . . influencing" unconstitutionally vague for defining an expenditure by persons or organizations not already political committees. The Court reinterpreted the term "expenditure" to be limited to communications that included explicit words of advocacy of election or defeat of a candidate. In a footnote, the Court provided examples of such words, including "vote for," "elect," "support," "defeat," and "reject."[68] Those phrases quickly became known in the world of campaign finance law as *Buckley*'s "magic words."

From the 1976 *Buckley* decision until Congress's adoption of BCRA in 2002, a nonfederal committee advertisement was not subject to federal campaign finance laws unless it contained express advocacy using the magic words or similar language with a clear and unmistakable meaning. Instead, such an advertisement would be deemed issue advocacy and not subject to federal campaign finance laws, even if broadcast in the midst of an election campaign with the only visible "issue" being a candidate's competence for office. This legal distinction between express and issue advocacy had at least two significant consequences in federal elections.

First, although federal law prohibited corporations and unions from making express advocacy expenditures from treasury funds, they could spend unlimited treasury funds on issue advocacy. Second, federal laws requiring disclosure of expenditures did not apply to issue advocacy, so individuals, corporations, and labor unions were free to raise and spend undisclosed amounts of money from undisclosed sources by avoiding the use of magic words. In short, issue advocacy escaped federal regulation altogether.

Congress enacted BCRA in 2002 in part to address the problem of unregulated soft money issue advocacy spending and to restore efficacy to the long-standing ban on corporate and union expenditures. Congress repudiated the long-ineffective magic words test, enacting a new "bright-line" test—"electioneering communications"—to regulate corporate and union campaign spending.

When the Supreme Court in *McConnell* reviewed the constitutionality of BCRA's electioneering communications provisions, it upheld the provisions in their entirety. The Supreme Court acknowledged the uselessness of using the magic words test to distinguish between campaign speech that can and cannot be constitutionally regulated. The Court reasoned:

> Not only can advertisers easily evade the [*Buckley* bright] line by eschewing the use of magic words, but they would seldom choose to use such words even if permitted. And although the resulting advertisements do not urge the viewer to vote for or against a candidate in so many words, they are no less clearly intended to influence the election. *Buckley's* express advocacy line, in short, has not aided the legislative effort to combat real or apparent corruption.[69]

The Court observed "the overwhelming evidence that the line between express advocacy and other types of election-influencing expression is . . . functionally meaningless."[70]

The Court conclusively rejected the *McConnell* plaintiffs' central argument that the express advocacy test was a constitutional mandate, emphasizing that it was instead "an endpoint of statutory interpretation, not a first principle of constitutional law."[71] The Court said that in *Buckley* it had resorted to interpreting the statutory language at issue as limited in scope to express advocacy in order to save the statute from being held void for vagueness, but that case "in no way drew a constitutional boundary that forever fixed the permissible scope of provisions regulating campaign-related speech."[72] The Court continued:

> Nor are we persuaded . . . that the First Amendment erects a rigid barrier between express advocacy and so-called issue advocacy. That notion

cannot be squared with our longstanding recognition that the presence or absence of magic words cannot meaningfully distinguish electioneering speech from a true issue ad.[73]

In sum, the Supreme Court in *McConnell* made clear that individuals and organizations do not possess a First Amendment right to engage in unlimited advertising referring to federal candidates financed by undisclosed sources immediately before an election. The *McConnell* Court upheld the regulation of *all* electioneering communications even if they not always—but only *often*—are intended to influence an election. Electioneering communications that are not so intended—those that may be "genuine" issue ads—are nonetheless still permissibly regulated by the statute because they fall within the scope of the statutory bright-line test and because the statute provides acceptable alternatives (for example, a corporation's or union's connected political committee subject to contribution limits and disclosure requirements) that allow speakers to convey their messages.

The distinction between "express" and "issue" advocacy remains relevant during the periods not covered by BCRA's electioneering communication provisions (that is, more than sixty days before a general election or thirty days before a primary election or party convention), although the Supreme Court's attack on its literalness leaves open the possibility that the courts and the FEC may now take a broader view of what constitutes "expressly advocating" a candidate's election or defeat.

Another aspect of political advertising relates to expenditures and payments for electioneering communications coordinated between the advertiser and a candidate's campaign. Under federal law, an expenditure or payment for an electioneering communication that is controlled by or coordinated with a candidate is deemed a contribution to the candidate and is subject to the applicable federal contribution limit.

The Internet

As discussed in detail in chapter 9, the Internet and e-mail are relatively new but increasingly important platforms for campaign activity relating to federal elections and the expression of political opinion. Like businesses and the media, party committees, candidates, and issue groups are attracted to the Internet because it enables them to transmit information in the desired format quickly, to either broad or highly specific audiences, at relatively low cost. Indeed, campaigns have used e-mail and the Internet to solicit political contributions, mobilize voters, and recruit volunteers, among other things.[74] The Internet also facilitates the receipt of information from voters. Unsurprisingly, campaign websites now accept donations by credit card.[75]

The FEC has had to consider the applicability of the FECA—written long before the age of cyberspace—to Internet and e-mail communications. Its deliberations in this regard have affected not only parties and candidates but also private citizens and outside groups. For example, what if a private citizen operating his or her own website posts an express advocacy message ("Vote for Candidate X") on the site? Is that an "independent expenditure" costing more than $200, subject to reporting requirements under the FECA? Is it a "contribution" to the promoted candidate? What if a union provides a link to the website of a candidate whom it endorses for election—is that an illegal contribution to a candidate?

Until now, the FEC has proceeded in a piecemeal manner in this area—resolving discrete questions through advisory opinions and narrow rulemaking. In November 1999, the FEC issued a notice of inquiry regarding the use of the Internet for campaign activity and received more than 1,300 comments, most urging the commission not to subject Internet communications to any form of regulation.[76] The commission followed up by inviting public comment on a draft set of regulations dealing only with the issues of Internet activities of campaign volunteers and of links and candidate endorsements posted on corporate or labor websites.[77] However, the commission never voted on any version of the draft rules.

The FEC's advisory opinions in this area have on some occasions found Internet communications to trigger restrictions or reporting requirements under the FECA, though the trend seems to be toward resisting regulation of online campaigning. For example, the FEC ruled in 1998 that if an individual creates a website expressly advocating the election of a federal candidate, the costs of that website (for example, the fee to secure registration of the domain name) must be reported as an independent expenditure if they are greater than $250 per year. Moreover, the website would have to post a disclaimer indicating who paid for the advertisement and whether it was authorized by a candidate or the candidate's committee.[78] However, the commission has more recently held that the costs of websites or e-mails supporting a campaign prepared by campaign volunteers using their home computers (including the re-publication of candidate materials) did not result in a contribution to a campaign.[79] Along the same lines, websites (including those of corporations) that provide candidate-related content that is nonpartisan in nature would not be considered to have made an expenditure or contribution to mentioned candidates.[80]

Then, as part of its BCRA-required rulemaking, the FEC adopted a regulation defining "public communication" that excluded all Internet communications. That regulatory definition had great significance in the context of coordinated expenditures. Under the regulation, candidates would be free to coordinate with Internet advertisers without the coordinated advertising expenditures being deemed a contribution from the advertiser to the candidate. Further, state parties could spend unlimited soft monies on Internet communications, including advertisements. However, because of these consequences, the regulation was challenged and invalidated by the district court in *Shays* v. *FEC.*[81] The FEC currently is considering new rules that would deal with these and other Internet issues.

Other Players in the Arena

Other significant entities play a role in political campaigns, including unions, corporations, and section 501(c)(4), section 501(c)(3), and section 527 organizations.

Unions

Campaign finance law and FEC regulations treat corporate and union funds similarly. Like corporations, they may not contribute directly to federal candidates. However, they may create and administer a PAC, which they must use to finance any electioneering communications within thirty days of a primary and sixty days of a general election. The Supreme Court in *McConnell* upheld the ban on electioneering communications paid for with union treasury funds, thereby for the first time explicitly approving the equal treatment of unions and corporations, despite the argument that union funds are derived from association members rather than from the legally constructed corporate person.

As membership organizations, unions also may communicate with their members (numbering in the millions) on any subject (including by urging them to vote for specific candidates or parties) and may use union treasury funds to do so. In *Communications Workers of America* v. *Beck,* the Supreme Court determined that under the National Labor Relations Act, nonunion employees could prevent union use of their agency fees (sometimes required as a condition of employment) for political activity.[82] As a result, nonunion employees in closed-shop states cannot be required to fund political spending as a condition of their employment.

That decision has not reduced the political use of agency fees paid to unions by nonmembers to the extent desired and anticipated by union critics. Among other things, the critics attribute this shortcoming to alleged inadequacies in the notice given to nonmembers of their "*Beck* rights," which, under *Beck* and subsequent National Labor Relations Board decisions, unions must provide. However, successive presidential administrations have alternated positions on whether to require government contractors to inform employees of their "*Beck* rights" as well.

On April 13, 1992, President George H. W. Bush issued executive order 12800, which required government contractors to post notices informing their nonunion employees that they could object to use of their union dues for political purposes. On February 1, 1993, however, President Bill Clinton issued executive order 12836, rescinding Executive Order 12800, and referred the issue to the National Labor Relations Board for further consideration. On February 17, 2001, President George W. Bush issued an executive order requiring federal contractors again to post notices informing nonunion employees of their *Beck* rights. However, the U.S. District Court for the District of Columbia struck down the order on the grounds that it was inconsistent with the National Labor Relations Act.[83]

The broader question of the use of dues from union members themselves for political activity was not addressed in *Beck*. Republican party leaders have argued that union members should be given some mechanism for authorizing or restricting the use of their dues for political purposes (perhaps including issue advertising), claiming that a substantial number of union members disagree with the political choices made by union leaders. Proposals to implement this idea are commonly known as "paycheck protection." Democrats and unions have responded that union leaders are freely elected by the membership and thus are only exercising their representative authority. Besides, they add, corporate shareholders do not vote on whether to approve corporate political spending on issue advocacy either. Member dues in any case provide only a portion of the funds available to unions for such communications, so union leaders could probably use other funds for those activities if necessary—for instance, unions reportedly receive tens of millions of dollars annually in fees from members' "affinity" credit cards. During consideration of BCRA in the Senate in 2001, a "paycheck protection" amendment (which was seen as a "poison pill" impairing passage of the McCain-Feingold bill) was defeated.

Corporations

Corporations have been prohibited from contributing to federal candidates since the beginning of the twentieth century, when the first federal campaign finance restrictions were enacted by Congress (see chapter 1 for a detailed description of the history of the ban). However, like unions, corporations still participate in the political process in a variety of ways.

Most visibly, corporations may establish and pay the administrative costs of corporate political action committees (referred to in the law as "separate segregated funds") and may encourage employees and stockholders to contribute personal funds to those committees. In addition, corporations may communicate with their executives and management personnel, urging them to support and contribute to specific parties or candidates, and they may host visits by candidates at corporate facilities, subject to FEC rules. The most important aspect of such internal corporate activity is the ability of corporate executives and PACs to raise funds for federal candidates. The FEC has issued complicated regulations governing such corporate political activity, but fundraising by corporate executives under the rules remains a substantial source of money for federal candidates.

Corporations, like unions, are prohibited from using treasury funds to run electioneering communications thirty days before a primary and sixty days before a general election, but they can fund such advertisements through their affiliated PACs, using voluntarily contributed individual monies in the PAC accounts. Some corporations pay for electioneering-related activities through donations to other groups, such as industry associations—section 501(c)(6) tax-exempt organizations such as the U.S. Chamber of Commerce or Americans for Job Security—or issue-oriented section 501(c)(4)s, such as the Sierra Club or the NRA.

The Supreme Court has held it unconstitutional to prohibit corporations from spending funds to campaign for and against state ballot measures.[84] In states where ballot initiatives often are identified with particular candidates or political parties, that ruling can provide an avenue for a significant direct expenditure of corporate funds that may have the effect of influencing an election.

Section 501(c)(4) Organizations

Section 501(c)(4) of the Tax Code provides for the exemption of "social welfare organizations" from federal income tax. While such organizations must be operated for the promotion of the public social welfare and not for profit, they can engage in political activities as long as those activities do not become their primary purpose.

The Internal Revenue Service interprets that restriction to allow 501(c)(4) organizations to participate in an election by doing such things as rating candidates on a partisan basis.[85] They also may promote legislation.[86] Under FEC regulations, incorporated 501(c)(4)s that qualify as *MCFL* corporations may engage in independent political expenditures and electioneering communications. However, just as in the case of other corporations, campaign finance law prohibits incorporated 501(c)(4)s from making contributions to federal candidates, a ban upheld recently by the Supreme Court in *FEC* v. *Beaumont*.[87]

As more light has been shed on politically active 501(c)(4) organizations, there have been calls for limits on such activities by tax-exempt entities. For instance, the Christian Coalition, an entity that has long sought 501(c)(4) status, has at times played a highly visible role in state and national Republican Party politics, going so far as to claim credit for the Republican success in the 1994 elections and to create a multimillion-dollar war room at the 1996 Republican National Convention. The FEC sued the group, claiming it illegally coordinated its activities (particularly its "voter guide" activities) with federal candidates, resulting in prohibited and unreported contributions to candidates. In a 1999 decision, the U.S. District Court for the District of Columbia largely dismissed the FEC's enforcement action against the Christian Coalition on the grounds that the interactions between the coalition and federal candidates did not rise to the level of "coordination," as a matter of law.[88] Republicans argue that many other groups, especially labor unions, engage in similar activities on behalf of Democrats.

In addition, the IRS appears to be questioning whether some groups may become so partisan in nature or purpose that they advance a narrow private or partisan purpose rather than the general social welfare and thus are not entitled to tax-exempt status. Indeed, the IRS denied that status under section 501(c)(4) to the Christian Coalition, apparently on the grounds that it engaged in excessive partisan political activity (the organization later reorganized as a for-profit corporation known as Christian Coalition International). Likewise, the IRS denied tax-exempt status to the National Policy Forum, headed by former RNC chairman Haley Barbour, on the same basis. Traditionally, both major parties have benefited from such organizations: the Democratic Leadership Council (DLC) is a 501(c)(4) organization that obtained its exemption in the 1980s and was once headed by Bill Clinton, before he became president.

501(c)(3) Organizations

Section 501(c)(3) organizations are tax-exempt entities organized for charitable and other similar purposes and are prohibited by law from intervening in any political campaigns. Therefore the organizations cannot endorse candidates, contribute to campaigns, or organize a political action committee. However, they can conduct nonpartisan voter registration and get-out-the-vote efforts in accord with FEC regulations as well as participate in activities related to state and local ballot measures.[89] In addition, they may sponsor candidate forums on issues of public concern.[90]

Campaign finance laws prohibit party committees from soliciting hard or soft money from or transferring soft money funds to 501(c) tax-exempt organizations that engage in activities in connection with federal elections, including nonpartisan get-out-the-vote and voter registration efforts. The law does not restrict federal officeholders and candidates from raising funds for nonelectoral purposes on behalf of 501(c) tax-exempts that are not principally engaged in electoral activity. However, if a 501(c) organization is principally engaged in such activity (again including nonpartisan get-out-the-vote or voter registration efforts) or if the solicitation is for get-out-the-vote or voter registration activity, the federal officeholder may raise funds only from individuals (as opposed to groups, corporations, and unions) in limited amounts. A federal officeholder may not raise funds for a 501(c) tax-exempt group to engage in issue advocacy advertisements.[91]

Many well-known think tanks are 501(c)(3) organizations, including Brookings, the American Enterprise Institute, Heritage, Cato, the Family Research Council, and the Progressive Policy Institute (associated with the DLC). Some are genuinely nonpartisan, while others appear to be close to one party or group of candidates. In addition, many organizations maintain a collection of entities under one umbrella, such as the Sierra Club (which has a 501(c)(3), a 501(c)(4), and a PAC) and the Club for Growth (which has a 501(c)(4), a PAC, and a section 527 organization). Many of the ethics charges against former House Speaker Newt Gingrich related to his use of just such a collection of organizations, including charitable and educational groups, for political purposes.

527 Organizations

As discussed above, the IRS has sometimes denied 501(c) tax-exempt status to certain organizations because of their partisan political activity. Furthermore, large donations to 501(c)(4)s may be subject to a gift tax. Accordingly, some entities intending to engage in substantial amounts of electioneering have instead organized under section 527 of the Internal Revenue Code. Section 527 provides beneficial tax treatment (that is, exemption from tax except for investment income) for "political organizations"—defined as organizations formed primarily for "the function of influencing or attempting to influence the selection, nomination, election, or appointment of any individual to any federal, State, or local public office or office in a political organization, or the election of Presidential or Vice-Presidential electors."[92]

When Congress wrote section 527 of the Tax Code to clarify that political organizations were not subject to tax, the organizations that fell into that category were political committees—parties, candidate committees, and political action committees at the federal, state and local levels. However, by claiming that their primary purpose is to influence elections in general but not any *specific* election, certain organizations have been able to enjoy the tax benefits of section 527 status without having to register as a federal or state political committee. This mismatch between the Internal Revenue Code and campaign finance laws has spurred the creation of certain types of 527 organizations (sometimes registered as political committees at the state level) that raise unlimited soft money donations and spend them on candidate-specific issue advocacy ads clearly designed to affect federal races. Prominent and well-funded 527s were active at both ends of the ideological spectrum during the 2004 election cycle, from America Coming Together and the Media Fund on the left to Progress for America and the Swift Boat Veterans and POWs for Truth on the right.

Congressional sponsors of reform bills like the section 527 legislation and BCRA and other reform groups have taken the position that any 527 group whose major purpose is to influence federal elections—and that spends more than $1,000 doing so—must register as a political committee with the FEC and use only federal funds for its election activities.

Federal statutory law defines the term "political committee" to mean "any committee, club, association or other group of persons which receives contributions aggregating in excess of $1,000 during a calendar year or which makes expenditures aggregating in excess of $1,000 during a calendar year."[93]

In *Buckley*, the Supreme Court narrowly construed the statutory definition of "political committee" to "only encompass organizations that are under the control of a candidate or the major purpose of which is the nomination or election of a candidate."[94] In *FEC* v. *GOPAC*, a single federal district court further narrowed the "major purpose" test to encompass only "the nomination or election of *a particular candidate or candidates* for federal office"[95] Though many believe that the district court in *GOPAC* misinterpreted the law and incorrectly narrowed the test for qualifying as a "political committee" as set forth by the Supreme Court in *Buckley*, the FEC deadlocked on whether to appeal the district court's decision.

The Supreme Court in *McConnell* restated the "major purpose" test for political committee status as iterated in *Buckley* and made no mention of the *GOPAC* requirement that a *particular* candidate be identified.[96]

Prior to 2000, the Internal Revenue Code did not require section 527 organizations to disclose their contributors and spending. Accordingly, organizations that avoided federal political committee status by engaging solely in electioneering issue advocacy were not subject to meaningful disclosure requirements. Congress intervened, passing legislation requiring 527s (except for federal political committees, state candidate committees, and organizations with less than $25,000 in estimated gross receipts) to disclose to the IRS the names of those who contributed at least $200 to the organization a year, as well as their disbursements to a single person of over $500 a year.[97] The enactment of those requirements reportedly caused certain 527 organizations—such as Citizens for a Better Medicare—to switch to 501(c)(4) tax-exempt status to avoid disclosure.[98]

Congress passed an amendment to the section 527 law on November 2, 2002, that exempted from IRS contributor and expenditure disclosure requirements state PACs that focused exclusively on state-level elections and that already disclosed their contributions and expenditures to state election oversight agencies.

The section 527 law has come under attack from various observers for being either too narrow or too broad. On the other hand, certain public interest groups believe the law must be strengthened to require groups to declare the purpose of each expenditure over the $500 threshold and to impose an electronic filing requirement on 527 organizations receiving or spending $50,000 or more a year.

A number of section 527 organizations were established during the 2004 election cycle. Groups like those mentioned above (ACT, Swift Boat, and others) raised and spent millions of dollars to affect the outcome of the hotly contested presidential race between President George W. Bush and Senator John Kerry. Reform groups estimate that Democratic Party–oriented 527 organizations spent nearly $185 million while Republican-oriented 527 organizations spent $77 million. (Republican-oriented 527s became active only in the last three months of the campaign.) One important element of the 2004 campaign was the amount of money raised and spent by these

Table 2-1. *Summary of Campaign Finance Law, 2005*

Contributors	Federal candidates	National and state party committees	Independent expenditures and express advocacy (not coordinated)	Electioneering communications
Individuals (excluding foreign nationals without U.S. residency permit)	$2,100 per election (subject to aggregate limit)[a]	$26,700 per year and $61,400 per cycle to national committees; $10,000 per year and an aggregate $37,500 per cycle to state party federal accounts (and federal PACs)	Unlimited but must be disclosed to the FEC	Unlimited but must be disclosed to the FEC
Corporations and unions	Prohibited	Prohibited in the case of national committees; prohibited to state party federal accounts	Prohibited	Prohibited
PACs	$5,000 per year	$15,000 per year to national committees; $5,000 per year to state committee federal accounts	Unlimited but must be disclosed	Unlimited but must be disclosed
National party committees	$37,300 to Senate candidates per cycle; $5,000 to presidential and House candidates	Unlimited transfers to other party committees	Unlimited but must be disclosed[b]	Unlimited but must be disclosed
Section 527 organizations not registered with the FEC	Prohibited	Prohibited	Prohibited if incorporated	Prohibited if incorporated. If not incorporated, unlimited[c]
501(c)(4)s and 501(c)(6)s	Prohibited	Prohibited	Prohibited except for qualifying 501(c)(4) *MCFL* corporations	

a. (All figures are indexed for inflation for 2005.) Individuals are subject to an aggregate limit of $101,400 per two-year election cycle. Of that limit, there is a $61,400 limit on federal noncandidate contributions, including no more than $37,500 to PACs and to state/local parties' federal accounts, and a $40,000 limit on federal candidate contributions.

b. The national party can make unlimited independent expenditures for the party's candidate if the national party committee is *not* the designated campaign committee.

c. If not incorporated, unlimited so long as the only funds used are those contributed by individuals and disclosed to the FEC if more than $10,000.

organizations that came from a limited number of very wealthy donors. Forty-one percent (nearly $85 million) of the funding of Democratic-leaning organizations involved with federal elections came from just fourteen wealthy donors. Fifty-two percent ($41.5 million) of the funding of Republican-leaning organizations involved with federal elections came from only eleven wealthy donors.[99]

During the 2004 election cycle, with its multimillion-dollar donations to section 527 organizations and heightened public scrutiny of the problem, congressional sponsors urged the FEC to write regulations to define these 527s as federal political committees subject to "hard money" rules. The FEC reopened a dormant rulemaking, accepted public comment, and held hearings. In the end, after a postponement of ninety days by the FEC on the matter (until it was too late for any rules to apply to the 2004 election cycle), the FEC finally rejected its own staff recommendation regarding the regulation of 527 organizations, and it has taken no action to bring 527s into compliance with the law. It deadlocked 3-3 on whether to continue exploring the issue in its last vote in August 2004, but it did establish allocation ratios for 527 spending that took effect in January 2005.

The inaction of the FEC spurred the filing of two lawsuits against the agency for failure to promulgate new rules regarding the definition of "political committee." Representatives Marty Meehan (D-Mass.) and Christopher Shays (R-Conn.) and President Bush filed suit in the D.C. District Court in the fall of 2004 to force the FEC to address the matter and bring all section 527 organizations under campaign finance regulations. The litigation is ongoing.

Enforcement

The Federal Election Commission

The federal campaign finance laws are enforced by the FEC in the case of civil violations and by the Department of Justice when a criminal violation is charged. The FEC itself has no independent authority to impose penalties except for administrative fines for reporting violations.[100] If, after an investigation, alleged violators of federal campaign finance law are unwilling to sign a settlement agreement and pay a monetary penalty to the U.S. Treasury, then the FEC can vote to sue the offender in federal court, present the evidence to a judge, and ask the court to find a violation and impose a fine.[101]

Penalties sought by the FEC range from a few hundred dollars to hundreds of thousands of dollars, depending on the size and nature of the violation. The law restricts penalties to $5,000 per violation or the amount at issue, whichever is larger, and doubles those sums in the case of knowing and willful violations.[102] (For a detailed discussion of the FEC, see chapter 8.)

When the FEC Deadlocks or Fails to Act

Campaign finance law contains a provision allowing persons whose complaints have been dismissed or otherwise not acted on by the FEC to file suit against the FEC in federal court alleging that the FEC's failure to act was arbitrary and capricious. If successful, the person can obtain a court order requiring the FEC to act on the complaint in accord with the law. If the FEC does not follow the court order within thirty days, the party may sue the alleged campaign law violator directly.[103] A rare recent example of the use of this provision is *Democratic Senatorial Campaign Committee* v. *Federal Election Commission,* when a federal judge held that the FEC had failed in its statutory duty to investigate a Democratic complaint against Republican campaign activity in a number of Senate campaigns in 1992.[104] The judge ruled that the commission's inability to complete its investigative process after four and a half years was an abdication of its enforcement role and as a result gave the Democratic Senatorial Campaign Committee (DSCC) the right to sue the National Republican Senatorial Committee directly in federal district court over the alleged violations. On remand from the appeals court, the district court found that the DSCC lacked standing (see *Akins* discussion to follow) but reconfirmed its prior order finding that the commission unreasonably delayed action on the DSCC complaint.[105]

The statutory right to challenge FEC action or inaction is an unusual provision that has served as the basis for a number of successful challenges to FEC enforcement decisions in the past. However, the right to seek judicial review of FEC actions requires a high standard of proof—that the FEC decision was "arbitrary and capricious"—and is in any case subject to the complainant having "standing" in federal court. As recent D.C. Circuit Court decisions make clear, complainants seeking judicial review of FEC action or nonaction must meet federal requirements regarding standing (the right to file suit) under Article III of the Constitution. They must suffer an "injury-in-fact" caused by the FEC's action (or failure to act) that may be redressed by the court's order. In *FEC* v. *Akins,* the Supreme Court held that if the FEC's failure to bring an enforcement action in a particular case deprived complainants, as voters, of *legally required* information about campaign-related activities, that failure constituted an injury sufficient to confer standing under the FECA (even though the harm may be widely shared).[106] However, the assertion that the FEC's acts deprived voters of information generally is not sufficient to convey standing.[107] In *Common Cause* v. *FEC*, Common Cause was denied the right to challenge the FEC's conclusion of an investigation of Republican Party spending in Montana, even though Common Cause had filed the original complaint with the FEC. The D.C. Circuit held that Common Cause could not secure standing by alleging that it was deprived of knowledge of whether a violation of the FECA had occurred, for the FECA does not require that such information concerning violations be disclosed to the public.[108] Similarly, in *Wertheimer* v. *FEC,* the D.C. Circuit Court rejected arguments from various reform groups that they were given standing by the FEC's failure to identify party spending that was coordinated with presidential candidates as "contributions" and "expenditures."[109] The Court noted that the transactions in question were reported in some form and that appellants were actually seeking a "legal conclusion" rather than disclosure of additional facts.

The FEC may not make public "any notification or investigation" without the consent of the person who receives such notification or who is under investigation.[110] The FEC interpreted the confidentiality provision as allowing it to publicly include exhibits pertaining to an ongoing investigation in a subpoena enforcement action and to make public complete enforcement action files upon termination of a case. Both interpretations were rebuffed in the courts. Indeed, the D.C. Circuit ruled in *In re Sealed Case* that documents relating to an ongoing FEC enforcement case must remain under seal, even when the FEC institutes a court action to enforce a subpoena.[111] The FEC voted unanimously not to appeal the D.C. Circuit Court's ruling but instead to adopt the court's position on the issue. In *AFL-CIO* v. *FEC,* the U.S. District Court for the District of Columbia overturned the FEC's practice of making entire case files public upon termination of a case.[112] The court found that the federal campaign finance law did not support the idea that the confidentiality requirement lapsed once the FEC terminated an investigation and suggested that case file disclosure could chill the free exercise of political speech. The FEC has adopted policies that limit what materials may be made public at the conclusion of enforcement matters.[113]

The Justice Department—Criminal Prosecutions

The Justice Department pursues criminal violations of the campaign finance laws either after referral from the FEC or upon independent discovery. U.S. Attorneys or the department's Public Integrity Section may investigate alleged violations, using FBI assistance and grand juries. Cases are tried in federal court, and allegations may include ancillary mail or wire fraud and conspiracy to violate the laws. Penalties may include jail terms and substantial monetary penalties.

Aggravated and intentional campaign finance crimes may be prosecuted either as misdemeanor violations of the act or as felonies under the conspiracy and false statement provisions.[114] Prosecution under the mail or wire fraud statutes also may be available in some cases.[115] The law that allows prosecution of fraudulent schemes "to deprive another of the intangible right of honest services"[116] has also been employed to enforce campaign contribution violations.[117] The Department of Justice pursues campaign finance crimes involving up to $10,000 as FECA misdemeanors and considers for felony prosecution only those involving more than $10,000.[118]

Criminal prosecution of federal election law violations is pursued in cases demonstrating "willful violation of a core" provision, involving "a substantial sum of money" ($2,000 or more) and resulting "in the reporting of false campaign information to the FEC."[119] The core provisions of the law include the following:

—the contribution limits
—the ban on corporation and labor contributions
—the ban on contributions from federal contractors
—the ban on contributions from foreign nationals
—the prohibition against making contributions in the name of another
—the avoidance of FEC disclosure requirements.

Schemes used to disguise illegal contributions also have been prosecuted as conspiracy to obstruct the lawful functioning of a government agency and submitting false information to a federal agency.[120]

Defendants convicted of campaign finance misdemeanors may receive sentences of imprisonment, and corporate defendants may receive large fines for misdemeanor FECA violations.[121]

Significant sentences have been applied to felony campaign finance crimes prosecuted under the conspiracy to obstruct or false statements provisions. The theory behind conspiracy prosecutions is explained in the Justice Department's handbook on election law crimes: "A scheme to infuse patently illegal funds into a federal campaign, such as by using conduits or other means calculated to conceal the illegal source of the contribution, thus disrupts and impedes the FEC in the performance of its statutory duties."[122] To obtain a conviction under the conspiracy to obstruct provision, the evidence must show that the defendant intended to disrupt and impede the lawful functioning of the FEC (such as by causing false information to be provided to the FEC by the recipient committee, thereby "misleading the public as to the actual source of the contribution"). Successful prosecution of violations of the false statements and false papers provisions requires a showing "that the defendant knew that statements [being] made were false" and "that the defendant intentionally caused such statements to be made by another," not proof that the defendant knew acts to be unlawful.[123] Similarly, conduits serving as intakes are significantly restricted by the fact that a "committee may not report that a signer is the actual source of funds if it is aware that the signer is not the source."[124] Thus the "simple interposition of conduits to sign" checks is sufficient to result in false reports by committees.[125] Taken together, the false statements and false papers provisions criminalize acts that cause another person (that is, a campaign treasurer) to submit false information to the FEC.[126]

Statute of Limitations Issues

In 2002, BCRA increased the statute of limitations for prosecution of criminal violations of campaign finance law from three to five years.[127] With that change, the Justice Department no longer needs to rely on the five-year statute of limitations for ancillary criminal provisions (conspiracy, fraud, and so forth), though such provisions remain available for prosecution of campaign finance violations. [128] However, the law does not specify the statute of limitations for *civil* enforcement actions. A number of courts have concluded that the general federal default five-year statute of limitations applies to civil actions.[129]

Some courts have found that the statute of limitations period commences when the violation is committed. In *FEC* v. *Williams*, the court rejected the FEC's argument that the period should be "tolled" (with the clock not started) until the violation is discovered.[130] The FEC also contended that the period should be tolled or frozen under the doctrine of "equitable tolling" for fraudulent concealment. Tolling a limit under this theory requires a showing that the defendant fraudulently concealed operative facts that the FEC failed to discover in the limitation period and that the FEC pursued the facts diligently until discovery of the facts. The court rejected that argument also, determining that the FEC had the facts it needed in campaign finance reports filed by recipient committees to discover the operative facts.[131] The practical effect of those decisions was to make it significantly more difficult for the FEC to pursue allegations of campaign finance violations and to cause the commission to close a number of high-profile investigations that were past or near the five-year limit. Especially in the case of presidential campaigns, which undergo a multiyear audit before the commission even authorizes the opening of an enforcement matter, the combination of the FEC's current capabilities and the five-year statute of limitations means that many investigations will as a practical matter be aborted without a resolution.

Notes

1. Bipartisan Campaign Reform Act of 2002 (BCRA), P. L. 107-155 (codified as amended at 2 U.S.C. 431 et seq.).

2. *Buckley* v. *Valeo,* 424 U.S. 1 (1976).

3. *McConnell* v. *FEC,* 124 S. Ct. 619 (2003).

4. 2 U.S.C. sec. 431(8)(A).

5. 2 U.S.C. sec. 441a(a)(1)(A); Federal Election Commission, "New Federal Contribution Limits Announced," press release, February 3, 2005.

6. 2 U.S.C. sec. 431(1)(A).

7. 2 U.S.C. sec. 441a(a)(1)(B); FEC, "New Federal Contribution Limits Announced."

8. 2 U.S.C. sec. 441a(a)(1)(C).

9. In certain circumstances, when a local committee can sufficiently demonstrate its independence, it will not be considered part of a state committee.

10. 2 U.S.C. sec. 441a(a)(3); FEC, "New Federal Contribution Limits Announced." New campaign finance laws set the aggregate limit on contributions by individuals to federal candidates at $37,500 over two years (starting with an odd-numbered year), indexed for inflation. BCRA, secs. 307(b), (d)(1). Likewise, contributions to multicandidate committees by individuals are always counted toward the indexed $37,500 aggregate limit of the year in which the contributions are made. 2 U.S.C. sec. 441a(a)(3); BCRA secs. 307(b), (d)(1).

11. 2 U.S.C. sec. 431(4).

12. *Buckley,* 424 U.S. at 79.

13. 11 C.F.R. sec. 100.5(e)(3).

14. 11 C.F.R. secs. 100.5(g)(2) and 110.3(a).

15. 11 C.F.R. sec. 100.5(9)(5).

16. 11 C.F.R. sec. 100.5(e)(4).

17. 11 C.F.R. sec. 110.2(e); FEC, "New Federal Contribution Limits Announced."

18. "Levin funds" are funds raised and spent by state, district, and local party committees for federal election activity, subject to a combination of state and special federal restrictions rather than the federal hard money restrictions that apply to all other federal election fundraising. State, district, and local party committees raise Levin funds according to state campaign finance laws. However, under no circumstances may Levin fund contributions to a state, district, or local party committee exceed a federal law limit of $10,000 per person per calendar year. Furthermore, federal election activities paid for with Levin funds may not refer to a clearly identified candidate for federal office.

19. 2 U.S.C. sec. 431(9).

20. See 2 U.S.C. sec. 441a(d).

21. *Colorado Republican Federal Campaign Committee* v. *FEC,* 518 U.S. 604 (1996).

22. *Colorado Republican Federal Campaign Committee* v. *FEC,* 533 U.S. 431 (2001).

23. See 11 C.F.R. sec. 109.1(d) (campaign literature); FEC Advisory Opinions 1982-30 and 1979-80. All FEC advisory opinions since 1977 are available on the FEC's website (www.fec.gov/law/advisoryopinions.shtml). Each opinion is identified by the year it was filed and the order in which it was received—for example, Advisory Opinion 1999-01 refers to the first opinion received by the FEC in 1999

24. *FEC* v. *Christian Coalition*, 53 F. Supp. 2d 45 (D.D.C. 1999).

25. See former 11 C.F.R. secs. 109.1(b)(4) and 100.23.

26. BCRA sec. 214. For a discussion of the legal implications of coordinating issue advocacy advertising with candidates and parties, see chapter 7.

27. *Shays* v. *FEC*, 337 F. Supp. 2d 28, 56–71 (D.D.C. 2004).

28. *McConnell*, 124 S. Ct. at 697.

29. See *FEC* v. *Massachusetts Citizens for Life, Inc.,* 479 U.S. 238 (1986) (*MCFL*). See also *McConnell*, 124 S. Ct. at 698–99 (citing MCFL).

30. "Promotion of political ideas" is defined as "issue advocacy, election influencing activity, and research, training or educational activity that is expressly tied to the organization's political goals." 11 C.F.R. sec. 114.10(b)(1).

31. Examples of such benefits are credit cards, insurance policies, savings plans or training, education, or business information supplied by the corporation. 11 C.F.R. sec. 114.10(c)(3)(ii)(A) and (B).

32. A nonprofit corporation can show through its accounting records that this criterion is satisfied or that it will meet this requirement if it is a qualified 501(c)(4) corporation and has a written policy against accepting donations from business corporations or labor organizations. 11 C.F.R. sec. 114.10(c)(4)(iii).

33. 11 C.F.R. sec. 114.10.

34. 2 U.S.C. sec. 431(9)(B)(i) (expenditure) and sec. 434(f)(3)(B)(i) (electioneering communication).

35. U.S. House of Representatives, Report 1239, *A Legislative History*, 93 Cong. 2 sess., p. 4.

36. See FEC Advisory Opinions 2004-7, 2003-34, 2000-13, 1998-17, 1996-48, 1996-41, 1996-16, 1982-44. See also *Readers Digest Association* v. *FEC*, 509 F. Supp. 1210, 1215 (S.D.N.Y. 1981); *FEC* v. *Phillips Publishing*, 517 F. Supp. 1308, 1312–13 (D.D.C. 1981).

37. 11 C.F.R. sec. 114.3(a).

38. 2 U.S.C. sec. 431(9)(B)(iii).

39. Amendments to Foreign Agents Registration Act, Pub. L. no. 89-486, sec. 4(e), 80 Stat. 244, 248 (1966).

40. Federal Election Campaign Act Amendments of 1976, Pub. L. no. 94-283, sec. 324, 90 Stat. 475, 493.

41. 2 U.S.C. sec. 441e (a)

42. Donations to a building fund of a national or state political party committee were specifically excepted from treatment as a "contribution" under the FECA. 2 U.S.C. sec. 431(8)(B)(viii). BCRA deleted that exception for donations to a national party building fund and, as discussed above, amended the foreign national prohibition to cover not merely a "contribution" but also a "donation of money or other thing of value . . . in connection with a Federal, state or local election" and a "contribution or donation

to a committee of a political party." BCRA secs. 103(b)(1), 303. Therefore a foreign national may no longer make donations to a building fund of a national or state political party committee.

43. 22 U.S.C. sec. 611(b) provides:

(b) The term "foreign principal" includes—

(1) a government of a foreign country and a foreign political party;

(2) a person outside of the United States, unless it is established that such person is an individual and a citizen of and domiciled within the United States, or that such person is not an individual and is organized under or created by the laws of the United States or of any State or other place subject to the jurisdiction of the United States and has its principal place of business within the United States; and

(3) a partnership, association, corporation, organization, or other combination of persons organized under the laws of or having its principal place of business in a foreign country.

44. 8 U.S.C. sec. 1101(a)(20) provides:

(20) The term "lawfully admitted for permanent residence" means the status of having been lawfully accorded the privilege of residing permanently in the United States as an immigrant in accordance with the immigration laws, such status not having changed.

In her testimony before the Senate Judiciary Committee on April 30, 1997, former U.S. attorney general Janet Reno indicated that the Department of Justice was interpreting Section 441e to prohibit soft money contributions to party committees from foreign nationals. See Hearing of the Senate Judiciary Committee, "Department of Justice Oversight," Federal News Service, April 30, 1997 (responses to questions from Senator Fred Thompson). Senator Thompson asserted in his questioning of Attorney General Reno that her interpretation that "soft money" was never a "contribution" under the act would make acceptance of soft money contributions from foreign sources legal. The attorney general disagreed, stating that "441e prohibits contributions from foreign nationals in connection with all elections, state and federal, and thus they can't use soft money from foreign sources for issue ads by political parties."

45. 11 C.F.R. sec. 110.4(a)(2) and (3).

46. 11 C.F.R. sec. 100.20(i).

47. 2 U.S.C. sec. 441c.

48. 2 U.S.C. sec. 441f.

49. 2 U.S.C. sec. 441e (foreign contributions) and sec. 441b (reimbusement).

50. See generally 11 C.F.R. sec. 9033.1.

51. Individuals may still contribute to a special fund that campaign committees may establish under FECA limits or restrictions to pay for legal and accounting compliance expenses.

52. 2 U.S.C. sec. 441a(d)(2).

53. See 26 U.S.C. sec. 9008.

54. See 11 C.F.R. 9008.52.

55. See 11 C.F.R. 9008.53.

56. See 11 C.F.R. sec. 9004.3.

57. See 11 C.F.R. sec. 9004.2.

58. BCRA sec. 101(a).

59. 18 U.S.C. sec. 601 (threat of firing), sec. 602 (solicitation from a federal employee), sec. 603 (contribution to employer's campaign), sec. 604 ("work relief" entitlement), and sec. 606 (demotion).

60. 18 U.S.C. sec. 607.

61. Robert Suro, "Reno Decides against Independent Counsel to Probe Clinton, Gore," *Washington Post*, December 3, 1997, p. A1.

62. BCRA sec. 302 (amending 18 U.S.C. sec. 607).

63. BCRA sec. 101.

64. U.S. House of Representatives, Committee on Standards of Official Conduct, "Memorandum for All Members, Officers, and Employees," April 25, 1997.

65. See U.S. Senate, Select Committee on Ethics, *Senate Ethics Manual*, S. Pub. 106-40 (September 2000), pp. 139–47.

66. 5 U.S.C. sec. 7322.

67. *Buckley*, 424 U.S. at 13 and 63, respectively.

68. Id. at 42–44 and 44 n. 52, respectively.

69. *McConnell*, 124 S. Ct. at 689.

70. Id. at 703.

71. Id. at 687.

72. Id. at 688.

73. Id. at 688–89.

74. See Rebecca Fairley Raney, "Candidates Try Asking for Money via E-Mail," *New York Times*, July 15, 1999 (http://nytimes.com/library/tech/99/07/cyber/articles/15campaign.html [May 17, 2005]); Leslie Wayne, "E-Mail Used to Mobilize Voters," *New York Times*, November 6, 2000 (www.nytimes.com/2000/11/06/technology/06MAIL.html [May 17, 2005]).

75. In fact, the FEC permits matching of credit card contributions received by presidential primary candidates. 11 CFR secs. 9034.2, 9034.3; FEC Advisory Opinion 1999-36. Some analysts suggest, however, that for online fundraising to succeed, it must be stimulated or supplemented by more traditional fundraising activities, such as phone calls or events. See Rebecca Fairley Raney, "Volunteers' Actions Lead Skeptics to Question McCain's Online Donations," *New York Times*, February 12, 2000 (www.nytimes.com/library/tech/00/02/cyber/articles/12campaign.html [May 17, 2005]).

76. "Notice of Inquiry: Use of Internet for Campaign Activity," 64 *Federal Register* 60360 (November 5, 1999).

77. "The Internet and Federal Elections: Candidate-Related Materials on Web Sites of Individuals, Corporations, and Labor Organizations," 66 *Federal Register* 50358 (proposed Oct. 3, 1999), to be codified at 11 C.F.R. parts 100, 114, and 117.

78. FEC Advisory Opinion 1998-22.

79. FEC Advisory Opinion 1999-17.

80. FEC Advisory Opinions 1999-7, 1999-24, and 1999-25.

81. *Shays,* 337 F. Supp. 2d at 65–71.

82. *Communications Workers of America* v. *Beck*, 487 U.S. 735 (1988).

83. *UAW-Labor Employment and Training Co.* v. *Chao*, No. Civ. A. 01-00950, 2002 U.S. Dist. LEXIS 50 (D.D.C. Jan. 2, 2002).

84. See *First National Bank of Boston* v. *Bellotti*, 435 U.S. 765 (1978); document 3.2.

85. U.S. Department of the Treasury (Treasury Department), Rev. Rul. 67-368, 1967-2 *Cumulative Bulletin* 194.

86. Treasury Department, Rev. Rul. 71-530, 1971-2 *Cumulative Bulletin* 237 (July), and Rev. Rul. 67-293, 1967-2 *Cumulative Bulletin* 185.

87. *FEC* v. *Beaumont*, 123 S.Ct. 2200, 556 (2003).

88. *FEC* v. *Christian Coalition*, 53 F. Supp. 2d 45 (D.D.C. 1999).

89. See 11 C.F.R. sec. 114.4.

90. Treasury Department, Rev. Rul. 86-95, 1986-2 *Cumulative Bulletin* 73.

91. BCRA sec. 101.

92. 26 U.S.C. sec. 527(e)(2).

93. 2 U.S.C. sec. 431(4); see also 11 C.F.R. sec. 100.5(a).

94. *Buckley,* 424 U.S. at 79.

95. *FEC* v. *GOPAC,* 917 F. Supp. 851, 859 (D.D.C. 1996) (emphasis added).

96. *McConnell,* 124 S.Ct. at 675, n. 64.

97. 26 U.S.C. sec. 527(j).

98. Campaign Finance Institute, data as of November 11, 2004.

99. Ibid.

100. 2 U.S.C. sec. 437g(a)(4)(A) and (C).

101. 2 U.S.C. sec. 437g(6).

102. Id.

103. 2 U.S.C. sec. 437g(a)(8).

104. *Democratic Senatorial Campaign Committee* v. *FEC*, Civil Action No. 96-2184 (JHG), (D.D.C. May 30, 1997).

105. See FEC Case Abstracts at www.fec.gov/pdf/cca.pdf.

106. *FEC* v. *Akins*, 524 U.S. 11 (1998).

107. *Common Cause* v. *FEC*, 108 F.3d 413 (D.C. Cir. 1997).

108. Id. at 418.

109. *Wertheimer* v. *FEC*, No. 00-5371 (D.C. Cir. Oct. 28, 2001), http://pacer.cadc. uscourts.gov/common/opinions/200110/00-5371a.txt.

110. 2 U.S.C. sec. 437g(a)(12).

111. In re Sealed Case, 237 F.3d 657, 667 (D.C. Cir. 2001).

112. *AFL-CIO* v. *FEC,* Civil Action No. 01-1522 (D.D.C. December 19, 2001), www.fecwatch.org/law/court/opinions/AFL-CIO.DDC.pdf.

113. 2 U.S.C. sec. 437g(a)(12).

114. 2 U.S.C. sec. 437g(d); 18 U.S.C. sec. 371, 1001. See generally Laura A. Ingersoll, ed., *Federal Prosecution of Election Offenses*, 6th ed. (Department of Justice, January 1995), pp. 133–35.

115. See 18 U.S.C. secs. 1341 and 1343.

116. 18 U.S.C. sec. 1346.

117. *United States* v. *Sun-Diamond,* 138 F.3d 961 (D.C. Cir. 1998).

118. Ingersoll, p. 115.

119. Ingersoll, p. 93.

120. 18 U.S.C. secs. 371 and 1001, respectively.

121. See *United States* v. *Goland*, 959 F.2d 1449 (9th Cir. 1992) (ninety days' imprisonment); *United States* v. *Fugi Medical Systems*, C.R. No. 90-288 (S.D.N.Y., sentencing proceedings, August 15, 1990).

122. Ingersoll, p. 109.

123. 18 U.S.C. secs. 1001 and 1002, respectively. See *United States* v. *Hsia*, 176 F.3d 517 (D.C. Cir. 1999).

124. *United States* v. *Kanchanalak*, 192 F.3d 1037 (D.C. Cir. 1999).

125. *Hsia*, 176 F.3d at 523.

126. See *United States* v. *Curran*, 20 F.3d 560 (3d Cir. 1994).

127. 2 U.S.C. sec. 455(a).

128. See 18 U.S.C. sec. 3282.

129. *FEC* v. *Williams*, 104 F.3d 237, 240 (9th Cir. 1996); *FEC* v. *National Right to Work Committee*, 916 F. Supp. 10 (D.D.C. 1996); *FEC* v. *National Republican Senatorial Committee*, 877 F. Supp. 15 (D.D.C. 1995).

130. *Williams*, 104 F.3d at 240.

131. Id. at 241.

3

The First Amendment and the Limits of Campaign Finance Reform

DANIEL R. ORTIZ

One would search the Constitution in vain for any mention of "campaign finance," let alone "contributions," "expenditures," "soft money," "issue advocacy," or any of the other specialized terms in today's campaign finance vocabulary. Yet despite that silence the Supreme Court has firmly and repeatedly held that the Constitution greatly limits what Congress and the states can do in this area. Believing that campaign finance regulations can restrict political expression and so implicate the First Amendment, which says only that "Congress shall make no law . . . abridging the freedom of speech," the Court has subjected them to searching review. In a series of cases that have sparked much public discussion, the Court has developed an often conflicted set of rules and principles.

The Supreme Court at Work

The Supreme Court did not develop a specialized campaign finance jurisprudence until fairly recently. When deciding cases before the 1970s, it applied more or less straightforwardly rules it had developed elsewhere. In the 1970s, however, it made an important turn. In the course of reviewing a growing number of cases, it started developing a body of rules that while based on traditional First Amendment concepts was quite autonomous.

Buckley *v.* Valeo

In *Buckley* v. *Valeo,* the first and most important of the campaign finance cases, the Supreme Court created a framework that still guides analysis.[1] In response to Watergate, Congress amended the Federal Election Campaign Act (FECA) in 1974 to close several loopholes that had made the FECA largely ineffective. In particular, Congress tightened the regulation of the financing of federal primary and general elections by

—restricting the amount of money individuals and entities could contribute to political campaigns

—restricting the amount candidates could contribute to their own campaigns

—restricting the amount individuals and entities could expend on behalf of candidates

—requiring disclosure of all sizable contributions

—restricting the amount of money that could be spent by or on behalf of a candidate

—providing for public financing of presidential primaries and elections. The 1974 amendments constituted the most wide-ranging and ambitious attempt to regulate money in federal elections up to that point.

In *Buckley* v. *Valeo,* the Supreme Court considered challenges to all the major provisions of the 1974 amendments. While upholding most of the provisions—including contribution limitations (except when candidates contribute to themselves), the overall presidential campaign spending limitations, the disclosure provisions, and the public financing scheme for presidential elections—it struck down one of the central features of the revised act: the limitation on so-called "independent expenditures"—that is, money spent by an individual or entity without coordination with a political campaign. At first, the Court's decision to uphold contribution limitations while invalidating expenditure limitations seems surprising. Do both types of spending not have similar effects—promotion of a particular candidate or set of views?

The Court defended treating contributions and expenditures differently on two grounds. First, the Court argued, contributions pose a threat of political corruption that expenditures do not. Simply put, the Court believed that a candidate could become beholden to a contributor but not to someone who merely expended monies on his or her behalf. If expenditures could not indebt a candidate to a voter, they could never give rise to even the appearance of corruption; regulating them therefore could not be claimed to protect the integrity of the political process.

Second, the Court saw contributions and expenditures as two quite different kinds of speech. To the Court, contributions serve only a signaling function. They indicate to the candidate and perhaps to others that the contributor supports the candidate's views; they have no greater communicative content. As the Court put it, "[a] contribution serves as a general expression of support for the candidate and his views, but does not communicate the underlying basis for the support." Since a contribution signals only the presence of a symbolic bond, its expressive content does not vary with its size. A small contribution expresses a contributor's political identification with the candidate just as effectively as a large one. If one believes, as the Court said it did, that "[t]he quantity of communication by the contributor does not increase perceptibly with the size of his contribution, since the expression rests solely on the undifferentiated, symbolic act of contributing," then capping contributions at any amount above the threshold at which this signal can be perceived does not impair communication. In contrast, to the Court's mind, expenditure limitations do significantly affect speech. Since expenditures serve to communicate one's own ideas rather than the mere fact of one's support for the views of another, limiting them poses much greater First Amendment problems. Expenditure regulations, in particular, affect both the quantity and content of political discourse.

Both grounds of the Court's distinction between contributions and independent expenditures have sparked much criticism—on and off the Court. First, might candidates not feel just as beholden to someone who expended sums on their behalf as to someone who actually gave them money? Contributions may produce a somewhat greater degree of indebtedness, but expenditures too can create at least the appearance of a quid pro quo.

Second, contributions serve to communicate much more than the mere fact of an individual's political "identification" with a particular candidate. If that were all contributions expressed, candidates presumably would spend less time and effort garnering them and contributors would seldom give more than symbolic amounts. After all, anything above the signaling threshold would be wasted. The importance of contributions to contributors and candidates alike lies rather in their ability to magnify the voice of the candidates. Few people contribute in order to express their own ideas directly. Many contribute, however, in order to allow a candidate to promote their personal views more effectively and to convince other voters of the wisdom of their values. To be sure, contributions are, as the Court has characterized them in another case, "speech by proxy," but speaking by proxy may heighten the effect of the communication. To discount the speech value of contributions because they allow the candidate but not the contributor to speak misses their point. If I give money to a candidate, I do so to better communicate and put into operation *my own* ideas—that is exactly what I hope the candidate will do. Most contributors would doubtless be surprised to learn that they contribute in order to express a symbolic connection between the candidate and themselves rather than to carry out their own ideas more effectively through the candidate's agenda.

Identifying a special First Amendment interest in independent expenditures did not by itself invalidate their regulation; all that it did was place on the government the burden of arguing a compelling governmental purpose for regulating them. Because the Court had characterized independent expenditures as inherently noncorrupting, however, the government had to argue a different purpose, and it did so. Congress argued that expenditure limitations were necessary in order to level the playing field for political competitors. If one person could expend much more than another, the argument went, that person could have much greater influence over the outcome of the election. Expenditure limitations thus served an egalitarian purpose: preventing undue influence in elections. The Court was skeptical. It doubted that equalizing people's ability to influence elections could ever be a legitimate, let alone a compelling, goal for government to pursue if it required restricting the speech of some:

> The concept that government may restrict the speech of some elements of our society in order to enhance the relative voice of others is wholly foreign to the First Amendment, which was designed to secure the widest possible dissemination of information from diverse and antagonistic sources and to assure unfettered interchange of ideas for the bringing about of political and social changes desired by the people.

With respect to political expression, the Court held, the more, the better.

One other move in *Buckley* has greatly shaped law in this area: the Court's emphasis on the need for clear rules. Worried that vagueness in some of the Federal Election Campaign Act's definitions might lead citizens to steer clear of speech that would be constitutionally permitted, the Court felt it necessary to interpret the statutory provisions quite specifically. Moreover, since the "bright-line" distinctions drawn had to avoid any potential constitutional problems in application, the Court "erred" on the side of free expression. As a result, the Court narrowed the statute's coverage quite dramatically. For example, the Court interpreted the act's central provision limiting "any expenditure . . . relative to a clearly identified candidate" to require mention of "explicit words of advocacy of election or defeat," such as "vote for," "elect," "vote against," and "defeat." These "magic words" protected free speech, to be sure, but they also failed to capture much spending clearly intended to benefit or harm particular candidates.

First National Bank of Boston *v.* Bellotti

The next major case in this area, *First National Bank of Boston* v. *Bellotti*, followed *Buckley* by two years.[2] It decided the constitutionality of a Massachusetts criminal statute prohibiting a corporation from spending money to influence referendums on questions that did not materially affect the property, business, or assets of the corporation. The First National Bank of Boston wanted to run an ad opposing a proposed state constitutional amendment that would have allowed a graduated state income tax. Massachusetts law clearly prohibited corporate expenditures on such campaigns by stating that "[n]o question submitted to the voters solely concerning the taxation of the income, property or transactions of individuals shall be deemed materially to affect the property, business or assets of corporation[s]." The bank sought a declaratory judgment from the state court invalidating the law on First Amendment grounds. The Massachusetts Supreme Judicial Court, however, upheld the law on the ground that a corporation's First Amendment rights extended no further than to issues affecting its property, business, and assets. The United States Supreme Court reversed that decision.

The Supreme Court found that the state court had approached the issue incorrectly. The issue was not whether and to what extent corporations had First Amendment rights, but rather whether the particular kind of speech involved was entitled to First Amendment protection. At bottom, the Court held, the state court had erred in looking at the issue from the speaker's rather than from the audience's perspective. Analysis had to proceed according to what was said, not who said it. "The inherent worth of the speech in terms of its capacity for informing the public does not depend upon the identity of its source."

The Court's approach is interesting not only because it so clearly identifies the listener's as the appropriate perspective for First Amendment analysis but also because it identifies the yardstick that the courts should use in measuring the value of different kinds of speech: "their capacity for informing the public." The Court found that yardstick so compelling that it used it not only to help decide the issue in *Bellotti* but also to justify large areas of existing First Amendment doctrine. Thus, in passing, the Court justified applying heightened scrutiny in its press cases because of the "role of that institution in informing and educating the public, offering criticism and providing a forum for discussion and debate" and justified its searching inquiry in cases involving entertainment or communication as "based not only on the role of the First Amendment in fostering individual self-expression but also on its role in affording the public access to discussion, debate, and the dissemination of information and ideas." Furthermore, the Court justified its controversial approach in commercial speech cases as following the principle that the First Amendment "prohibit[s] government from limiting the stock of information from which members of the public may draw. A commercial advertisement is constitutionally protected . . . [largely] because it furthers the societal interest in the 'free flow of commercial information.'" In *Bellotti* itself, applying that yardstick led the Court to see the Massachusetts law not as regulating campaign expenditures, but as "prohibiti[ng] . . . the 'exposition of ideas.'" From that perspective, of course, the law required compelling justification.

The Court then proceeded to reject Massachusetts's argument that allowing corporations to spend money on referendums might unduly influence the public. As the Court described the argument, Massachusetts claimed that "corporations are wealthy and powerful and [that] their views may drown out other points of view." The Court first rejected the argument for lack of legislative findings or support in the record but then went on to suggest, more ominously, that empirical evidence could *never* support it:

> Nor are appellee's arguments inherently persuasive or supported by the precedents of this Court. . . . To be sure, corporate advertising may influence the outcome of the vote; this would be its purpose. But the fact that advocacy may persuade the electorate is hardly a reason to suppress it . . . [T]he people in our democracy are entrusted with the responsibility for judging and evaluating the relative merits of conflicting arguments. They may consider, in making their judgment, the source and credibility of the advocate.

In other words, to the Court, corporate spending influences voters only insofar as the ideas and arguments it serves to communicate rationally persuade. Any difference advertising makes is a good one, for it leads people to change their choices on the basis of more information and more fully tested argument.

In short, the Court decided that a state could not treat individuals and corporations differently. A state could bar neither individual nor corporate expenditures. But the Court's holding was limited by the facts of the case: *Bellotti* concerned a referendum, not the election of a candidate. Since a corporation cannot seek a quid pro quo from a ballot measure, states did not need to ban corporate expenditures in referendum elections in order to prevent the one type of corruption that *Buckley* had identified as a constitutionally permissible concern. It left open the question of whether expenditures in candidate elections were different.

Massachusetts Citizens for Life, Inc., *v.* FEC *and* Austin *v.* Michigan State Chamber of Commerce

Not until 1986 did the Court begin to address the issue of expenditures in candidate elections. In two cases, *Massachusetts Citizens for Life, Inc.,* v. *FEC* (*MCFL*) and *Austin* v. *Michigan State Chamber of Commerce,* the Court developed some complex rules.[3] In *MCFL,* the Supreme Court held that the First Amendment barred the government from prohibiting ideological corporations—defined as corporations existing for the purpose of promoting their members' views on particular issues—from making independent expenditures. In this case, a group called Massachusetts Citizens for Life (MCFL), a pro-life advocacy group incorporated under Massachusetts law, published a special edition of its newsletter endorsing particular candidates in Massachusetts primary elections. The FEC claimed that the expenditure violated section 441b of the Federal Election Campaign Act, which prohibits corporations from expending funds from the corporate treasury for candidate elections. If a corporation wants to engage in political activity, the FECA allows it do so only through the use of a "separate segregated fund." The corporation can pay for the administration of the fund but cannot contribute directly to its resources, which must come from the corporation's "members," who are generally its board members, officers, shareholders, and employees.

The question was whether Massachusetts Citizens for Life could use its general corporate funds to endorse particular candidates or whether it was limited to administering a separate segregated fund. Because the FECA scheme limited the amount of money MCFL could expend and because running a separate segregated fund would have imposed many significant record-keeping, reporting, and personnel requirements, the Supreme Court thought that the FECA's direct expenditure prohibition posed a significant burden on the exercise of the corporation's First Amendment rights. That result was unsurprising, of course, given *Buckley*'s finding that "[t]he expenditure limitations . . . in the Act represent substantial rather than merely theoretical restraints on the quantity and diversity of political speech." The expenditure prohibition, then, penalized speech by forcing an organization that wanted to promote a particular candidate to forgo the advantages of the corporate form. The burden then shifted to the government to show a compelling interest for restraining an organization in such a fashion.

The FEC argued that the "importan[ce of] . . . protect[ing] the integrity of the marketplace of political ideas" justified any burden on the organization's First Amendment interests. As the Supreme Court redescribed that argument, "direct corporate spending on political activity raises the prospect that resources amassed in the economic marketplace may be used to provide an unfair advantage in the political marketplace." To the Court, the basic question in the case was whether the state's interest in preventing the transformation of economic into political power was strong enough to outweigh the burden on the exercise of the corporation's First Amendment rights.

The Court answered that question in a surprising way. It said:

> Political "free trade" does not necessarily require that all who participate in the political marketplace do so with exactly equal resources. Relative availability of funds is after all a rough barometer of public support. The resources in the treasury of the business corporation, however, are not an indication of the popular support for the corporation's political ideas. They reflect instead the economically motivated decisions of investors and customers. The availability of these resources may make a corporation a formidable political presence, even though the power of the corporation may be no reflection of the power of its ideas.

The Court's discussion is surprising because although it rejects the equalization rationale for regulation, just as it did in *Buckley* and *Bellotti*, it also rejects one of the rationales of *Buckley* itself. In that case, the Court argued that although money may have an influence apart from the power of the ideas it expresses, it cannot distort political outcomes since it reflects the amount of popular support the ideas have. That argument appears in the part of the opinion striking down the overall limitations on expenditures by individual campaigns, where the Court says that the goal of equalizing financial resources cannot justify capping overall campaign expenditures because "given the limitations on the size of outside contributions, the financial resources available to a candidate's campaign, like the number of volunteers recruited, will normally vary with the size and intensity of the candidate's support." In the Court's view, there is no reason to regulate campaign finance because it cannot bias politics. Any influence that money has on elections is proper because it reflects popular support. According to the Court in *MCFL*, however, corporate money's power to influence works in the opposite direction, because corporate support may not reflect popular support at all. Adopting that position, despite its problems with respect to individual expenditures, allows the Court to save the result in *Buckley* and *Bellotti* while embracing the opposite result with respect to most corporate expenditures.

The Court's discussion of the point is doubly odd since it is purely dictum. Since the Court found that the First Amendment forbids preventing ideological corporations like MCFL from making direct expenditures, its express "acknowledg[ment of] the legitimacy of Congress' concern that organizations that amass great wealth in the economic marketplace not gain unfair advantage in the political marketplace" is, technically speaking, unnecessary. Since MCFL was not a traditional economic corporation, the Court's discussion answered "a question not before [it]." Thus, although *MCFL*'s reasoning contradicted that underlying the earlier cases, its actual holding did not. It technically left open the larger question of whether the First Amendment similarly barred prohibiting expenditures by everyday "business" corporations.

In *Austin* v. *Michigan State Chamber of Commerce,* the Court took up that question. This case raised the same claim as *MCFL*, but this time the claim was made by an economic corporation. In *Austin*, Michigan law prohibited corporations from making independent expenditures. However, Michigan law did allow corporations to make expenditures from separate segregated funds created solely for political purposes. In essence, then, the Michigan scheme paralleled the federal one. The Michigan State Chamber of Commerce, a Michigan nonprofit corporation, brought suit seeking an injunction against enforcement of the expenditure prohibition. It put forward two primary claims. First, it argued, the First Amendment barred limitation of any corporation's campaign expenditures. That claim tried to extend *Bellotti* from referendum to candidate elections. Second, it argued that as a nonprofit trade association it represented an ideological corporation like MCFL.

The Court decided both claims against it. Although recognizing the chamber's nonprofit status, the Court found that the chamber satisfied none of the factors that it had laid out in *MCFL* for identifying ideological corporations. In particular, the chamber pursued many nonpolitical activities, it was structured so as to make it difficult for members who disagreed with its politics to withdraw, and it could serve as a conduit for economic corporations seeking to circumvent the limitation of expenditures. The Court made clear that a corporation's for-profit or nonprofit status did not determine its ideological or economic character. The chamber was a nonideological non-profit, which was to be considered an economic corporation for constitutional purposes.

As to the other claim, the one discussed extensively as dictum in *MCFL*, the Court held that the state could bar economic corporations from making independent expenditures in candidate elections. In fact, the Court simply quoted its reasoning from *MCFL* and thereby incorporated it as part of the holding of the new case. The Court described the evil Michigan sought to correct as "the corrosive and distorting effects of immense aggregations of wealth that are accumulated with the help of the corporate form and that have little or no correlation to the public's support for the corporation's political ideas." "The Act," the Court wrote, "does not attempt 'to equalize the relative influence of speakers on elections'; rather it ensures that expenditures reflect actual public support for the political ideas espoused by corporations." The Court thus refused to extend *Bellotti* and its assumptions about individual political decisionmaking. At the same time, however, the Court sought to minimize the conflict with *Buckley*, just as it had in *MCFL*. In an odd statement, it said that "[w]e emphasize that the mere fact that corporations may accumulate large amounts of wealth is not the justification for [the expenditure prohibition]; rather, the unique state-conferred corporate structure that facilitates the amassing of large treasuries warrants the limit."

The importance of the case lies not in its actual holding, which, after all, only made authoritative what *Massachusetts Citizens for Life* had strongly suggested. Rather, its importance lies in the Court's total departure from its earlier assumptions, which Justice Scalia's dissent makes clear. Justice Scalia reveals the fundamental contradiction between the Court's reasoning in *Massachusetts Citizens for Life* and its assumptions in *Buckley* and *Bellotti*. As he states it: "[T]hat corporations 'amas[s] large treasuries' . . . is . . . not sufficient justification for the suppression of political speech, unless one thinks it would be lawful to prohibit men and women whose net worth is above a certain figure from endorsing political candidates." If corporate expenditures are troubling because they do not reflect public support of the corporation's ideas, individual expenditures should be troubling as well, he argues. The same analysis applies to both.

To see that, it is helpful to reconsider the Court's reasoning in *MCFL* in terms of individual expenditures. First, individual expenditures, like the corporate expenditures discussed in *MCFL*, do not necessarily reflect the extent of public support for the ideas they convey because their amount depends in great part on the wealth of the people making them. Two candidates enjoying the complete support of similarly sized groups of very rich and very poor people respectively would not expect equal expenditures to be made on their behalf. Thus "relative availability of funds [from individuals] is" *not* "after all a rough barometer of public support," as the *MCFL* court suggested. The resources in a person's bank account, just like "[t]he resources in the treasury of a business corporation, . . . are not an indication of popular support for the [individual's] political ideas." They too "reflect instead . . . economically motivated decisions," like how hard one works, the type of job one has, and the success of one's investments. "The availability of these resources [, then,] may make [an individual] a formidable political presence, even though the power of the [individual] may be no reflection of the power of [his or her] ideas." As Justice Scalia points out, the Court cannot persuasively distinguish between individual and corporate expenditures:

> [The Court] does not endorse the proposition that government may ensure that expenditures "reflect actual public support for the political ideas espoused," but only the more limited proposition that government may ensure that expenditures "reflect actual support for the political ideas espoused *by corporations*." The limitation is of course entirely irrational. Why is it perfectly all right if advocacy by an individual billionaire is out of proportion with "actual public support" for his positions? There is no [satisfactory] explanation.

What's sauce for the goose is sauce for the gander.

The inconsistency, moreover, is not of just theoretical interest. As Justice Scalia argues forcefully in his dissent, *Austin* undermines a critical feature of *Buckley*. Such a broad interpretation of corruption effectively rehabilitates the equalization rationale rejected in *Buckley* as "wholly foreign to the First Amendment." *Austin*, in other words, seems to say that in some cases Congress may legislate to equalize just so long as it describes itself as doing something else. At the very least, the change has introduced great tension and some confusion into the jurisprudence.

Colorado I *and* II

In a single case, the Supreme Court has twice considered the constitutionality of congressional regulation of party spending on behalf of candidates. In 1986, before the Colorado Republican Party selected its own candidate for that fall's senatorial election, its federal campaign committee bought ads attacking the Democratic Party's likely candidate. The FEC eventually charged that the expenditure exceeded the limits that the FECA imposed on political party "expenditures in connection with" a "general election campaign" for congressional office. The Colorado Republican Party responded that the FECA's party expenditure provision violated the First Amendment both generally and as applied to the particular set of facts in its case. As a general matter, it argued, Congress could not limit any—coordinated or uncoordinated—party expenditures on behalf of candidates. More narrowly, it argued, Congress could not limit party expenditures, like its, that were truly uncoordinated with candidates.

In *Colorado Republican Federal Campaign Committee* v. *FEC* (*Colorado I*), decided in 1996, the Supreme Court addressed the narrower of the two claims.[4] Although the Court splintered four ways, with no opinion garnering the support of a majority of justices, it decided that the First Amendment did bar Congress from limiting party expenditures that truly were uncoordinated with party candidates. The principal opinion, written by Justice Breyer and joined by Justices O'Connor and Souter, found no reason to deviate from the Court's prior belief that the First Amendment generally protects independent expenditures from limitation. "We are not aware," Justice Breyer wrote, "of any special dangers of corruption associated with political parties that tip the constitutional balance in a different direction . . . [and t]he Government does not point to record evidence or legislative findings suggesting any special corruption problem in respect to independent party expenditures."

The only question, then, was whether the expenditure here was independent or not. The FEC argued that because parties and their candidates are so close, all party expenditures on behalf of candidates should be conclusively presumed to be coordinated. The principal opinion, however, disagreed. It found no factual or legal reason to make such a presumption, and without it the expenditure in the case could be classified only as independent. Although all six other justices would have ruled on the more general argument of whether the First Amendment bars limitation of truly coordinated party expenditures—four said that it would and two said that it would not—the principal opinion refused to address that question. As a result, the Court remanded the case to the lower courts to consider the broader claim.

In 2001, the broader claim returned to the Supreme Court in *Federal Election Commission* v. *Colorado Republican Federal Campaign Committee* (*Colorado II*).[5] This time a Court majority joined in a single opinion upholding congressional limitations on party expenditures coordinated with candidates. As the Court framed the inquiry:

The issue in this case is . . . whether a party is . . . in a different position from other political speakers, giving it a claim to demand a generally higher standard of scrutiny before its coordinated spending can be limited. The issue is posed by two questions: does limiting coordinated spending impose a unique burden on parties, and is there reason to think that coordinated spending by a party would raise the risk of corruption posed when others spend in coordination with a candidate?

The Colorado Republican Party's argument, the Court believed, boiled down to a factual one: "coordinated spending is essential to parties because 'a party and its candidates are joined at the hip.'" Because of that special relationship, the party argued, a party "cannot function . . . without coordinated spending, the object of which is a candidate's election" and a party is "uniquely able to spend in ways that promote candidate success."

The Court, however, rejected both arguments. It thought that "[p]arties . . . perform functions more complex than simply electing candidates; whether they like it or not, they act as agents for spending on behalf of those who seek to produce obligated officeholders." Since they perform that other function, "a party's efficiency in getting large sums and spending intelligently" is reason to be wary, not solicitous, of coordinated party expenditures. "If the coordinated spending of other, less efficient and perhaps less practiced political actors can be limited consistently with the Constitution," the Court asked, "why would the Constitution forbid regulation aimed at a party whose very efficiency in channeling benefits to candidates threatens to undermine the contribution (and hence coordinated spending) limits to which those others are unquestionably subject?"

The Court, in other words, was worried by the prospect of traditional, *Buckley*-type corruption. The fear was not that parties would influence candidates for the parties' own political purposes. Given parties' special role in the political process, that makes little sense as a form of corruption. Rather, the fear was that parties would exert influence over candidates on behalf of others. As the Court put it, "parties' capacity to concentrate power to elect is the very capacity that apparently opens them to exploitation as channels for circumventing contribution and coordinated spending limits binding on other political players." The Court accordingly applied the same level of constitutional scrutiny to coordinated expenditures by parties as to coordinated expenditures by other actors and found sufficient evidence to support the regulation in the acts of those who use parties to circumvent the nonparty contribution and coordinated expenditure limitations.

Together, *Colorado I* and *II* place political parties in exactly the same position as other political actors. Just as the First Amendment bars Congress from restricting uncoordinated party expenditures more than it restricts the uncoordinated expenditures of others (*Colorado I*), the First Amendment does not allow political parties to escape restrictions on coordinated expenditures that apply to other actors (*Colorado II*). One decision is the flip side of the other.

Nixon *v.* Shrink Missouri Government PAC

In 2000, between *Colorado I* and *Colorado II*, the Supreme Court decided another important campaign finance case: *Nixon* v. *Shrink Missouri Government PAC* (*Shrink Missouri*).[6] This case concerned a Missouri statute that imposed contribution limits ranging from $250 to $1,000 (depending on the particular state office and the size of the constituency) and provided for yearly inflation adjustments. The Court had little trouble upholding the limits and in the process clarified several important features of *Buckley*. Admitting that "[p]recision about the relative rigor of the standard to review contribution limits was not a pretense of . . . *Buckley*," the Court held that stricter standards governed expenditure than contribution limits and that both standards "bore more heavily on the associational right than on freedom to speak." Thus, if the Court could identify the standard that applied to claims that contribution limits violated associational rights and determined that the limits met that standard, it could uphold the limits without having to actually identify the standard of review that applied to free speech interests. That is exactly what it did. It held that under *Buckley* "a contribution limit involving 'significant interference' with associational rights could survive [only] if the Government demonstrated that the contribution regulation was closely drawn to match a 'sufficiently important interest,' though the dollar amount of the limit need not be fine tuned." Under that approach, in claims asserting both free speech and associational interests, free speech has no independent bite. As a practical matter, only the analysis of the burden on associational rights is important.

The Court further held that the state's interest in preventing corruption and the appearance of corruption was "sufficiently important" to support the contribution limit, just as it was in *Buckley* itself. The Court made clear, however, that that interest swept beyond the most traditional forms of corruption. The interest was "not confined to bribery of public officials, but extend[ed] to the broader threat from politicians too compliant with the wishes of large contributors." And the appearance of corruption was "almost equal" in concern to corruption itself. "Leave the perception of impropriety unanswered," the Court said, "and the cynical assumption that large donors call the tune could jeopardize the willingness of voters to take part in demo-cratic governance." To the Court's mind, *Buckley* clearly settled that much.

The question remained, however, of how much evidence of corruption and particularly of the appearance of corruption was necessary to support that rationale. Could a state limit contributions without citing hard evidence that its citizens thought large contributions corrupted the political process? The Court basically believed *Buckley* settled that question too: "The quan-tum of empirical evidence needed to satisfy heightened judicial scrutiny of legislative judgments will vary up or down with the novelty and plausibility of the justification raised [and] *Buckley* demonstrates that the dangers of large, corrupt contributions and the suspicion that large contributions are corrupt are neither novel nor implausible." The Court refused to define the minimum amount of evidence needed, finding simply that the evidence in the case—together with that in *Buckley* itself—supported the concern. But the evidence offered in the case, at least the evidence that the Court men-tioned, was somewhat slim. It consisted of an affidavit from a state senator stating that large contributions have "the real potential to buy votes"; several newspaper reports of large contributions that supported inferences of impro-priety; several questionable contributions mentioned in an unrelated Mis-souri case; and the popular vote in favor of a state initiative containing even stricter contribution limits. If that evidence is safely above the evidentiary threshold that *Buckley* requires, one of two things must be true—the *Buckley* evidentiary threshold is fairly low or the evidence offered in *Buckley* itself goes very far toward meeting the threshold in later cases. Either way the evi-dentiary standard is not as demanding as it might seem.

The Court also found that the particular limits in *Shrink Missouri*, although lower than those in *Buckley*, posed no constitutional problem. Although it stated that in *Buckley* the relevant test had been "whether there was any showing that the limits were so low as to impede the ability of candi-dates to 'amass the resources necessary for effective advocacy,'" it focused the test in *Shrink Missouri* in a way that made it much harder to find a constitu-tional violation—"whether the contribution limitation was so radical in effect as to render political association ineffective, drive the sound of a candi-date's voice below the level of notice, and render contributions pointless." Under that refashioned standard, it may be possible to set contribution limits very low indeed.

Although it settled many issues, *Shrink Missouri* is ultimately more inter-esting for what it suggested about *Buckley*'s future than for what it said about its current reach. The separate concurrences and dissents of six justices clearly indicated great doubts about *Buckley's* continued viability among two-thirds of the Court's membership. Justice Stevens, for example, stated that if there were to be a "new beginning . . . I make one simple point. Money is property; it is not speech." He would have offered campaign spending some protection but less than the degree accorded traditional speech, and he suggested that the source of that protection might lie in some constitutional provision other than the First Amendment. Justices Breyer and Ginsburg, by contrast, would have recognized a speech interest in campaign spending, but they believed that strict review is inappropriate because "this is a case where constitutionally protected interests lie on both sides of the legal equation." They believed that "a presumption against constitutionality was out of place" and went so far as to question the central justification of *Buckley* itself: "the concept that government may [not] restrict the speech of some elements of our society in order to enhance the relative voice of others." In passing, moreover, they suggested that their view would permit regulation of soft money; would leave open the constitutionality of many other reforms, particularly reduced-price media time; and might permit the Court to revisit in light of the post-*Buckley* experience some of the features of *Buckley* itself, most notably its rejection of limits on how much money wealthy candidates can contribute to their own campaigns. In addition, if *Buckley* did not permit "the political branches sufficient leeway to enact comprehensive solutions to the problems posed by campaign finance," they would overrule it.

Justices Thomas and Scalia also would overrule *Buckley*, but in the opposite direction. They would subject contribution limits to the same strict scrutiny that applied to expenditure limits, thereby invalidating contribution limits too. While Justice Kennedy largely agreed with Justices Thomas and Scalia, he would have taken a novel course. He "would overrule *Buckley* and then free Congress or state legislatures to attempt some new reform, if, based upon their own considered view of the First Amendment, it is possible to do so." In other words, he called for a fresh start. The nation should throw overboard *Buckley's* "misshapen system," go back to serious First Amendment principles, and see if a more sensible system of campaign finance regulation can survive serious First Amendment review.

McConnell *v.* FEC

In early 2002, Congress enacted and President Bush signed the Bipartisan Campaign Reform Act of 2002 (BCRA), known popularly as the McCain-Feingold or Shays-Meehan Act after its chief Senate and House sponsors. BCRA changed much of the legal landscape. Among other things, it

—raised contribution limits

—banned soft money contributions to influence federal elections

—regulated certain forms of so-called "issue advocacy."

Of all the changes, the regulation of soft money and of issue advocacy sparked the most debate. The first dried up a major source of funds for political parties, and the second barred some entities, most notably business corporations and labor unions, from funding certain kinds of political advertisements from their general treasuries and required individuals who ran such advertisements to disclose that they were doing so and how much they were spending. Legal challenges to BCRA focused primarily on those two provisions.

In *McConnell* v. *FEC,* the Supreme Court upheld nearly all the challenged provisions.[7] BCRA's soft money provisions are quite complex. The cornerstone provision, section 323(a), prohibits national party committees and their agents from soliciting, receiving, directing, or spending any soft money—that is, money raised outside the FECA's contribution rules, including any money from general corporate and union treasuries and money from individuals in excess of their contribution limits. The other soft money provisions are meant to reinforce the restrictions of section 323(a). As the Court described them:

> New FECA § 323(b) prevents the wholesale shift of soft-money influence from national to state party committees by prohibiting state and local party committees from using such funds for activities that affect federal elections. . . . New FECA § 323(d) reinforces these soft-money restrictions by prohibiting political parties from soliciting and donating funds to tax-exempt organizations that engage in electioneering activities. New FECA § 323(e) restricts federal candidates and officeholders from receiving, spending, or soliciting soft money in connection with federal elections and limits their ability to do so in connection with state and local elections. Finally, new FECA § 323(f) prevents circumvention of the restrictions on national, state, and local party committees by prohibiting state and local candidates from raising and spending soft money to fund advertisements and other public communications that promote or attack federal candidates.

In general, the Court thought that the various restrictions had "only a marginal impact on the ability of contributors, candidates, officeholders, and parties to engage in effective political speech." As "[c]omplex as its provisions may be," the Court found, "§ 323, in the main, does little more than regulate the ability of wealthy individuals, corporations, and unions to contribute large sums of money to influence federal elections, federal candidates, and federal officeholders."

The Court focused most of its attention on the "cornerstone" provision, which it believed fit squarely within the framework of *Buckley*. As a bar to certain types of *contributions*, section 323(a) did not significantly burden either speech or association, and "[b]oth common sense and the ample record" indicated that regulation of soft money was necessary to prevent corruption or its appearance. After looking at the record, the Court found "that candidates and donors alike have in fact exploited . . . soft money . . . , the former to increase their prospects of election and the latter to create debt on the part of officeholders, with the national parties serving as willing intermediaries." "[L]obbyists, CEOs, and wealthy individuals alike all have candidly admitted donating substantial sums of soft money to national committees not on ideological grounds, but for the express purpose of securing influence over federal officials." The Court found "[p]articularly telling . . . the fact that . . . more than half of the top 50 soft-money donors gave substantial sums to *both* major national parties, leaving room for no other conclusion but that these donors were seeking influence, or avoiding retaliation, rather than promoting any particular ideology."

Even more significant, the Court expanded its traditional notion of corruption. Although some dissenting justices argued that corruption should encompass only clear quid pro quo arrangements in which a candidate promises to take action in return for a contribution, the Court found that conception too narrow. As the Court put it,

> [m]any of the deeply disturbing examples of corruption cited by this Court in *Buckley* to justify FECA's contribution limits were not episodes of vote buying, but evidence that various corporate interests had given substantial donations to gain access to high-level government officials. Even if that access did not secure actual influence, it certainly gave the appearance of such influence.

Once the notion of corruption was thus expanded to encompass selling access, the record easily supported extensive soft money regulation. The record was "replete . . . with examples of national party committees peddling access to federal candidates and officeholders in exchange for large soft-money donations." The practice was so pervasive, in fact, "that the six national party committees actually furnished their own menus of opportunities for access to would-be soft-money donors, with increased prices reflecting an increased level of access." Given its low burden on speech and association and the high importance of Congress's goal, banning soft money contributions to the parties easily passed constitutional muster.

In passing, the Court's discussion of soft money appeared possibly to settle one important question that some thought had been left open. In an earlier case, *California Medical Association* v. *FEC* (*CalMed*),[8] the Supreme Court had upheld the FECA's $5,000 limit on individual contributions to political action committees but seemingly avoided considering "the hypothetical application" of the FECA to political committees that made independent expenditures but no contributions. Justice Blackmun, in fact, signaled misgivings about applying the limit to such committees. He wrote:

> [a] different result [sh]ould follow if [the $ 5,000 limit] were applied to contributions to a political committee established for the purpose of making independent expenditures, rather than contributions to candidates. . . . [Political action committees like the California Medical Association are] essentially conduits for contributions to candidates, and as such they pose a perceived threat of actual or potential corruption. In contrast, contributions to a committee that makes only independent expenditures pose no such threat.

Justice Blackmun, in other words, would seemingly distinguish between those organizations that make contributions to candidates and perhaps to parties and those that make only independent expenditures. Contributions to the former could be limited; contributions to the latter could not. His distinction, however, was technically dictum and would not have been controlling even if his opinion represented the views of a majority of the justices. Since the California Medical Association did make direct contributions to candidates, the facts of the case implicated only the first half of his distinction and that was all that was necessary for decision of the case. Thus, while the case made clear that Congress could limit contributions to political committees that made contributions to candidates, it appeared to leave unclear whether Congress could limit contributions to committees that made only independent expenditures.

In footnote 48 of *McConnell*, however, the Court appeared to take a clear stand on the issue. It mustered a particular interpretation of *CalMed* to reject Justice Kennedy's argument that only quid pro quo corruption should count. In the Court's view, *CalMed* itself foreclosed that position:

> [In *CalMed*], we upheld FECA's $ 5,000 limit on contributions to multicandidate political committees. It is no answer to say that such

limits were justified as a means of preventing individuals from using parties and political committees as pass-throughs to circumvent FECA's $1,000 limit on individual contributions to candidates. Given FECA's definition of "contribution," the $5,000 . . . limi[t] restricted not only the source and amount of funds available to parties and political committees to make candidate contributions, but also the source and amount of funds available to engage in express advocacy and numerous other noncoordinated expenditures. If indeed the First Amendment prohibited Congress from regulating contributions to fund the latter, the otherwise-easy-to-remedy exploitation of parties as pass-throughs (*e.g.*, a strict limit on donations that could be used to fund candidate contributions) would have provided insufficient justification for such overbroad legislation.

In other words, the Court believed that despite Justice Blackmun's stated misgivings and the plurality's stated avoidance of the issue, the Court in *CalMed* had necessarily held that Congress could limit contributions to entities that engaged solely in independent expenditures. If Blackmun's own stated view were controlling in that case, footnote 48 argues, then the only permissible goal of the $5,000 limit would have been to prevent parties from serving as "pass-throughs," a goal that could have been achieved through a much more limited form of regulation: "a strict limit on donations that could be used to fund candidate contributions." In that case, however, the Court would have struck down the FECA's $5,000 limit as overbroad. That the *CalMed* Court instead upheld it means, in the view of the *McConnell* Court, that Justice Blackmun—in broadly upholding limits on all donations to political committees that make contributions rather than forcing Congress to take the narrower approach and limiting the amount of money donated that the political committee could use to fund candidate contributions—undercut his own stated misgivings. And, since his misgivings were dictum while his bottom-line vote to uphold the limit at issue in *CalMed* itself was necessary for the decision, his bottom-line vote, not his misgivings, should control.

At first glance, footnote 48 seems arcane and hardly worthy of extended discussion. Why focus on a footnote? However, the Court's considered statement of the law in this area—if that is truly what it is—is tremendously important. It settles a question that the upholding of BCRA's soft money bans makes pressing. Before, in a world where political parties could accept unlimited amounts of soft money, donors seeking influence would give to the parties themselves. They had no reason to give to independent political committees since, as the Court found in *McConnell*, the parties were effective conduits of influence. Once BCRA's soft money provisions closed down that means of influence, however, independent committees became an attractive alternative, but only to the extent that the $5,000 limit on contributions to them did not apply. Justice Blackmun's opinion in *CalMed* seemingly left open the possibility that contributions to political committees that engaged solely in independent expenditures would, as a constitutional matter, have to be treated exactly the same as independent expenditures themselves. In other words, they could not be limited so long as they consisted of individual, rather than corporate or union, money. If that were the case, individuals could now circumvent the soft money bans by contributing unlimited amounts to committees that engaged solely in independent expenditures, even when everyone understood that those expenditures would be used to support or defeat particular candidates for federal office.

That, in a nutshell, is the current turmoil over the status of so-called "527 organizations," which has become the most important campaign finance issue since *McConnell*. Can individuals contribute unlimited amounts for other groups to spend to influence federal candidate elections, or, if they are going to spend unlimited amounts, do they have to spend it themselves? This is a big issue with real political consequences. In legal terms, the question is whether the Court meant what it said in footnote 48. If it did, individuals will not be able to contribute unlimited amounts to political committees that make only independent expenditures. If it did not, the question is still an open one. On that little footnote hangs much indeed.

The Court's treatment of BCRA's provisions regulating so-called "sham issue advocacy" is thankfully less complex. In *Buckley*, the Court held that in order to avoid concerns about vagueness, the FECA's central provision restricting expenditures "relative to a clearly identified candidate" should be construed as limited to expenditures on communications that included explicit words of advocacy of election or defeat of a candidate—words like "vote for," "elect," "support," "defeat," and "reject"—the so-called "magic words." BCRA, proceeding on the understanding that the Court's *particular* narrowing construction was not constitutionally required, adopted a different bright-line test to identify the relevant communications, which it called "electioneering communications." Its definition covered only broadcast, cable, and satellite communications that clearly identified a candidate for federal office, aired within sixty days before a general or thirty days before a primary election, and could be received by 50,000 or more people in the jurisdiction that the candidate sought to represent. BCRA then applied that definition in two different ways. It required disclosure of disbursements for electioneering communications by individuals totaling more than $10,000 in a calendar year and barred business corporations, unions, and any nonprofit that received any money from business corporations and unions from spending any general treasury funds on such communications.

BCRA's opponents attacked the provisions first by claiming that the definition itself was unconstitutional. They argued that use of the magic words was constitutionally required. The Court quickly rejected that argument. *Buckley*'s "express advocacy restriction," it noted, "was an endpoint of statutory interpretation, not a first principle of constitutional law." It was simply a way "to avoid problems of vagueness and overbreadth [and] we nowhere suggested that a statute that was neither vague nor overbroad would be required to toe the same express advocacy line." As a matter of constitutional law, the Court held, "*Buckley*'s magic-words requirement [wa]s functionally meaningless." And, whatever dangers the definition of "electioneering communications" posed, vagueness was not one of them.

The Court easily upheld the disclosure requirements placed on those engaging in electioneering communications. It simply noted that "the important state interests that prompted the *Buckley* Court to uphold the FECA's disclosure requirements—providing the electorate with information, deterring actual corruption and avoiding any appearance thereof, and gathering the data necessary to enforce more substantive electioneering restrictions— apply in full to BCRA" and then proceeded to quote a single paragraph in the lower court's opinion that documented how the magic words approach had allowed spenders to conceal their identities from the public—a practice that, in the Court's view, did "not reinforce the precious First Amendment values that Plaintiffs argue are trampled by BCRA."

The Court also upheld the prohibition against business corporations and unions spending from their general treasuries to fund electioneering communications—even with disclosure. The Court noted that the prohibition was not complete. Business corporations and unions could always spend for such advertising from their affiliated PACs, and they could spend from their general treasuries for political communications that fell outside that specific category of advocacy. The question was whether the bar was overbroad or underinclusive. BCRA's opponents challenged it as overbroad because they believed "that the justifications that adequately support[ed] the regulation of express advocacy [under the magic words test] do not apply to significant quantities of speech encompassed by the definition of electioneering communications."

The Court held that the argument failed to the extent that electioneering communications not containing express advocacy "are the functional equivalent of express advocacy." They are, the Court thought, "if the ads are intended to influence the voters' decisions and have that effect," which, the Court found, "the vast majority of [covered] ads" did. "Far from establishing that BCRA's application to pure issue ads is substantial, . . . the record," the Court found, "strongly supports the opposite conclusion."

The argument regarding underinclusiveness proved no better. Here the challengers argued that the exclusion of print and Internet ads from coverage invalidated the prohibition. The Court found, however, that the "record amply justifies Congress' line drawing" because business corporations and unions had primarily used the one type of media but not the others. As it held in *Buckley*, "reform may take one step at a time, addressing itself to the phase of the problem which seems most acute to the legislative mind."

The Larger Reform Debate

Few recent constitutional decisions have raised as much commentary as *Buckley* v. *Valeo* and its progeny. On one side, reformers attack the Supreme Court for misunderstanding both the First Amendment and how money works in politics. They read many of the cases prior to *Shrink Missouri* and *McConnell* as constitutional mistakes, as wrongheaded judicial meddling that magnifies the power of the rich and distorts politics. On the other side, deregulationists celebrate the Court in these cases for upholding the First Amendment against strong public opinion while criticizing it in other cases for not going far enough. In their eyes, the Court has acted bravely to save the American political system from misguided (albeit popular) reform. Many commentators, of course, see some wisdom in both positions and seek to defend a view somewhere between them.

Arguments in Favor of Reform

Four seemingly different concerns underlie the drive for campaign finance regulation. First, some reformers advocate regulation as a means to improve the day-to-day operation of legislative politics. Vincent Blasi, for example, has argued that the need to keep elected representatives' eyes on their jobs justifies some important campaign finance restrictions.[9] Since elected representatives feel that they need to spend a good deal of time raising money to protect their seats from challenge, they do not devote as much of their energy as they should to the job that their constituents elected them to do. As Blasi puts it:

As difficult as the general subject of representation can be, one does not need a sophisticated understanding of either republican theory or modern interest group politics to conclude that there is a failure of representation when candidates spend as much time as most of them now do attending to the task of fund-raising. This feature of modern representation should trouble those who favor close constituent control as well as those who favor relative independence for legislators; those who favor an "aristocracy of virtue" as well as those with more populist ideals regarding who should serve; those who conceive of representation as flowing exclusively from geographic constituencies as well as those who see a role for constituencies defined along other lines, be they racial, ethnic, gender, economic, religious, or even ideological. Whatever it is that representatives are supposed to represent, whether parochial interests, the public good of the nation as a whole, or something in between, they cannot discharge that representational function well if their schedules are consumed by the need to spend endless hours raising money and attending to time demands of those who give it.

In Blasi's view, fundraising is a form of shirking that impairs the quality of the officeholder's representation of his or her constituents. He believes that the state has an important interest in avoiding such behavior—an interest that supports some regulation of money in politics, particularly the imposition of campaign spending limits.

Second, many argue that regulating money in politics can help improve the quality of political discussion and debate. The two most notable proponents of this view, the late J. Skelly Wright and Cass Sunstein, believe that appropriate regulation can refocus political discourse on substantive ideas. Wright, for example, argued that unregulated spending leads to people voting according to what he called "intensities."[10] When candidates spend huge amounts of money on mass advertising, he argued, voters will follow the louder rather than more thoughtful voice. He also believed that restraining spending would improve discussion by encouraging retail rather than mass, wholesale politics. The giving and spending restrictions might cause candidates and other individuals to rely more on less expensive means of communication, but there was no reason to believe that such a shift in means would reduce the number of issues discussed in a campaign. And, by forcing candidates to put more emphasis on local organizing or leafleting or door-to-door canvassing and less on full-page ads and television spot commercials, the restrictions might well generate deeper exploration of the issues raised. To his mind, such a shift would mean that candidates would individually engage and address voters rather than treating them as mass consumers to target with affective advertisements, the same way a manufacturer interested in increasing demand for its deodorant might view them.

Similarly, Cass Sunstein hopes that campaign finance regulation will improve political debate, but he focuses on legislative rather than electoral politics.[11] As he puts it:

> Politics should not simply register existing preferences and their intensities, especially as these are measured by private willingness to pay. In the American constitutional tradition, politics has an important deliberative function. The constitutional system aspires to a form of "government by discussion." Grants of cash to candidates might compromise that goal by, for example, encouraging legislatures to vote in accordance with private interest rather than reasons.

By lessening legislators' incentive to serve contributors rather than constituents, campaign finance regulation may improve the chance that legislatures will function through discussion, reason-giving, and debate. Thus, according to Wright and Sunstein, campaign finance regulation is necessary to improve the quality of political decisionmaking on both the elective and representative levels of democratic politics.

Third, even more reformers argue that campaign finance regulation protects the political process from direct, quid pro quo corruption. Their view, like Sunstein's, maintains that without some forms of regulation, particularly limitations on individual direct contributions to political candidates, candidates become so beholden to contributors that they follow the contributors' rather than the voters' interests. Many, including the Supreme Court, agree that this is a serious danger and that even its appearance can seriously weaken politics. Fred Wertheimer and Susan Weiss Manes have catalogued remarks and testimony from people as diverse as the late senator Barry Goldwater ("To be successful, representative government assumes that elections will be controlled by the citizenry at large, not by those who give the most money. . . . Elected officials must owe their allegiance to the people, not to their own wealth or to the wealth of interest groups who speak only for the selfish fringes of the whole community") to former senator Dale Bumpers ("[E]very Senator knows I speak the truth when I say bill after bill after bill has been defeated in this body because of campaign money"). The late senator Paul Douglas, they believe, summed up this view well:

What happens is a gradual shifting of a man's loyalties from the community to those who have been doing him favors. His final decisions
are, therefore, made in response to his private friendships and loyalties
rather than to the public good. Throughout this whole process, the
official will claim—and may indeed believe—that there is no causal
connection between the favors he has received and the decisions which
he makes. He will assert that the favors were given and received on the
basis of pure friendship unsullied by worldly considerations. He will
claim that the decisions, on the other hand, will have been made on the
basis of the justice and equity of the particular case. The two series of
acts will be alleged to be as separate as the east is from the west. Moreover, the whole process may be so subtle as not to be detected by the
official himself.[12]

The pivotal questions concern how great a danger corruption and its appearance actually present and how well alternative means of regulation, like
bribery laws, can control it.

Fourth, and most controversial, many reformers argue that regulation is
necessary to maintain political equality. They all start with the belief that
democracy demands formal equality in the political sphere. Some voters' candidates may win, and some may lose, but each voter should have an equal
chance to affect the ultimate decision. That principle represents the democratic norm of equal political entitlement reflected in such legal rules as "one
person, one vote," the Fifteenth and Nineteenth Amendments, and the Voting
Rights Act of 1965. To this group of reformers, problems arise from democracy's tolerance of great economic inequality. The danger is that some of the
rich will try to stretch their economic advantage into the political sphere. If
the rich do convert economic into political power, they violate the norm of
equal political entitlement. Many reformers believe that campaign finance regulation is necessary to help keep the inequality accepted in the economic
realm from infecting politics, where inequality is not as tolerated. Proposals
limiting individual spending, for example, often are defended as a way of preventing the wealthy from exerting a disproportionate influence on politics.

Ronald Dworkin presents a strong version of this reform argument.[13] He
begins by asking whether *Buckley* was wrongly decided and ends by calling
for the Court to overrule it. Cutting through to the Court's central justification, he finds that *Buckley* stands on an "individual-choice" model of politics.
By that he means that its overall stance, which is deeply suspicious of government regulation, rests ultimately on the view that the First Amendment

allows people to hear whatever they want, at least in the realm of politics. Although that notion may be attractive (especially to people who believe in a bustling, free marketplace of ideas), Dworkin considers it fundamentally mistaken. To his mind, it misunderstands not only free speech but also "what it really means for free people to govern themselves." The result is not just legal error but the weakening of democratic politics.

The mistake that Dworkin finds in this view is that it sees equality as necessary to only one aspect of democracy. Although the individual-choice model gives each voter one vote and thus makes each an equally powerful judge of competing candidates and positions, the model ignores equality among citizens in another important respect. It allows some people more power than others as participants in the contest of forming political opinion. Wealthy individuals can "command [more] attention for their own candidates, interests, and convictions" than can others. As Dworkin puts it:

> When the Supreme Court said, in the *Buckley* case, that fairness to candidates and their convictions is "foreign" to the First Amendment, it denied that such fairness was required by democracy. That is a mistake because the most fundamental characterization of democracy—that it provides self-government by the people as a whole—supposes that citizens are equals not only as judges but as participants as well.

According to Dworkin, citizens must have equal power not only to judge among the views presented—as the rule of "one person, one vote" seeks to guarantee—but also to draw the attention of others to their own views. Such equality does not, of course, require others to find those arguments persuasive, but it does demand that each citizen be able to compete on equal terms for every other citizen's attention.

Dworkin believes that such equality justifies regulating some spending in elections and thus necessitates overruling *Buckley*. But he sees little prospect of that—at least anytime soon. Instead, Dworkin argues a more realistic strategy: we should simply declare *Buckley* a mistake, even if the Supreme Court will not admit it, and do everything we can to avoid its implications. He thus advocates reform that pursues the second type of equality to the full extent that *Buckley* permits and urges us to challenge *Buckley* whenever we can.

Arguments against Reform

Like the arguments in favor of campaign finance reform, those against it are many and diverse. First, some deregulationists argue that the reformers' basic descriptive theories about how money works in politics are wrong. Bradley Smith, for example, lays out four major descriptive assumptions reformers make about money in politics: that too much money is spent, that smaller contributions are better than larger ones, that money buys elections, and that money corrupts politicians.[14] All four, he argues, are wrong or at least unsupported. Smith argues against the first by comparing political and product advertising. As large as the amounts spent in political advertising may be, he points out, they are dwarfed by the amounts spent in advertising products. When viewed as cost per voter, moreover, they look reasonably small. Smith challenges the second assumption—that when it comes to contributions, smaller is better—by pointing out that too few Americans actually make contributions to support adequate political debate. Moreover, those candidates who can garner widespread small contributions are usually those who excite the passions of supporters on the extremes of political debate. The mainstream appears to be poorly stocked with small contributors. Smith contests the third assumption—that money buys elections—by arguing that money may follow success more than success follows money. And finally, he uses empirical arguments to fight the view that money corrupts candidates. Money affects few votes in the legislature, he claims, and "the available evidence simply does not show a meaningful, causal relationship between campaign contributions and legislative voting patterns." That empirical claim, of course, has quite far-reaching implications for the anticorruption rationale that *Buckley* upheld.

Smith does not rest there. He goes on to argue that the consequences of reform are just as bad as its assumptions. To his mind, the reformers have it exactly backward. Far from shoring up democracy, reform undermines it in several particular ways. First, Smith argues that campaign finance reform entrenches the status quo. It necessarily favors incumbents by making it harder for challengers to raise money. Second, he believes that campaign finance reform promotes influence peddling in the legislature; by restricting contributions, reform restricts people's ability to monitor their representatives and so keep them from shirking. Bad enough by itself, decreased monitoring also makes bribery, which Smith sees as a "substitute" for contributions, more likely.

Third, Smith argues that campaign finance reform favors "select elites." To the extent that reform decreases the power of money to influence elections, it increases the power of elite attributes (like name recognition and celebrity status) to influence them. That change simply redistributes power from wealthy individuals to select elites without making its overall distribution more equitable. In addition, Smith contends that campaign finance reform favors wealthy candidates. Additional regulation only increases the advantage *Buckley* gave to such candidates when it struck down restrictions on candidates contributing to their own campaigns. Finally, Smith argues that campaign finance reform favors special interest over grassroots activity. Because it requires lawyers and others with specialized knowledge to navigate through the shoals of legal requirements, regulation "professionalizes" politics and thus distances it from ordinary citizens.

Samuel Issacharoff and Pamela Karlan attack reform differently.[15] They lay out two different reform critiques—one consequential and one normative. "Because," they believe, many reformers "are relatively unfamiliar with the more general history of electoral reform or are largely uninterested in the practical details of political regulation," reform strategies have largely led to "perverse consequences." As they colorfully argue,

> [Reform has] produced a system in which candidates face an unlimited demand for campaign funds (because expenditures generally cannot be capped) but a constricted supply (because there is often a ceiling on the amount each contributor can give). As in all markets in which demand runs high but supply is limited, the value of the good rises. In campaigns, the result is an unceasing preoccupation with fundraising. The effect is much like giving a starving man unlimited trips to the buffet table but only a thimble-sized spoon with which to eat: chances are great that the constricted means to satisfy his appetite will create a singular obsession with consumption. If candidates are unable to rely on large contributions, the rather predictable outcome is that they will spend all their time having to chase smaller contributions to fill their giant-sized appetites.

The more serious perverse consequence that they see is that since the "money that reform squeezes out of the formal campaign process must go somewhere," power will move away from more accountable political actors, like candidates and parties, toward less accountable actors like individuals and special interest groups.

Their normative critique attacks the vision of politics that they see underpinning the reformers' case. To their minds, reform necessarily rests on an "idealistic" or a "republican-communitarian perspective" that is wrongheaded as a normative matter and unrealistic as a descriptive one. Reformers, they believe, think politics should be thoughtful, deliberative, and aimed at the public good. Such a view, they argue, violates equality because it devalues the ways many ordinary people actually make decisions and would shift power "towards those individuals who are good at making political arguments for themselves and away from individuals who depend on others to make their arguments for them. . . . [I]t is hardly surprising that the scholarly argument for campaign reform would produce a world in which intellectuals would have more influence and the persons they have chosen not to be— businessmen or the people who devote their working hours to earning a living in a fashion that does not involve having and disseminating deep political thoughts—will have less."

In two different short pieces, Kathleen Sullivan argues against the dangers that reformers fear and the legal arguments that they muster to defend campaign finance regulation. In one article she attacks the "seven . . . supposedly deadly sins of unregulated political money," which run from political inequality in voting, distortion of public policy, corruption, carpetbagging, diversion of legislative and executive energies, and enervation of political debate to lack of competitiveness in elections.[16] Each, she claims, is overstated, misconceived, or otherwise wrong. As a result, the reform movement needs to narrow its ambitions to disclosure. Only in that way can it avoid perverse, unintended consequences and a cure that is worse than the disease.

In the other article Sullivan attacks reformers' legal arguments.[17] To her mind, they make four different arguments for why limits should escape the strict bite of the First Amendment: that money is not speech, that elections are different from other occasions of speech, that campaign finance restrictions are content-neutral, and that compelling interests justify limits. The first argument, she believes, rests on a mistaken "ontological approach" that is notoriously slippery and which the Court has largely rejected in other areas. The second argument "is odd and maybe backwards [in] privileg[ing] non-campaign over campaign debate" and leads to unacceptable difficulties in administration. The third she rejects as resting on an indefensible form of structural redistribution among speakers. And the fourth she rejects for the reasons given in the first article: the compelling interests that reformers assert are misguided.

Finally, Lillian BeVier takes on the reformers' central constitutional argument—that courts should not employ strict scrutiny.[18] They are mistaken, she argues, for two reasons. First, reformers fail to realize the great injury that most campaign finance reforms do to critical First Amendment interests. In particular, "limitations on giving and spending burden certain forms of political participation rather than regulating the entire range of political activities [and t]he political realities of campaign finance reform . . . suggest that these activities are the target of regulation at least in part because they are closely tied to political agendas that reformers oppose." Second, reformers get the institutional concerns exactly backward when they suggest that courts should exhibit great deference to Congress's judgments in campaign finance matters. In few other areas, BeVier argues, is there less reason to trust congressional judgment. Campaign finance, like election law generally, offers unique opportunities for incumbents to bias the system in their own favor.

These writers offer a fair sample of the many different positions political and legal commentators take on campaign finance law reform. The great differences of opinion spring not just from different notions of what the Constitution requires, but also from different normative and descriptive assumptions about democratic politics. The debate is complex and fascinating, and so long as such robust and differing ideas abound about how democracy should and does function it will remain irresolvable.

Notes

1. *Buckley* v. *Valeo,* 424 U.S. 1 (1976).

2. *First National Bank of Boston* v. *Bellotti,* 435 U.S. 765 (1978).

3. *Massachusetts Citizens for Life, Inc.,* v. *FEC,* 479 U.S. 238 (1986); *Austin* v. *Michigan State Chamber of Commerce,* 494 U.S. 652 (1990).

4. *Colorado Republican Federal Campaign Committee* v. *FEC,* 518 U.S. 604 (1996).

5. *FEC* v. *Colorado Republican Federal Campaign Committee,* 533 U.S. 431 (2001).

6. *Nixon* v. *Shrink Missouri Government PAC,* 528 U.S. 377 (2000).

7. *McConnell* v. *FEC,* 124 S.Ct. 619 (2003).

8. *California Medical Association* v. *FEC,* 453 U.S. 182 (1981).

9. Vincent Blasi, "Free Speech and the Widening Gyre of Fund-Raising: Why Campaign Spending Limits May Not Violate the First Amendment after All," *Columbia Law Review* 94, no. 4 (May 1994): 1281–325.

10. J. Skelly Wright, "Politics and the Constitution: Is Money Speech?" *Yale Law Journal* 85 (July 1976): 1001.

11. Cass R. Sunstein, "Political Equality and Unintended Consequences," *Columbia Law Review* 94. no. 4 (May 1994): 1390–414.

12. Fred Wertheimer and Susan Weiss Manes, "Campaign Finance Reform: A Key to Restoring the Health of Our Democracy," *Columbia Law Review* 94, no. 4 (May 1994): 1126–59.

13. Ronald Dworkin, "The Curse of American Politics," *New York Review of Books,* October 17, 1996, p. 19.

14. Bradley A. Smith, "Faulty Assumptions and Undemocratic Consequences of Campaign Finance Reform," *Yale Law Journal* 105, no. 4 (January 1996): 1049–91.

15. Samuel Issacharoff and Pamela S. Karlan, "The Hydraulics of Campaign Finance Reform," *Texas Law Review* 77, no. 7 (June 1999): 1705–38.

16. Kathleen M. Sullivan, "Political Money and Freedom of Speech," *U.C. Davis Law Review* 30, no. 3 (Spring 1997): 663–90.

17. Kathleen M. Sullivan, "Against Campaign Finance Reform," *Utah Law Review* (1998): 311–29.

18. Lilian BeVier, "Money and Politics: A Perspective on the First Amendment and Campaign Finance Reform," *California Law Review* 73 (July 1985): 1045.

4

Campaign Finance Disclosure Laws

Trevor Potter

Sunlight is . . . the best . . . disinfectant.
—Justice Louis Brandeis, quoted in *Buckley* v. *Valeo*[1]

Mandatory public disclosure of basic information about the ways in which election campaigns are funded has long been a fundamental aspect of the nation's campaign finance law. Indeed, disclosure has often been called its cornerstone, an essential element in any effort to guarantee a relatively open, transparent democratic process.[2] Transparency, in turn, is intended to give citizens access to the information that they need to make informed political choices and to stem political corruption.

Disclosure requirements historically have had the strong support of both the public and policymakers, and that support continues into the present. The first federal campaign disclosure laws were enacted nearly 100 years ago, and today's requirements were put into place by the Federal Election Campaign Act (FECA) and its 1974 amendments. In the past several years, Congress

The author wishes to acknowledge Daniel Manatt for his work on early drafts of this chapter and Kirk Jowers, Mark Glaze, Glen Shor, and Diana Hartstein for their significant editorial assistance in the chapter's preparation.

enacted three major additions to the federal regime, including new electronic filing requirements;[3] disclosure requirements for so-called 527 organizations, or stealth PACS;[4] and several substantial disclosure provisions in the Bipartisan Campaign Reform Act of 2002 (the Reform Act, or BCRA).[5]

Still, the support for campaign disclosure measures is less monolithic than it appears.[6] The near-unanimous public approval of disclosure in the abstract sometimes breaks down when attention turns to particular, often contentious issues. For example, disclosure requirements for candidate-specific "issue advertising," campaign activity on the Internet, and spending by nonprofit organizations continue to cause considerable controversy. Also, the government's ability to enforce disclosure requirements and its appetite for doing so remain in question. The investigation of fundraising in the 1996 presidential election by the Senate Committee on Government Affairs (detailed in what is commonly known as the Thompson Committee Report) indicated a troubling, persistent culture of evasion of disclosure requirements,[7] and the Supreme Court itself has repeatedly noted the skill with which political operatives avoid the requirements altogether.[8]

Disclosure remains a contested area of election law. The Supreme Court's jurisprudence here is complex and sometimes contradictory. While the Court has generally upheld laws requiring disclosure of campaign contributions and expenditures, it also has ruled that disclosure can violate the First Amendment in certain contexts; for example, when it is applied to anonymous speech by individuals concerning ballot initiatives, when it is seen to create severe regulatory burdens, or when it exposes citizens to politically motivated threats, harassment, and reprisals.[9]

This chapter first outlines the nation's federal and state campaign disclosure regimes, particularly the FECA and the new Reform Act, and discusses the means of enforcing those laws. It then surveys the Supreme Court's disclosure cases and assesses the lower federal and state courts' application of the Supreme Court's rulings. The chapter concludes with a review of proposals for future reform of the disclosure regime.

Throughout, this chapter will emphasize the key issues underlying the debate over disclosure policy, especially the following:

—*What are the main purposes of disclosure laws?* To deter and detect corruption, inform voters, or promote accountability and civility? Are some of those purposes constitutionally invalid?

—*Who should be required to disclose?* Candidates, parties, and PACs only? Donors and fundraisers? Other speakers, including nonprofit organizations?

—*What information should be disclosed?* Contributions? Expenditures? Contracts for future advertising? At what level of specificity?

—*When should disclosure be made?* How quickly and often? Electronically?

—*To whom should disclosure be made?* To media outlets like television stations airing political advertisements? To voters themselves, by way of disclaimers within political communications? To government agencies?

—*What limitations and exceptions apply to disclosure laws?* Time limitations, dollar thresholds, and small donor exceptions? Exemptions when disclosure imposes undue burdens on or danger to citizens?

—*Whose rights and which rights are at stake in the constitutional debate over disclosure?* The candidate's right to free speech? The voter's right to information? The third party's right to criticize politicians? Do some of those rights take precedence over others?

At all times, this chapter seeks to examine the inherent tension between competing First Amendment values animating the disclosure debate: the right to free, private, and even *secret* speech and association; the public's right to information about candidates; and the great importance of an informed electorate in a democratic society.[10]

The Disclosure Framework

Today's campaign disclosure framework has its roots in laws enacted at the turn of the twentieth century, most specifically the Publicity Act of 1910. Generally, those early laws fell short of their goals; candidates and political committees seldom complied with them, and the entities charged with enforcing the laws rarely did so.[11]

The modern disclosure regime began with the passage of the FECA and its amendments in 1974 and 1976. The FECA updated and expanded requirements for disclosing campaign contributions and expenditures and gave responsibility for collecting the data to the newly created Federal Election Commission (FEC).[12] The federal campaign finance disclosure regime was greatly strengthened by a 2002 law requiring disclosure by 527 organizations—nonfederal, nonprofit political committees dubbed stealth PACs—and was further strengthened by BCRA in 2002.[13] The technological and procedural aspects of disclosure were likewise transformed in 1996, when the FEC first authorized voluntary electronic filing of reports required by the FECA.[14] Congress began requiring electronic or Internet-based filing of campaign reports in 1999, though the requirement was not implemented until 2001.[15]

Even before these recent legislative changes, the volume of data disclosed to the FEC—which did not include "electioneering communications" for candidate-specific "issue advertising" until the 2004 cycle—had vastly increased. In the 2000 election cycle, through electronic filings alone, the FEC received reports disclosing $1 billion in campaign transactions from more than 1,000 federal filers and entered 2,390,837 detailed records in its database, which is available to the public through the Internet.[16]

The Federal Scheme: The FECA, BCRA, and Related Laws

The FECA and related federal campaign disclosure laws include three core areas:

—parties that are required to disclose their funding and its sources, including individuals, federal political committees (candidate campaign committees, political parties, political action committees), bundlers or conduits, 527 organizations and nonfederal political action committees, corporations, labor unions, and nonprofit organizations

—political advertising that is required to disclose its funding sources under the FECA, BCRA, Federal Communications Commission (FCC), and even U.S. Postal Service laws that target the type of communication, rather than the type of communicator

—laws designed to combat "political money laundering"— that is, laws proscribing circumvention of disclosure laws.

Individuals

Individuals are required to disclose the following types of independent federal campaign spending to the FEC:

"Independent expenditures" (express advocacy). If an individual spends more than $250 in a calendar year on "independent expenditures" in connection with a given election, the individual must report it to the FEC.[17] If an individual makes or contracts to make "independent expenditures" aggregating $10,000 or more in connection with a given election at any time up to the twentieth day before the election—or aggregating $1,000 or more within twenty days of a given election—additional FEC reporting is required.[18]

Electioneering communications. An individual who spends in aggregate excess of $10,000 in any calendar year on the direct costs of producing or airing an "electioneering communication" must file a report with the FEC within twenty-four hours of the communication's public airing.[19] The report must disclose the amount of each disbursement of more than $200 during the period covered by the report.[20]

Federal Political Committees

At its most basic level, FEC disclosure requirements involve a two-step process: registration and reporting. Federal political committees—a category that includes candidate campaign committees, political parties, and federal political action committees (PACs)—must register with the FEC upon their organization.[21] Candidates are required to file disclosure reports quarterly even during nonelection years;[22] national parties are required to file reports monthly in every calendar year;[23] and federal PACs are required to disclose spending quarterly or monthly depending on whether they are reporting in an election year or a nonelection year.[24]

The reports must identify each donor who has given $200 or more to the organization in a calendar year.[25] Committees must also make their "best efforts" to secure the name, mailing address, occupation, and employer of each contributor.[26]

As elections approach, reporting requirements increase substantially. Entities must file pre- and postelection reports twelve days before and twenty days after an election, and in the final days of a campaign, contributions of $1,000 or more must be reported within forty-eight hours.[27]

Electioneering Communication Disclosure

BCRA created a disclosure requirement for "electioneering communications," television and radio advertising that refers to a federal candidate, that is broadcast within thirty days of a primary or sixty days of a general election, and that targets the relevant electorate.[28]

Under BCRA, corporate and labor treasury funds may not be used for electioneering communications. In order to finance such communications, corporations (including most incorporated nonprofit organizations) and unions have to use a separate, segregated fund that is registered as a federal political committee and can contain only limited contributions from individuals. Other persons or entities, including unincorporated section 501(c)(3) or (c)(4) organizations, may not use donations from corporations or unions to finance electioneering communications, but they may use donations from individuals for such purposes. In that event, the act requires disclosure when their spending on electioneering communications aggregates to more than $10,000 in a calendar year.[29]

State Party Disclosure

Under the Reform Act, nonfederal funds raised by state political parties are subject to federal disclosure requirements in certain circumstances.

Specifically, any state party funds spent on voter registration or voter mobilization or get-out-the-vote activities—categorized as "Federal election activity" under BCRA because they affect federal elections as well as state and local elections in some instances—must be disclosed to the FEC.[30]

Disclosure by 527 Organizations

Technically, all political organizations are "527 organizations"—nonprofit political organizations exempt from income tax under section 527 of the Tax Code.[31] However, as the term is commonly used, 527 entities are organizations subject only to Internal Revenue Service rather than FEC disclosure requirements because their activities do not require them to register with the FEC as a federal political committee. Under the 527 disclosure law—enacted in 2000 after the presidential primary campaigns, in which such entities were very active—these organizations must file reports with the IRS that largely mirror the reporting requirements for federal political committees filing with the FEC. Under the law, 527s must register with the IRS and file reports on a semiannual or quarterly basis disclosing the names and addresses of all persons who contribute $200 or more to them and of all persons or entities that receive $500 or more from them. An amendment to the 527 law was passed by Congress on November 2, 2002, exempting from the additional disclsoure requirements state PACs that focus exclusively on state-level elections and that already disclose their contributions and expenditures to state election oversight agencies.

The constitutionality of the IRS disclosure provisions applicable to 527 organizations was challenged in litigation shortly after the disclsoure law was enacted.[32] In 2002, the Mobile Republican Assembly and other parties brought suit to invalidate the contribution and expenditure disclosure requirements for 527 organizations on the grounds that they violated the groups' right to free speech and that the imposition of the requirements on state and local organizations violated principles of federalism. On December 24, 2003, the U.S. Court of Appeals for the Eleventh Circuit upheld a critical aspect of the nation's disclosure regime, ruling that Congress may require 527 political organizations to publicly disclose information about their contributors and expenditures. The Eleventh Circuit Court unanimously held that the disclosure requirements, rather than imposing an unconstitutional penalty, were merely a condition placed on the voluntary receipt of a government subsidy, a tax exemption. The court noted that any political organizations uncomfortable with expenditure or contribution disclsoure may decline to file for the exemption and avoid the requirements. Further, the court reasoned that "the fact that the organization might then engage in somewhat less speech because of stricter financial constraints does not create a constitutionally mandated right to the tax subsidy."[33]

Media Disclaimers

All "public communications"[34] by *federal PACs* must bear an advertising "disclaimer."[35] The following public communications by *individuals* also must bear a disclaimer:

—public communications expressly advocating a federal candidate's election or defeat

—public communications that also are electioneering communications

—public communications that solicit federal campaign contributions.[36]

Exceptions to the disclaimer regulations include the following:

—buttons, bumper stickers, pins, and similar items on which the disclaimer cannot be easily or conveniently printed

—skywriting, water towers, or other larger-scale advertisement displays wherein the inclusion of a disclaimer would be impracticable

—checks, receipts, and other items of minimal value that are purely administrative and lack a political message[37]

—permissible solicitations of funds for a corporate or union federal PAC by its connected corporation or union or by the PAC itself

—permissible communications by a union or corporation (or its affiliated federal PAC) to its restricted class.[38]

General Disclaimer Requirements. If the public communication is not authorized by a federal candidate (or campaign or agent), the disclaimer must, in a clear and obvious manner, state the full name and permanent address, telephone number, or World Wide Web address of the person or organization that paid for the communication. The disclaimer also must state that the communication is not authorized by any federal candidate (or by a candidate's campaign committee).[39]

Printed Communications. In addition to the general disclaimer requirements noted above, the disclaimer on a printed public communication must be clearly readable, set apart from other contents of the communication, and printed with a reasonable degree of color and font size.[40]

Television and Radio Communications. Additional "stand by your ad" requirements apply to television and radio communications.[41] Such ads must include an audio statement, indicating that "[name of the political committee or individual] is responsible for the content of this advertising."[42] The statement may be conveyed either in a voice-over or an unobscured full-screen view of a representative of the candidate.[43] For a television ad, the disclaimer must also appear in writing at the end of the advertisement, in letters equal to or greater than 4 percent of the vertical picture height, for at least four seconds, with a reasonable degree of color contrast from the background.[44]

Other Federal Disclosure Requirements

Political committees and other entities or persons are subject to a range of disclosure requirements.

Fundraising Solicitation Disclaimers. The FECA also requires that political fundraising solicitations through certain media—whether or not they feature the language of express advocacy—must include a disclaimer disclosing whether they were paid for or authorized by the candidates that they support.[45] Moreover, the Internal Revenue Code requires political organizations whose gross proceeds exceed $100,000 to indicate on solicitations that contributions to such entities are not tax deductible.[46]

Independent Expenditures and Express Advocacy Communications. Political committees also must report independent expenditures, which by definition include only express advocacy communications.[47] Non-PACs making independent expenditures, such as individuals or nonprofits legally permitted to do so,[48] also must file a report with the FEC, similar to those required of political committees.[49] Any independent expenditure of $1,000 or more made within twenty days of an election must be reported within twenty-four hours of the expenditure.[50] The Reform Act adds a new requirement that any independent expenditure of $10,000 or more during an election cycle must be reported within forty-eight hours of the expenditure.[51]

Bundler or Conduit Disclosure. Disclosure to the FEC is also required of all entities serving as conduits or "bundlers"—people or groups that make fundraising solicitations on behalf of a campaign or political committee, then receive and forward the contributions to the campaign or committee.[52] Campaign officials and other committee agents are exempt from this reporting requirement, although some campaigns have voluntarily reported the names of their fundraisers and the amounts raised. The Bush-Cheney 2004 campaign, for example, posted its top fundraisers, the Pioneers and Rangers, on the campaign website.[53]

Contribution Laundering and Contributing in the Name of Another. The FECA forbids "contribution laundering" and other evasions. The act proscribes making "contributions in the name of another," which includes making or allowing someone else to make a contribution and falsely identifying the contributor.[54]

Federal Communications Commission Political Advertising Disclosure. The Federal Communications Act of 1934 requires that all commercial and political broadcast advertising identify the advertisement's sponsor.[55] For political advertising, special rules apply.[56] For instance, sponsors of political advertising must disclose certain information about the sponsors' leadership and the "true identity" of the sponsor.[57]

BCRA amends the FCC disclosure requirements to require television and radio stations to maintain records of all requests for political advertising time relating to candidates or legislative issues. The records must include the person or entity buying the time, the candidate or issue concerned, and the date and time the ad runs, if at all.[58]

U.S. Postal Commission Political Disclosure. Under U.S. Postal Service disclosure rules, political parties, certain nonprofit organizations, and sponsors of bulk mailings also are subject to disclosure rules. A sponsor of nonprofit mailings, including political mailings, must identify itself on each mail piece that it sends. False representation of the mailing group's true identity is prohibited; an organization may not identify itself by using "pseudonyms or bogus names of persons or organizations."[59]

Additional Disclosure by Nonprofits, Corporations, and Unions

Nonprofit Disclosure: Section 501(c)(3) and (c)(4) Organizations. Form 990, the annual information return filed by 501(c)(3) and (c)(4) tax-exempt organizations, reports organizational income, budget, officer salaries, general budget categories, and other information. Portions of the report must be made public; however, contributions to the organization are exempt from the public reporting requirement Nonprofits also must make public their application for tax-exempt, nonprofit status (on IRS Forms 1023 or 1024) and related documents.[60]

Corporate and Labor Internal Communications. Under the FECA, corporations, labor unions, and other organizations must disclose to the FEC all expenditures of more than $2,000 for "internal communications" made to stockholders, employees, or members expressly advocating the election or defeat of a particular candidate.[61] Those communications, though subject to disclosure requirements, are an exception to the general ban on corporate and union expenditures in connection with federal elections.

Labor Disclosure. Under the Labor Management Reporting and Disclosure Act of 1959, labor unions with annual receipts of $200,000 or more must disclose their internal finances to the Labor Department on Form LM-2 (Labor Organization Annual Report).[62] The Labor Department revised Form

LM-2, mandating that the form be filed electronically, that unions "identify 'major' receipts and disbursements," and that labor organizations report the "assets, liabilities, receipts, and disbursements . . . that meet the statutory definition of a 'trust in which a labor organization is interested.'"[63] The regulations were challenged in court, and on January 22, 2004, the U.S. District Court for the District of Columbia found the rule implementing the revised LM-2 reasonable and upheld it in *AFL-CIO* v. *Chao*.[64] The rule is now in full effect.[65]

Federal Disclosure Technology and Public Access

Perhaps as significant as the substantive disclosure reforms in BCRA is the new requirement that statements and reports filed with the FEC must be posted for public access on the Internet within forty-eight hours of receipt by the commission.[66] Implementation of electronic filing, while not perfect, has generally won praise from the regulated community, incuding skeptics who now embrace electronic filing as a vast improvement in efficiency. As noted earlier, the only federal candidates not now filing electronically are those for the U.S. Senate, as Senate leaders continue to refuse to require electronic filing for incumbent senators and their challengers.

BCRA also includes a number of noncontroversial but significant disclosure provisions. The act directs the FEC to create a central website not only for reports and statements required to be filed with the commission but also for any election-related information publicly disclosed by other agencies.[67] The website could, and should, feature links to reporting by 527 organizations to the IRS, as well as lobbying, labor, and FCC disclosures, among other types.[68] The act also requires the FEC to develop free software with specific, disclosure-enhancing functionalities, such as the capacity for candidates and committees to file in real time, with instantaneous public availability on the web.[69] It also requires that presidential inaugural committees disclose any donations of more than $200.[70]

State Disclosure Innovations

In the early to middle 1970s, most states enacted campaign finance disclosure statutes modeled on the FECA.[71] The majority of those states, however, began making that information available to the public over the Internet only in the last five years.

The scope and quality of state disclosure regimes range from very good— approaching the federal standard (state money websites for Idaho, Colorado, Ohio)—to nonexistent (Montana, Tennessee, Alaska, Minnesota, South

Carolina, and Wyoming). The fact that in many states, even those with comprehensive disclosure requirements and full Internet access to information, only scanned images of required disclosure forms are available, usually in PDF files, is a major stumbling block. Data from such documents do not become part of a searchable database; instead, the forms must be inspected one by one, which substantially hampers research efforts. Similarly, some states have important disclosure measures on the books that nevertheless fall far short of the federal standard. California, for instance, requires broad disclosure of campaign contributors but provides only summaries, rather than information about actual contributors, to the public. Also, as legislators cut budgets, disclosure programs sometimes have been targets of legislators who believe that such programs do not serve their political interests.

While the FECA disclosure framework served as the substantive model for nearly all the states that established disclosure regimes, the requirements of some differ from—and even exceed, in certain areas—the federal model. Some examples:

Fundraiser Disclosure (Kentucky). Under Kentucky law, fundraisers are required to report contributions received and expenditures made on behalf of gubernatorial candidates. Any persons who directly solicit and receive contributions must register with the state election registry once their fundraising exceeds $3,000 in any election.[72]

Banking-Based Disclosure (Massachusetts). Massachusetts requires banking institutions used by candidates to file reports reflecting all deposits (contributions) and withdrawls (expenditures).[73] The banking-level disclosure is meant to ensure more accurate and verifiable disclosure.

Financial Instrument and Transaction Restrictions (California and New Jersey). Under California law, contributions must be made by written instrument containing the name of the donor and the name of the payee.[74] New Jersey forbids cash payment of any campaign obligation and requires any payment by a campaign or political committee—including payments for voter mobilization efforts, historically made in cash—to be made by check.[75]

Donor-Specific Disclosure Laws (Connecticut, California, and Hawaii). Under Connecticut law, special disclosure must be made of lobbyists' donations. Lobbyists and their spouses and dependents who contribute to candidates or committees have a legal obligation to inform the recipient that they have made the donation. The recipient must indicate which contributions originated with lobbyists when filing state disclosure forms.[76] California requires that disclosure reports be filed not only by candidates and committees but by certain donors as well. This "major donor" disclosure provision applies to donors who donate $10,000 or more in contributions to state or local candidates or committees in a calendar year and continues for all periods in which the donor exceeds the $10,000 threshold.[77] Finally, some state codes contain statutes requiring special disclosure by state contractors to prevent quid pro quo arrangements between businesses and state officeholders. Hawaii's disclosure law, for example, provides that state contractors who receive $50,000 or more in state contracts in a year must register and report their campaign contributions to the state election commission.[78] Disclosure must include the donor and candidate's name, total amount of state contracts, and an itemization of each state contract awarded to the donor.[79] If the contractor is a corporation, the disclosure also must include the names of the company's principal officers and directors.[80]

Enforcement of Disclosure Laws

FEC Enforcement and Administrative Fines

Enforcement of the FECA's disclosure provisions is a multifaceted process. First, the FEC may begin an investigation based on information that it has obtained in carrying out its supervisory responsibilities or when a complaint is filed by a third party alleging that a violation has occurred.[81] The commission's conventional investigation and enforcement process is very time consuming, and historically disclosure violations have not been given high priority. An administrative fines system was established in 2000 to provide an alternative to the conventional enforcement process and thereby ensure relatively swift and certain sanctions for nonfiling and late filing.[82] Under the program, entities failing to file or filing late are automatically fined and given forty days to either pay the penalty or submit a written explanation and begin the conventional dispute resolution procedure. Through 2002, the FEC had issued 519 administrative fines and collected a total of $722, 221 in fines.[83]

The commission recently adopted a new rule modifying the administrative fines program. Among other changes, the rule reduces the fines assessed on political committees that have less than $50,000 in financial activity in a reporting period.[84]

Justice Department Prosecution of Disclosure Violations: The False Statements Act

FECA disclosure violations are prosecuted either by the FEC pursuant to its civil enforcement authority[85] or by the Justice Department's Public

Integrity Section or U.S. Attorneys when the violation, by being a knowing and willful act, becomes a federal crime.[86]

BCRA increased the penalties for serious knowing and willful violations. In addition to increasing the criminal statute of limitations for violations of federal campaign finance law from three years to five years (as for most federal crimes),[87] it increased criminal penalties for knowing and willful violations of federal campaign finance law involving amounts aggregating more than $25,000 in a calendar year while maintaining the previous $2,000 "floor" for criminal prosecutions.[88] The act also directs the U.S. Sentencing Commission to promulgate a specific sentencing guideline for federal campaign finance offenses.[89] Previously, there was no specific sentencing guideline for campaign finance offenses, though some were dealt with under the general fraud guideline. In compliance with the act, the commission approved a new guideline specific to violations of provisions of federal campaign finance law.[90]

In addition to bringing actions under the FECA against knowing and willful violators, the Justice Department and U.S. Attorneys can prosecute FECA disclosure violations under a statute forbidding false statements to government agencies. The False Statements Act applies to individuals who have a legal responsibility to file reports with the government—in the FECA context, campaign or political committee treasurers.[91] Quite often campaign treasurers are not the actual "bad actors" when disclosure rules are violated; rather they merely convey false information provided by other campaign officials or by contributors. Prosecutions therefore often are based not only on the false statement itself but also on the original wrongdoing by use of theories of vicarious culpability, such as when someone "causes" the filing of false statements by providing false information to the committee knowing that it will be filed with the FEC.[92] The federal conspiracy statute can also be used to reach those who conspire with "straw donors" or others to carry out a scheme that violates disclosure requirements.[93]

Campaign Disclosure and the Constitution

Political disclosure laws can implicate core constitutional rights and values, including the rights of free speech and free association and the public interest in an informed electorate and an accountable government. It is therefore useful to understand the Supreme Court's disclosure decisions and its First Amendment jurisprudence more generally.

The Supreme Court has concluded that disclosure requirements both infringe on First Amendment freedoms and promote First Amendment interests. Mandatory disclosure infringes on those rights to the extent that it necessarily imposes regulatory burdens on speech and associational activities like political advertising and organizing. Conversely, disclosure greatly enhances the "marketplace of ideas" by furnishing important information about the nation's democratic processes. In particular, disclosure provides information that is essential if voters are to make informed political decisions and hold officeholders responsible for their actions. Thus, to the extent that a main purpose of the First Amendment is to facilitate open, effective democratic governance, disclosure is thought to promote that end.

Understanding this tension—what might be termed disclosure's constitutional paradox—is the key to understanding the Supreme Court's disclosure jurisprudence. A close examination reveals that this paradox has resulted in inconsistent rulings at all levels of the federal and state judiciaries.

Supreme Court Disclosure Jurisprudence: The Buckley Framework

The Supreme Court has developed a complex constitutional framework for analyzing disclosure provisions. As with most areas of campaign finance law, the lodestar of its analysis is the seminal 1976 case, *Buckley* v. *Valeo*.[94]

Threshold Question: Are Disclosure Laws Subject to Intermediate or Strict Judicial Scrutiny?

When the Supreme Court considers the constitutionality of a law touching on activity protected by the First Amendment, it often employs a balancing test, considering whether the justification for the law outweighs the potential impact of the statute on the protected freedoms. A first step in the analysis involves determining the degree of constitutional protection the activity at issue commands and the risk that the law under consideration poses to the protected activity. In cases in which the asserted freedom lies near the heart of First Amendment rights, the Court conducts a searching analysis of the law and its potential effects, demanding that the law be narrowly tailored to serve compelling state interests. Conversely, where the asserted activity has traditionally been afforded less constitutional protection, as with commercial speech, or is not placed at substantial risk by the asserted category of regulation, the Court applies a lower degree of scrutiny and may require only that the law serve an interest that the legislature involved was rational in asserting.

Accordingly, the Court in *Buckley* began its analysis by determining the appropriate level of "judicial scrutiny" to apply to the FECA's disclosure provisions. Reasoning that "compelled disclosure in itself can seriously infringe on privacy of association and belief,"[95] the Court concluded that the risk to those important rights posed by the disclosure provisions was sufficient to require courts reviewing the regulations to apply "exacting scrutiny."[96] In order to be upheld, the Court reasoned, a disclosure provision must be justified by *important public interests* and have a *relevant correlation* or *substantial relation* to the public interest being served. This level of scrutiny is generally referred to as "intermediate scrutiny," as opposed to the higher standard of "strict scrutiny," under which a statute must be *narrowly tailored* to promote a *compelling state interest.*[97]

What Public Interests Justify Disclosure?

Applying intermediate scrutiny to the facts of the case, the Court sought to identify important interests served by campaign finance disclosure law and to determine whether the FECA's disclosure provisions were drawn with sufficient care to have a relevant correlation or substantial relation to those interests.[98]

The "Anti-Corruption Interest." The *Buckley* Court observed that mandatory campaign finance disclosure, by exposing campaign fundraising and spending to public scrutiny, deters both actual and apparent corruption in the nation's democratic processes. The Court also noted that disclosure is helpful in detecting and prosecuting violations of federal contribution limits.[99]

The "Informational Interest." In addition to the anticorruption utility of disclosure, the Court recognized also that disclosure provides valuable information to voters and therefore contributes substantially to the maintenance of an informed electorate. Campaign information, according to the Court, enables the public to better evaluate candidates and "to place more precisely each candidate along the political spectrum."[100] The Court continued, "knowledge of a candidate's financial sources permits voters to predict future performance in office by identifying the interests to which a candidate is most likely to be responsive." Disclosure also "increases the fund of information concerning those who support the candidates . . . [and] helps voters define more of the candidates' constituencies."[101] In a significant finding, the *Buckley* Court concluded that the informational interest could be as important as the anticorruption interest and that disclosure statutes can be justified by the informational interest in cases in which the implicated anticorruption interest alone provides insufficient justification.[102]

The importance of the informational interest was ratified and expanded in the subsequent *First National Bank of Boston* v. *Bellotti,* in which the Court suggested that disclosure may enable voters to evaluate a political speaker's credibility better and thus the credibility of his or her political communications.[103] However, in *McIntyre* v. *Ohio Board of Elections,* discussed below, a different majority of justices concluded that the informational interest may not be compelling in certain circumstances.[104]

The Narrow Tailoring Test: Vagueness and Overbreadth. In the intermediate scrutiny analysis, a disclosure statute must have a relevant correlation or substantial relation to the interests it is intended to protect. That is, the statute must be carefully drawn to serve the asserted interests, and it must not be so vague or so broad as to be unconstitutional.[105]

The original Federal Election Campaign Act disclosure provisions raised vagueness issues. As written, the act required disclosure of all independent spending "for the *purpose of influencing* a Federal election."[106] Because that definition was almost entirely subjective, the Court held that it was overly vague and thus "could be interpreted to reach groups engaged purely in issue discussion."[107]

In order to avoid declaring the statute unconstitutionally vague, the Court applied two "narrowing constructions," interpretations meant to save a statute from being held unconstitutional. First, the Court narrowed the definition of "political committees" subject to disclosure to apply only to organizations that are under the control of a candidate or whose major purpose is the nomination or election of a candidate.[108]

Second, and more famously, it narrowed the disclosure provision to cover only express advocacy independent expenditures.[109] As discussed in chapter 7, the Supreme Court in *McConnell* held that the *Buckley* express advocacy standard was merely a saving of poorly drafted statutory language, neither constitutionally required nor particularly useful.

Buckley also addressed whether the FECA's disclosure provisions were overbroad because they applied to donors who made very small contributions. The FECA had two thresholds, or "triggers," that determined whether an entity was required to disclose information. First, political committees were required to disclose names and addresses of individuals contributing more than $10.[110] Second, for individuals making aggregate contributions of more than $100, the committees also were required to disclose the donor's occupation and place of business. While the *Buckley* Court upheld those threshold provisions, it noted that the "thresholds are indeed low."[111] Taking its cue from the Court, Congress raised the contributor disclosure thresholds to $200 in the 1979 amendments to the FECA. Since then, lower courts have generally upheld even lower thresholds.[112]

The Harassment Exemption. The *Buckley* Court did indicate a circumstance in which the FECA's disclosure requirements might pose such an undue burden that they would be unconstitutional. The Court opined that disclosure could be unconstitutional if disclosure would expose groups or their contributors to threats, harassment, and reprisals.[113] To address that concern, the Court suggested a "hardship" exemption from disclosure requirements for groups and inviduals able to demonstrate a reasonable probability that their compliance would result in such adverse consequences.[114]

In establishing the exemption, *Buckley* drew heavily on the 1958 case *NAACP* v. *Alabama*.[115] There, the Court considered a demand by Alabama authorities for extensive disclosure of NAACP records, including a complete list of all NAACP members in the state, to determine whether the group was violating the state's business corporation law. The NAACP—while substantially complying with court orders to produce evidence—sought to block disclosure of some of the information requested, saying that disclosing its membership list would expose members to physical danger. Applying exacting scrutiny, the Supreme Court unanimously blocked the disclosure, stating that Alabama had not demonstrated that its asserted interest—proving that the NAACP was engaged in "business" activity in Alabama—was substantially related to the information sought in the subpoenaed membership lists.[116] In addition, the Court found that the NAACP had empirically proven, through evidence of violence against its members in the segregationist South of the 1950s, that "revelation of the identity of rank-and-file members has exposed these members to economic reprisal, loss of employment, threats of physical coercion, and other manifestations of public hostility."[117] The Court consequently upheld the FECA's disclosure requirements but ruled that parties should be exempt if they could demonstrate a reasonable probability that disclosure would result in threats, harassment, and reprisals against members or the organization itself.[118]

Six years after *Buckley*, the Court granted such an exemption in *Brown* v. *Socialist Workers Party '74 Campaign Committee*.[119] In that case, the Court found that the Workers Party had proven that members had suffered the sort of threats, harassment, and reprisals that the *Buckley* Court had contemplated. Specifically, the Court noted that Workers Party members had been subjected to threatening phone calls, hate mail, police harassment, FBI surveillance, the firing of gunshots at a party office, and the dismissal of several party members from their jobs because of membership.[120] The Court consequently ordered that they be granted an exemption from the FECA's disclosure requirements.[121]

Disclosure by Certain Nonprofits (The MCFL "Exception"). In *Massachusetts Citizens for Life* (MCFL), a nonprofit corporation challenged the FEC's requirement that corporations, including nonprofits, must form a PAC in order to engage in campaign activity.[122] A grassroots pro-life group contended that the strict accounting, disclosure, and reporting requirements imposed on PACs were prohibitively burdensome for small, nonprofit organizations. The Supreme Court agreed, ruling that ideological nonprofits like MCFL, as long as they accept no corporate or union funds, could engage in campaign activity—even express advocacy—without having to comply with all PAC disclosure requirements:

> The administrative costs of complying with such increased responsibilities may create a disincentive for the organization itself to speak. . . . Detailed record-keeping and disclosure obligations . . . impose administrative costs that many small entities may be unable to bear. . . . Faced with the need to assume a more sophisticated organizational form, to adopt specific accounting procedures, to file periodic detailed reports . . . it would not be surprising if at least some groups decided that the contemplated political activity was simply not worth it.[123]

The Court emphasized how burdensome the requirements would be if applied to small entities whose activities consist predominantly of grassroots activities like "garage sales, bake sales, and raffles."[124] The Court therefore created a special exception whereby these so-called "MCFL organizations" would have to report specific independent expenditures but would not have to comply with the FECA's other disclosure and organizational requirements.[125]

In the lower courts, however, actions to invalidate disclosure on the basis of regulatory burden have failed when the party challenging disclosure has been a large organization—namely, a national political party and a coalition of television broadcasters.[126]

Supreme Court Cases in the 1990s: McIntyre, Akins, *and* ACLF

The *Buckley* Court, in sum, narrowed but substantially upheld the FECA's disclosure framework. In the 1970s and 1980s, the Court frequently upheld disclosure provisions. In the 1990s, however, the High Court's disclosure opinions followed a more erratic path.

McIntyre *v.* Ohio Board of Elections: *Overbreadth Analysis Redux,
or a New Right to Anonymous Speech?*

In the 1995 case *McIntyre* v. *Ohio Elections Commission,* the Supreme
Court, after tipping the scale in favor of disclosure in *Buckley,* seemed to
reverse direction and reveal a new skepticism.[127] In *McIntyre,* the Court
appeared to assert that disclosure laws were subject to *strict scrutiny* and in
particular to searching overbreadth analysis. Under its new approach, statutes
would have to be narrowly tailored to support compelling interests, a much
more difficult test than intermediate scrutiny.

The Ohio disclosure law at issue in *McIntyre* required all materials relating
to ballot initiatives or referendum pamphlets to include source identification disclaimers disclosing the name of the entity producing the literature.[128]
The defendant in the case, Mrs. McIntyre, an elderly taxpayer, had hand-
distributed leaflets opposing a school tax levy, which was the subject of an
initiative election. Some leaflets had no source identification disclaimer,
while others included the pseudonymous disclaimer "Concerned Parents and
Taxpayers."[129] The Ohio Elections Commission fined Mrs. McIntyre $100
for violating the source identification disclaimer law.

In defending the statute, Ohio asserted public interests analogous to those
approved in *Buckley*: providing the electorate with relevant information and
preventing fraud and libelous statements. The Court summarily dismissed
the informational interest, reasoning that few members of the public would
know the defendant and thus disclosure of her name revealed little. The
Court also rejected the antifraud and misinformation interest, saying that the
disclosure requirements duplicated several more specific prohibitions in
Ohio's election code against making or disseminating false statements during
political campaigns. The Court thus found that the purpose was served better
by other provisions and that the statute was redundant, overbroad, and
unconstitutional.[130]

In doing so, the Court appeared to apply strict, not intermediate, scrutiny,
requiring Ohio to show that the law promoted compelling state interests and
was narrowly tailored.[131] The Court seemed to weigh two considerations
most heavily. First, the Court extolled the historical importance of anonymous speech, citing such illustrious anonymous works as the *Federalist
Papers.*[132] Second, it was plainly concerned with the breadth of the statute.
Regarding the latter, the Court said that the Ohio law

> applies not only to the activities of candidates and their organized sup-
> porters, but also to individuals acting independently and using only

their own modest resources. It applies not only to elections of public officers, but also to ballot issues that present neither a substantial risk of libel nor any potential appearance of corrupt advantage. It applies not only to leaflets distributed on the eve of an election, when the opportunity for reply is limited, but also to those distributed months in advance. It applies no matter what the character or strength of the author's interest in anonymity. We recognize that a State's enforcement interest might justify a more limited identification requirement, but Ohio has shown scant cause for inhibiting the leafleting at issue here.[133]

It is important to note that the decision is written so as to apply only to ballot issues, and the Court expressly distinguished ballot initiatives from candidate elections.[134]

McIntyre's *Impact on Disclosure Laws: Broad or Narrow?*

The lower courts are split on *McIntyre's* reach. Several courts have interpreted the ruling broadly, asserting that the Court actually created a constitutional right to anonymous speech. Among those cases are *West Virginians for Life, Inc., v. Smith, Yes for Life PAC v. Webster,* and *Stewart v. Taylor.*[135] The district court in *Stewart* went even farther, construing *McIntyre* to recognize a right to engage in anonymous political speech that extended to candidates engaging in express advocacy on their own behalf, despite the *McIntyre* Court's language to the contrary.[136]

However, a number of other courts have held that *McIntyre* did not establish a right to anonymous speech but merely applied standard overbreadth analysis to a particular statute. Among them are the Second and the Sixth Circuit Court in *FEC* v. *Survival Education Fund* and *Kentucky Right to Life* v. *Terry,* respectively; the California, Texas, and Connecticut Supreme Courts in *Griset v. Fair Political Practices Commission, Osterberg v. Peca,* and *Seymour* v. *Elections Enforcement Commission,* respectively; and the U.S. District Court for Southern Alabama in *Richey* v. *Tyson.*[137]

In these cases, the courts opined that *McIntyre* did not fundamentally change *Buckley's* disclosure framework and suggested that narrowly crafted disclosure statutes, including source disclosure laws, still can withstand constitutional scrutiny. Specifically, *Seymour* held that the Supreme Court had limited *McIntyre's* reach to ballot issues and was inapplicable to candidate elections. *Osterberg* likewise analyzed *McIntyre* to hold merely that disclosure requirements may be unconstitutional if they violate the overbreadth test.[138] *Survival Education Fund* differentiated the facts in that case from those in

McIntyre, concluding that the government's interest in regulating fundraising is sufficiently compelling to withstand a constitutional challenge.[139] Finally, *Richey* concluded that the Court in *McIntyre* had not treated advocacy of the passage or defeat of a ballot measure or referendum as "automatically beyond the reach of government regulation."[140]

FEC v. Akins: *New Life for the "Informational Interest"?*

Another significant post-*Buckley* case is 1998's *FEC* v. *Akins*.[141] In that case, the Supreme Court held that private citizens may sue the FEC to enforce the FECA's disclosure provisions. The *Akins* Court reasoned that citizens suffer an "informational injury" when political groups fail to make disclosures—a holding that suggests that the informational interest, *McIntyre* notwithstanding, may be alive and well.

According to the *Akins* Court, "[Citizens'] failure to obtain relevant information—is an injury of a kind that FECA seeks to address." It added, "The 'injury in fact' that respondents have suffered consists of their inability to obtain information—lists of . . . donors . . . and campaign-related contributions and expenditures—that, on respondents' view of the law, the statute requires that [PACs] make public. There is no reason to doubt their claim that the information would help them (and others to whom they would communicate it) to evaluate candidates for public office, especially candidates who received assistance from [PACs], and to evaluate the role that [PACs'] financial assistance might play in a specific election." It concluded, "[The] informational injury at issue here, directly related to voting, the most basic of political rights, is sufficient . . . to authorize its vindication in the Federal courts."[142]

American Constitutional Law Foundation (ACLF): *A Fractured Court and Jurisprudence*

The most recent Supreme Court ruling on disclosure came in 1999 with *Buckley* v. *American Constitutional Law Foundation (ACLF)* (commonly referred to as *Buckley II*).[143] This case addressed compelled disclosure in the context of ballot initiative petitions. The Court reviewed two Colorado statutory provisions governing the ballot initiative petition process: a provision requiring all petition circulators to wear name badges while soliciting signatures for the initiatives and a provision requiring that the names and addresses of all paid petition circulators be disclosed.

The Court unanimously struck down the name badge requirement, saying that the requirement constituted compelled disclosure likely to chill speech

without a sufficient state interest. Five justices also found the petition's circu-
lator reporting provisions unconstitutional, noting that the Colorado statute
at issue already contained sponsor disclosure provisions that promoted the
asserted antifraud and informational interests.[144] Justice Ginsburg, writing for
the majority, wrote that "the added benefit of revealing the names of paid circulators . . . is hardly apparent and has not been demonstrated." The Court
also noted that "ballot initiatives do not involve the risk of *'quid pro quo'* corruption present when money is paid to, or for, candidates."[145]

Justice Sandra Day O'Connor (who was joined by Justice Stephen Breyer)
and Chief Justice Rehnquist each wrote strong dissents concerning the
reporting portion of the decision. O'Connor termed the majority's opinion a
"disturbing" invalidation of "vitally important" disclosure regulations.
O'Connor said that the antifraud interest provided a sufficient basis to
uphold the reporting requirement. O'Connor also forcefully argued for the
provision based on the informational interest in disclosure:

> Colorado's disclosure reports provide facts useful to voters who are
> weighing the options. Member of the public deciding whether to sign a
> petition or how to vote on a measure can discover who has proposed it,
> who has provided funds for its circulation, and to whom these funds
> have been provided. Knowing the names of paid circulators and the
> amount paid to them also allows members of the public to evaluate the
> sincerity or, alternatively, the potential bias of any circulator that
> approaches them.[146]

Disclosure in the State and Federal Courts

As the cases described above make clear, the Supreme Court has left a
somewhat erratic path for lower courts to follow. Consequently, lower courts
have had to confront numerous specific issues without direct Supreme Court
precedent and with rather conflicted guidance on basic questions.

Disclosure and Issue Advocacy prior to McConnell

The exact scope of *Buckley's* disclosure holding may be the most liti-
gated—yet least settled—election law issue in the quarter century since
Buckley.[147] In particular, disclosure of candidate-specific "issue advocacy,"
often in the form of so-called "sham issue ads," has emerged as one of the
most contentious areas of election law. The debate was finally resolved by the
Supreme Court in *McConnell* v. *FEC*.

Strict View Prior to McConnell: *Disclosure Is Restricted to "Magic Words" Express Advocacy.* Prior to *McConnell*, several courts had struck down disclosure provisions if they regulated any communications that were not "express advocacy" using the so-called "magic words" set forth in *Buckley*.[148]

Courts taking that approach include the Second Circuit Court in the 1980 case *FEC* v. *Central Long Island Tax Reform Immediately Committee* and the 2002 case *Vermont Right to Life* v. *Sorrell*.[149] In *Sorrell*, the court concluded that *Buckley*'s express advocacy standard was the appropriate constitutional test for disclosure provisions and accordingly struck down a Vermont law requiring disclosure for advertising that "*explicitly or implicitly*"—rather than "*expressly*"—advocated a candidate's election or defeat. The Fourth Circuit Court, in *North Carolina Right to Life Inc.* v. *Bartlett,* similarly held that a state disclosure law "subject[ed] groups engaged in only issue advocacy to an intrusive set of reporting requirements."[150]

In *Kansans for Life, Inc.,* v. *Gaede,* a federal district court held that a television ad that "contrasts the positions of two candidates on the issue of abortion and asserts that one candidate is honestly stating his position on the issue while the other candidate is not" was issue advocacy rather than express advocacy of a candidate's defeat or election and that it could not be held subject to a disclosure requirement. The court wrote that although an ordinary, reasonable person would understand that the ad was *intended to*—and *did*—favor one candidate over the other, the ad did not *expressly* advocate the election or defeat of a candidate because it did not use the magic words set forth in *Buckley* and therefore could not be regulated.[151] The Eighth Circuit Court addressed the questions of the "intent" and "effect" of ads in *Iowa Right to Life* v. *Williams.* There, the court opined that such questions should be excluded from court analysis because an ad's sponsors cannot reasonably be asked to predict how anything the ad might say would be understood by others.[152] The Fifth Circuit Court in *Chamber of Commerce* v. *Moore* similarly held that disclosure requirements were impermissible if the magic words of express advocacy were absent. In doing so, the court reversed a district court opinion concluding that *MCFL* had broadened *Buckley*'s definition of express advocacy to include communications "marginally less direct" than those usually defined as "express advocacy."[153]

In *Planned Parenthood Affiliates of Michigan* v. *Miller,* a federal district court in Michigan invalidated a state rule "prohibit[ing] the use of a candidate's name or likeness in communications made by a corporation forty-five days prior to an election" as "overbroad and [likely to] chill the exercise of constitutionally protected 'issue advocacy.'"[154] Finally, the Fourth Circuit Court in *Perry* v. *Bartlett* invalidated a statute that required disclosure of advertisements in which the sponsoring entity admitted its intent to advocate the election or defeat of a clearly specified candidate. The Court held that it would not recognize an exception to the "express advocacy" test even when the entity admits, outside of the advertisement, that it is trying to defeat a particular candidate.[155]

Middle View: Disclosure Is Restricted to Express Advocacy, but Express Advocacy May Extend beyond Magic Words. In interpreting and applying campaign finance disclosure provisions, some courts prior to *McConnell* construed express advocacy to encompass some language extending beyond the magic words. Those courts gave great weight to the anticorruption and informational interests in disclosure.

FEC v. *Furgatch,* the most prominent case to adopt a broad express advocacy standard, was a disclosure case.[156] Under that decision, speech need not contain the magic words listed in *Buckley* to constitute express advocacy. Rather, express advocacy extends to speech that "when read as a whole, and with limited reference to external events, [is] susceptible of no other reasonable interpretation but as an exhortation to vote for or against a specific candidate."[157] The *Furgatch* court emphasized the strength of the public interest in disclosure:

> One goal of the First Amendment . . . *is to ensure that the individual citizen has available all the information necessary to allow him to properly evaluate speech.* . . . Disclosure requirements, which may at times inhibit the free speech that is so dearly protected by the First Amendment, are indispensable to the proper and effective exercise of First Amendment rights. . . . Properly applied, [disclosure has] only a "reasonable and minimally restrictive" effect on the exercise of First Amendment rights.[158]

Broad View: Narrow Tailoring, Not Express Advocacy, Is the Constitutional Requirement. Several cases cast doubt on whether disclosure must meet any express advocacy test at all, whether broad or narrow. Instead, they suggested that the express advocacy test is merely one way to ensure that disclosure laws are narrowly tailored. In their view, other standards for determining what constitutes a campaign communication properly subject to regulation (including disclosure requirements) may also be narrowly tailored.

For example, the district court's decision in *McConnell* v. *FEC* endorsed the proposition that express advocacy was not constitutionally required for a communication to be subject to funding source prohibitions or disclosure requirements.[159] Those prohibitions and requirements could apply to other communications, so long as they are narrowly tailored to serve compelling government interests. In that case, the court upheld funding source prohibitions and disclosure requirements relating to disbursements for non–express advocacy "electioneering communications" that promoted, supported, attacked, or opposed federal candidates, regardless of whether they expressly advocated a specific election result.

Moreover, in *Wisconsin Realtors* v. *Ponto,* the U.S. District Court for the Western District of Wisconsin rejected plaintiffs' claim that a statute imposing funding source prohibitions and disclosure requirements with respect to advertisements that appear within sixty days of an election and feature a clearly identified candidate is unconstitutional on its face because of its alleged departure from the Buckley definition of express advocacy. In doing so, the court indicated that "in Buckley, the Supreme Court 'stopped short of grounding [the express advocacy test] in the Constitution.'"[160] In *National Federation of Republican Assemblies* v. *United States,* the U.S. District Court for the Southern District of Alabama likewise disputed the notion that a political organization's avoidance of express advocacy placed it beyond the reach of any constitutional disclosure requirement, stating that "*Buckley* did not hold that disclosure requirements [as applied to even organizations that are not political committees] are unconstitutionally overbroad to the extent they reach beyond express electoral advocacy."[161]

Disclaimers in Political Communications

Disclosure requirements requiring disclaimers for political communications often are attacked not only on overbreadth grounds (the basis for the *McIntyre* decision) but also on the theory that they violate the First Amendment prohibition against compelled speech. Under that analysis, disclosure regulations force speakers to make a statement—the disclaimer itself—that they wish to omit. The case law in this area is mixed. In *RNC* v. *FEC* and *FEC* v. *Survival Education Fund,* the District of Columbia District Court and the Second Circuit Court, respectively, rejected "compelled speech" challenges to statutes requiring disclaimers on fundraising solicitations.[162] In *Kentucky Right to Life* v. *Terry* and *KVUE* v. *Moore*, the Sixth and the Fifth Circuit Court upheld the use of disclaimers in express advocacy communications and "advertising concerning state elections and campaigns" respectively.[163] Most recently, the Connecticut Supreme Court in *Seymour* v. *Elections Enforcement Commission* upheld a disclaimer provision.[164]

However, disclaimer requirements for campaign advertising were struck down by U.S. District Courts in Arkansas in *Arkansas Right to Life* v. *Butler;* in Indiana in *Stewart* v. *Taylor;* and in Maine in *Yes for Life PAC* v. *Webster.*[165]

Advance Notice Laws and Prior Restraint Analysis

Advance notice requirements, also called "no-ambush" laws, require that political advertisers give notice to candidates that they plan to target or criticize in their ads. At least one court has struck down such a law as unconstitutional under the First Amendment *prior restraint* doctrine.[166] Under that doctrine, laws that limit or censor speech before a statement is actually made are given more exacting judicial scrutiny than regulations or punishments imposed after a statement is made.[167] In *Florida Right to Life* v. *Mortham,* a federal district court struck down a disclosure provision requiring individuals making independent expenditures on behalf of candidates to provide advance notice to opposing candidates within twenty-four hours of signing a contract for media time with a broadcaster.[168] Similarly, in *North Carolina Right to Life* v. *Bartlett,* a federal district court struck down a statute requiring PACs to tell their donors, at the time of the fundraising solicitation, the names of candidates the PAC intends to support. The Fourth Circuit Court affirmed that ruling.[169]

Future Issues

The resurgence of the practice of "bundling" hard money (especially in fundraising for presidential campaigns), may result in renewed calls for enforcement of existing bundling and conduit disclosure requirements or for new disclosure or prophylactic measures.[170] More generally, calls for greater disclosure by persons who serve as fundraisers are likely to become more common.

Beyond BCRA's changes, many proposals for disclosure reform remain. Corporations and unions, whose political activities now go largely undisclosed, continue to be the subject of disclosure proposals.[171] Other key disclosure proposals target telephone communications,[172] get-out-the-vote spending (so-called street money),[173] and "no disclosure, no deposit" rules.[174]

Also notable is an encouraging trend toward candidates' institution of voluntary disclosure programs for their own campaigns that go beyond what is required by law. In the 2000 presidential election, several presidential candidates voluntarily disclosed information about their major fundraisers.[175]

George W. Bush, for example, disclosed all of his contributors on his campaign website, in addition to the required FEC reports.[176] In the 2004 presidential election both President Bush and his Democratic challenger, Senator John Kerry, followed that practice. Finally, it is worth noting that some of the greatest advances in disclosure have come from nongovernmental websites, including those maintained by watchdog and media organizations, which use the information in the government databases but reformat them in ways that make the information more useful to the public.[177]

Notes

1. *Buckley* v. *Valeo,* 424 U.S. 1, 67, n. 80 (1976), quoting Louis Brandeis, *Other People's Money* (National Home Library Foundation, 1933), p. 62.

2. See *Buckley* v. *American Constitutional Law Foundation,* 525 U.S. 182, 223 (1999), Justice O'Connor dissenting: "[I]n the United States, for half a century compulsory publicity of political accounts has been the cornerstone of legal regulation. Publicity is advocated as an automatic regulator, inducing self-discipline among political contenders and arming the electorate with important information," quoting Herbert E. Alexander and Brian A. Haggerty, *The Federal Election Campaign Act: After a Decade of Political Reform* (The Foundation, 1981), p. 37. See also Herbert E. Alexander, *Financing Politics: Money, Elections and Political Reform,* 4th ed. (CQ Press, 1992), p. 164: "'total disclosure' has been recognized as the 'essential cornerstone' to effective campaign finance reform and 'fundamental to the political system.'"

3. 2 U.S.C. sec. 434(a)(11).

4. Internal Revenue Code—Amendment, Pub. L. 106-230, 114 Stat. 477 (2000); amended by Income Tax Notification and Return Requirements—Political Committees, Pub. L. 107-276, 116 Stat. 1929 (2002).

5. Bipartisan Campaign Reform Act of 2002, Pub. L. 107-155, 116 Stat. 181 (2002).

6. See my discussion of congressional debate over Pub. L. 106-230 below.

7. See U.S. Senate, Report 105-167, vols. 1–6 (1998) ("Thompson Committee Report"), available at www.senate.gov/~gov_affairs/sireport.htm [January 2005]). The Thompson Committee Report studied the federal elections of 1996 to demonstrate the frequency with which campaign finance laws, including disclosure provisions, are evaded or ignored. Among many other topics, the report demonstrates how campaign money laundering, the use of front groups to hide political operatives' true identities, and other means of evasion of disclosure rules are widespread (pp. 15981–82).

8. See *FEC* v. *Colorado Republican Federal Campaign Committee,* 533 U.S. 431, 462 (2001) (*Colorado II*), noting the "practical difficulty of identifying and directly combating circumvention under actual political conditions"; *Buckley,* 424 U.S. at 76: "Efforts . . . had been [made] in the past . . . to avoid the disclosure requirements by routing financial support of candidates through avenues not explicitly covered by [disclosure]."

9. See, respectively, the discussions of *McIntyre* v. *Ohio Elections Commission, FEC* v. *Massachusetts Citizens for Life,* and *Brown* v. *Socialist Workers '74 Campaign Committee* below.

10. As the Court itself has noted, application of First Amendment scrutiny "does not allow us to avoid the truly difficult issues involving the First Amendment. Perhaps foremost among these serious issues are cases that force us to reconcile our commitment to free speech with our commitment to other constitutional rights." *Burson* v. *Freeman,* 504 U.S. 191, 198 (1992). Justice Cardozo also famously echoed that sentiment. As he wrote, "The reconciliation of the irreconcilable, the merger of the antitheses, the synthesis of opposites, these are the great problems of the law." Benjamin N. Cardozo, *The Paradoxes of Legal Science* (Columbia University Press, 1928), p. 4.

11. Political scientist Louise Overacker described the state of the disclosure program in the House Clerk's office in 1932 in this way: "[O]ne is taken into a tiny washroom, where a series of dusty paper-covered bundles repose upon an upper shelf. By climbing upon a chair and digging about among the bundles one usually finds what one wants . . . but there is no file and no system." Robert E. Mutch, *Campaigns, Congress and Courts: The Making of Federal Campaign Finance Law* (New York: Praeger, 1988), p. 26.

12. Federal Election Campaign Act of 1971 (FECA), Pub. L. 92- 225, 86 Stat. 3 (1972); amended by Pub. L. 93-443, 88 Stat 1263 (1974); subsequently amended and codified at 2 U.S.C. secs. 431 et seq.

13. Pub. L. 106-230, 26 U.S.C. sec. 6012 (2000); amended by Pub. L. 107-276, 116 Stat. 1929 (2002).

14. 2 U.S.C. sec. 434(a)(11). See also "Electronic Filing of Reports by Political Committees," available at www.fec.gov/pdf/nprm/mandatory_electronic_filing/mandatory effinal.pdf [January 2005]).

15. Ironically, the only federal political organizations *not* required to file electronically are campaigns for the U.S. Senate, because the Senate leadership has steadfastly refused to adopt that requirement.

16. See FEC, *Annual Report* (2000), p. 5.

17. 2 U.S.C. sec. 434(c); 11 C.F.R. sec. 109.10(b).

18. 2 U.S.C. sec. 434(g); 11 C.F.R. secs. 109.10(c)–(d).

19. 2 U.S.C. secs. 434(f)(1), (2), (4), and (5); 11 C.F.R. sec. 104.20.

20. 2 U.S.C. sec. 434(f)(2)(C); 11 C.F.R. sec. 104.20(c)(4).

21. 2 U.S.C. sec. 433. The registration statement is a simple initial disclosure document or "statement of organization" that describes basic information about the committee, such as who serves as the committee's treasurer, the bank that holds the committee's accounts, and so forth. For a detailed description of registration requirements, see FEC campaign guides (available at www.fec.gov/general/library.shtml [January 2005]). See also Forms FEC-3 (campaign committees) and FEC-3x (PACs and other committees) (available at www.fec.gov/info/forms.shtml [January 2005]).

22. Pub. L. 106-230, sec. 503; 2 U.S.C. sec. 434(a)(2)(B).

23. 2 U.S.C. sec. 434(e)(1), BCRA sec. 103(a).

24. 2 U.S.C. sec. 434(a)(4); 11 C.F.R. sec. 104.5(c).

25. 2 U.S.C. sec. 434(b).

26. 2 U.S.C. sec. 432(i); 11 C.F.R 104.7 (2003). However, contributors are not required by law to provide that information to candidates or PACs.

27. 2 U.S.C. sec. 434.

28. 11 C.F.R. sec. 104.20.

29. 2 U.S.C. sec. 434(f), BCRA sec. 201.

30. 2 U.S.C. sec. 434(3)(2)(B), BCRA sec. 103.

31. Pub. L. 106-230, 26 U.S.C. sec. 6012. This law grew out of activity in the 1998 and 2000 election cycles, when an increasing number of section 527 political organizations began sponsoring issue advertising campaigns and other political activities. However, because they were not considered to have engaged in express advocacy of a federal election result, they did not have to register with the FEC or potentially even state election agencies. The most spectacular of the groups was Republicans for Clean Air, which ran millions of dollars of advertising attacking John McCain and praising George Bush immediately prior to the Super Tuesday Republican presidential primaries. Press investigators discovered that the group was a front for Texas supporters of Governor Bush's campaign. Congress responded quickly to the new "stealth PAC" section 527 phenomenon by enacting a disclosure bill. Political organizations established under section 527 of the IRS Tax Code file annual tax returns on IRS form 1120-POL.

32. *Mobile Republican Assembly* v. *United States,* No. 02-16283 (11th Cir., December 24, 2003); see also *National Federation of Republican Assemblies* v. *United States,* 218 F.Supp. 2d 1300 (S.D. Ala. 2002); both available at www.campaignlegalcenter.org/cases-48.html [January 2005]).

33. *Mobile Republican Assembly,* No. 02-16283.

34. The FEC's regulations define "public communications" to include "a communication by means of any broadcast, cable or satellite communication, newspaper, magazine, outdoor advertising facility, mass mailing or telephone bank to the general public" (see 11 C.F.R. sec. 100.26), as well as unsolicited e-mail of more than 500 substantially similar communications and political committee Internet websites available to the general public. See 11 C.F.R. sec. 110.11(a).

35. 2 U.S.C. sec. 441d(a); 11 C.F.R. sec. 110.11(a)(1). In addition to these requirements, federal PACs must comply with the requirement that they employ their "best efforts" to maintain and report the name, address, occupation, and employer of contributors who give more than $200 in a calendar year and specifically request such information in their solicitations and inform contributors that they are required to use "best efforts" to collect and report it; 11 C.F.R. sec. 104.7(a). Moreover, the Internal Revenue Code requires that political committees with gross receipts normally exceeding $100,000 disclose in their solicitations that contributions to such committees are not tax deductible; 26 U.S.C. sec. 6113. For an excellent discussion of source identification statutes and court rulings on them, see Malcom A. Heinicke, "A Political Reformer's Guide to McIntyre and Source Disclosure Laws for Political Advertising," Note, *Stanford Law and Policy Review* 8 (1997): 139.

36. 2 U.S.C. sec. 441d(a); 11 C.F.R. secs. 110.11(a)(2)–(4). "Qualified non-profit corporations" (QNCs) must include disclaimers on the same communications for which individuals must include disclaimers. See 11 C.F.R. sec. 114.10(g).

37. 11 C.F.R. sec. 110.11(f)(1).

38. 11 C.F.R. sec. 110.11(f)(2).

39. 2 U.S.C. sec. 441d(a)(3); 11 C.F.R. secs. 110.11(b)(3), 110.11(c)(1). If the communication is authorized by a candidate, the disclaimer must clearly state that it is paid for by the PAC or person and is authorized by the candidate. 2 U.S.C. sec. 441d(a)(2); 11 C.F.R. sec. 110.11(b)(2).

40. 2 U.S.C. sec. 441d(c). 11 C.F.R. sec. 110.11(c)(2).

41. See 2 U.S.C. sec. 441d(d)(1); 11 C.F.R. sec. 110.11(c)(3).

42. 2 U.S.C. sec. 441d(d)(2); 11 C.F.R. sec. 110.11(c)(4)(i). The name of a connected organization paying for such advertising also must be included in the audio statement, unless its name already is provided in the audio statement identifying the PAC. 2 U.S.C. sec. 441d(d)(2); 11 C.F.R. secs. 110.11(c)(4)(i).

43. 2 U.S.C. sec. 441d(d)(2); 11 C.F.R. sec. 110.11(c)(4)(ii).

44. 2 U.S.C. sec. 441d(d)(2); 11 C.F.R. sec. 110.11(c)(4)(iii). If the advertising is authorized by a federal candidate, the candidate is required to convey that he or she has approved the communication. For radio advertising, an audio statement by the candidate to this effect is required. 2 U.S.C. sec. 441d(d)(1)(A); 11 C.F.R. sec. 110.11(c)(3)(i). For television advertising, the statement can be conveyed through either a voice-over by the candidate (accompanied by a photograph of the candidate occupying at least 80 percent of screen height) or full-screen view of the candidate making the statement. 2 U.S.C. sec. 441d(d)(1)(B); 11 C.F.R. sec. 110.11(c)(3)(ii).

45. 2 U.S.C. sec. 441d.

46. 27 U.S.C. sec. 6113.

47. 2 U.S.C. secs. 434(b)(4)(H)(iii), (6)(B)(iii). The term "independent expenditure" means an expenditure by a person expressly advocating the election or defeat of a clearly identified candidate that is made without cooperation or consultation with any candidate or any authorized committee or agent of any candidate; and that is not made in concert with or at the request or suggestion of any candidate or any authorized committee or agent of any candidate. See 2 U.S.C. sec. 431(17). In *Buckley* v. *Valeo,* the Supreme Court introduced the notion of "express advocacy" and provided the following examples: "'vote for,' 'elect,' 'support,' 'cast your ballot for,' 'Smith for Congress,' 'vote against,' 'defeat,' 'reject.'" *Buckley,* 424 U.S. at 43, n. 52.

48. 11 C.F.R. sec. 114.10 (2003) (codification of the Supreme Court's carve-out for political nonprofit associations, as stated in *FEC* v. *Massachusetts Citizens for Life,* discussed below).

49. 2 U.S.C. sec. 434(c), BCRA sec. 212 (a)(2).

50. 2 U.S.C. sec. 434(g)(1), BCRA sec. 212(a)(2).

51. 2 U.S.C. sec. 434(g)(2), BCRA sec. 212(a)(2).

52. 2 U.S.C. sec. 441a(a)(8).

53. 11 C.F.R. sec. 110.6.

54. 2 U.S.C. sec. 441f.

55. 47 U.S.C. sec. 317. A number of states have political broadcast advertising disclosure rules as well. See, for example, that of Kentucky: Ky. Rev. Stat. Ann. sec. 121.180(11)(b) (2003).

56. 47 U.S.C. sec. 317(a)(2).

57. 47 C.F.R. 72.1212(e) (2003).

58. BCRA sec. 504.

59. See U.S. Postal Service *Domestic Mail Manual,* Forms 3615, 3624 (www.usps.com/forms/allforms.htm [January 2005]).

60. For background on tax-exempt organizations, see "Tax-Exempt Status for Your Organization," IRS publication 557 (www.irs.gov/pub/irs-pdf/p557.pdf [January 2005]).

61. 2 U.S.C. sec. 431(9)(B)(iii).

62. Pub. L. 86-257, 73 Stat. 519 (1959), codified as amended at 29 U.S.C. secs. 151–69 (1994).

63. For a description of the proposed rule, see "Labor Organization Financial Reports, Proposed Rule Stage," 67 *Federal Register* 74749 (www.dol.gov/esa/regs/unifiedagenda/ 1215-AB34.htm [January 2005]).

64. AFL-CIO v. Chao (D.D.C., January 22, 2004).

65. The new LM-2s are available at www.dol.gov/esa/regs/compliance/olms/ Form%20LM-2%20Final.pdf.

66. BCRA sec. 501.

67. BCRA sec. 502.

68. The efficacy of the website will ultimately lie in the FEC's implementation of the provision and other agencies' cooperation, inasmuch as the provision appears to leave substantial discretion for actual application.

69. BCRA sec. 306.

70. 36 U.S.C. sec. 510(b).

71. For guides to state election laws and disclosure laws, see FEC, "Campaign Finance Law 2000: A Summary of Campaign Finance Laws" (www.fec.gov/pubrec/cfl/cfl00/ cfl00.htm [January 2005]); FEC, "Combined Federal/State Disclosure and Election Directory 2005" (www.fec.gov/pubrec/cfsdd/cfsdd.shtml [January 2005]). See also "Grading State Disclosure 2004," a report by the UCLA School of Law, the Center for Governmental Studies, and the California Voter Foundation (www.campaigndisclosure. org [January 2005]).

72. Ky. Rev. Stat. Ann. secs. 121.170(2), 180(3)(a) (Michie 2005).

73. Mass. Gen. Laws, ch.55, secs. 19(e)-(f) 92005).

74. Cal. Gov't Code sec. 84300(c) (2002).

75. N.J. Stat. Ann., sec. 19:44a-11.7 (2005).

76. Conn. Gen. Stat. sec. 9-333j(c)(1) (2002).

77. Cal. Gov't Code sec. 82013(c) (West 2005).

78. Haw. Rev. Stat. sec. 11-205.5 (2002).

79. Id. sec. 11-205.5(b)(3).

80. Id. sec. 11-205.5(b)(4).

81. 2 U.S.C. sec. 437g(a)(1). FEC enforcement actions often result from scrutiny of disclosure records by others. The 1996 foreign contributions scandal, for instance, began not with FEC enforcement action but because of press investigations into FEC reports filed by the Democratic National Committee. Those investigations revealed funds raised from foreign citizens, companies, and governments. See, for example, Alan C. Miller, "Democrats Return Illegal Contribution; South Korean Subsidiary's $250,000 Donation Violated Ban on Money from Foreign Nationals," *Los Angeles Times,* September 21, 1996, at A16.

82. Until recently, violations such as late filing and failure to file were dealt with the same way that campaign finance violations were—through a time-consuming investigation or litigation.

83. See Press Release, "Committees Fined for Filing Reports Late," March 25, 2003 (www.fec.gov/press/20030325late.html [January 2005]). Random audits were included in the original FECA; Congress then repealed the provision, following complaints by members that such audits adversely affected incumbents seeking reelection. Congress did,

however, leave the presidential audits in place. See 26 U.S.C. secs. 9007, 9038. Congress also retained "for cause" audits of other political committees. 2 U.S.C. sec. 438(b).

84. See Federal Election Commission, *Record* 29 (April 2003): 1–2 (www.fec.gov/pdf/record/2003/apr03.pdf [January 2005]).

85. 2 U.S.C. sec. 437(g).

86. Craig C. Donsanto and Nancy S. Stewart, *Federal Prosecution of Election Offenses,* 6th ed. (U.S. Department of Justice, 1995), p. 106.

87. BCRA sec. 313.

88. BCRA sec. 312.

89. BCRA sec. 314.

90. See "Report to the Congress: Increased Penalties for Campaign Finance Offenses and Legislative Recommendations," May 2003 (www.ussc.gov/r_congress/camp2003.pdf [January 2005]).

91. 18 U.S.C. sec. 1001.

92. 18 U.S.C. sec. 2(b), providing that any person who causes another to commit an act "which if directly performed by him or another would be an offense . . . is punishable as a principal." For key cases concerning the False Statements Act and 18 U.S.C. secs. 2 and 371 as they relate to the act, see *United States* v. *Hansen,* 772 F.2d 940 (D.C. Cir. 1985), *cert. denied,* 475 U.S. 1045 (1986); *United States* v. *Curran,* 20 F.3d 560 (3rd Cir. 1994); *United States* v. *Hopkins,* 916 F.2d 207 (5th Cir. 1990); *Hsia* v. *United States,* 176 F.3d 517 (D.C. Cir. 1999), *cert. denied,* 528 U.S. 1136 (2000); *United States* v. *Kanchanalak,* 192 F.3d 1037 (D.C. Cir. 1999).

93. Many of the prosecutions arising out of the 1996 fundraising scandals were based in part on 18 U.S.C. secs. 1001 and 371. See, for example, *Hsia,* 176 F.3d at 517.

94. *Buckley,* 424 U.S.

95. Id. at 64.

96. Id.

97. Recent cases have been inconsistent in the level of scrutiny used to analyze disclosure statutes. For example, the Supreme Court applied "intermediate scrutiny" in its most recent case, *American Constitutional Law Foundation,* 525 U.S.. However, in *McIntyre,* the Court articulated "exacting scrutiny" but in fact applied classic "strict scrutiny." *McIntyre* v. *Ohio Elections Commission,* 514 U.S. 334, 345–46 (1995).

98. A possible public interest, not mentioned in *Buckley,* that may justify certain disclosure requirements is the utility of disclosure provision in enabling candidates and the media to evaluate false or misleading political communications. The Court in *McIntyre* acknowledged that interest, noting "false statements [in a campaign] may have serious adverse consequences . . . and give rise to a 'legitimate' justification for disclosure requirements." *McIntyre,* 514 U.S. at 349. Nevertheless, the *McIntyre* court held that the antifraud/misinformation interest was unnecessary in the context of the Ohio election laws analyzed in that case because Ohio's political libel and slander laws served the same function, making disclosure laws unnecessary. Id. at 344. Other Court cases and considerations, however, cast doubt on that portion of *McIntyre.* See, for example, *State ex rel. Public Disclosure Commission* v. *119 Vote No! Committee,* 957 P.2d 691 (Wash. 1998), striking down campaign libel law on First Amendment grounds.

99. *Buckley,* 424 U.S. at 67.

100. Id.

101. Id. at 81.

102. Id.

103. *First National Bank of Boston* v. *Bellotti,* 435 U.S. 765 (1978). According to the majority decision in *Bellotti,* "the people in our democracy are entrusted with the responsibility for judging and evaluating the relative merits of conflicting arguments. *They may consider, in making their judgment, the source and credibility of the advocate. . . . Identification of the source of advertising may be required as a means of disclosure, so that the people will be able to evaluate the arguments to which they are being subjected* [emphasis added]." Id. at 791.

104. *McIntyre,* 514 U.S. at 349.

105. *Buckley,* 424 U.S. at 76.

106. 2 U.S.C. sec. 434(e) (1976).

107. *Buckley,* 424 U.S. at 79.

108. Id. at 80. In *FEC* v. *GOPAC,* the FEC asked a district court to declare that GOPAC, a political organization run by former U.S. House Speaker Newt Gingrich, was subject to the FECA's disclosure requirements. *FEC* v. *GOPAC,* 917 F.Supp. 851 (D.D.C. 1996). GOPAC argued that it did not fall under the FEC's purview because its major purpose was to support *state* and *local* candidates, not *federal* candidates. The district court hearing the case agreed, observing that while GOPAC's ultimate and indirect purpose may have been to help bring about the eventual election of Republicans to Congress, its operational function was to elect Republicans at the state and local level. GOPAC wanted to use state and local officials as a "farm team" from which to later recruit candidates to run for Congress. Id. at 854. The Court found that purpose was too indirect and remote to trigger disclosure obligations under the FECA. Similarly, the Court found that GOPAC mailings referring to electing a Republican majority in Congress were mere fundraising hyperbole and not evidence of the organization's major purpose. Id. at 858–59. Consequently, GOPAC was not considered a federal "political committee" supporting federal candidates and not subject to the FECA's disclosure requirements. The FEC deadlocked on whether to appeal the decision. The district court's interpretation of the definition of federal political committee has never been reviewed.

109. *Buckley,* 424 U.S. at 76.

110. Id. at 82.

111. Id. at 83.

112. In an early post-*Buckley* case, *Oregon Socialist Workers 1974 Campaign Committee* v. *Paulus,* 432 F. Supp 1255 (D. Or. 1977), a three-judge panel upheld a disclosure law that had no minimum threshold. By contrast, in *Vote Choice, Inc.,* v. *DiStefano,* 4 F.3d 26 (1st Cir. 1993), the First Circuit Court struck down a similar statute. The court, however, held that "first-dollar disclosure is not, in all cases, constitutionally proscribed." Rather, the court faulted the statute for its disparate (and allegedly discriminatory) treatment of PACs and individuals, since the first-dollar provision applied to PACs only. Id at 33.

113. *Buckley,* 424 U.S. at 69.

114. Id. at 74.

115. *NAACP* v. *Alabama,* 357 U.S. 449 (1958).

116. Id. at 466.

117. Id. at 462.

118. *Buckley,* 424 U.S. at 74.

119. *Brown* v. *Socialist Worker's Party '74,* 459 U.S. 87 (1982).

120. Id. at 99.

121. Lower courts have likewise deemed certain organizations exempt from disclosure requirements by reason of harassment, threats, or reprisals. See, for example, *FEC* v. *Hall-Tyner Election Campaign Committee,* 678 F.2d 416 (1982).

122. *Massachusetts Citizens for Life, Inc.* v. *FEC,* 479 U.S. 238 (1986) (*MCFL*). The Court rejected MCFL's assertion that it engaged only in issue advocacy. Id. at 250–51.

123. *Buckley,* 479 U.S. at 255.

124. Id.

125. The FEC has codified the *MCFL* exemption into its regulations. See 11 CFR 114.10. The Texas Supreme Court recently ruled that a husband and wife did not have to register and form a political committee in order to make an independent expenditure but that they did have to file independent expenditure reports. *Osterberg* v. *Peca,* 12 S.W. 3d 31 (Tex. 2000).

126. The D.C. Circuit, in *RNC* v. *FEC,* rejected the RNC's claims that the FEC's "best efforts" regulations constituted an undue administrative burden on the RNC. Analyzing whether compliance with the requirement imposed a severe burden on the RNC, the court found that the burden was slight and rejected the claim. *RNC* v. *FEC,* 76 F.3d. 400, 409 (D.C. Cir. 1996), *cert. denied,* 519 U.S. 1055 (1997). See also *Adventure Communications* v. *Kentucky Registry of Election Fin.,* 191 F.3d 429 (4th Cir. 1999).

127. *McIntyre,* 514 U.S. at 334.

128. Id. at 338, n.3, reciting Ohio disclosure statute.

129. Id. at 337, n.2.

130. Id. at 356.

131. Id. at 346.

132. Id. at 342.

133. Id. at 353.

134. As the *McIntyre* Court noted, "Not only is the Ohio statute's infringement on speech more intrusive than the Buckley disclosure requirement, but it rests on different and less powerful state interests. The Federal Election Campaign Act of 1971, at issue in *Buckley,* regulates only candidate elections, not referenda or other issue-based ballot measures; and we construed 'independent expenditures' to mean only those expenditures that 'expressly advocate the election or defeat of a clearly identified candidate.' . . . In candidate elections, the Government can identify a compelling state interest in avoiding the corruption that might result from campaign expenditures. Disclosure of expenditures lessens the risk that individuals will spend money to support a candidate as a *quid pro quo* for special treatment after the candidate is in office. Curriers of favor will be deterred by knowledge that all expenditures will be scrutinized by the Federal Election Commission and by the public for just this sort of abuse. Moreover, the federal Act contains numerous legitimate disclosure requirements for campaign organizations; the similar requirements for independent expenditures serve to ensure that a campaign organization will not seek to evade disclosure by routing its expenditures through individual supporters. . . . In short, although *Buckley* may permit a more narrowly drawn statute, it surely is not authority for upholding Ohio's open-ended provision." Id. at 356. Thus, whatever interests states have

in regulating referendum and initiative campaigns, deterring corruption of elected officials is not as clearly at stake as it is with candidate elections.

135. *West Virginians for Life, Inc., v. Smith,* 919 F. Supp. 954 (S.D.W.Va. 1996), granting preliminary injunction; see also *West Virginians for Life, Inc., v. Smith,* 952 F. Supp. 342, awarding fees and costs; and *West Virginians for Life, Inc., v. Smith,* 960 F. Supp. 1036, decision on summary judgment motion. *W. Virginians for Life* held that *McIntyre* "based its holding on the First Amendment's protection of the right to publish anonymous issue advocacy"; *W. Virginians for Life,* 960 F. Supp. at 1042. *Yes for Life PAC* v. *Webster,* 84 F. Supp. 2d 150 (D. Me. 2000). *Stewart* v. *Taylor,* 953 F. Supp. 1047 (S.D. Ind. 1997).

136. *Stewart,* 953 F. Supp. at 1055.

137. *FEC* v. *Survival Education Fund,* 65 F.3d 285 (2d Cir. 1995). *Kentucky Right to Life* v. *Terry,* 108 F.3d 637 (6th Cir. 1997). *Griset* v. *Fair Political Practices Commission,* 23 P.3d 43 (Cal. 2001); *Griset* was originally decided before the 1995 *McIntyre* decision, and then was reaffirmed on *res judicata* grounds. *Osterberg* v. *Peca,* 12 S.W.3d 31 (Tex. 2000), *cert. denied,* 530 U.S. 1244 (2000). *Seymour* v. *Elections Enforcement Commission,* 762 A.2d 880 (Conn. 2000), *cert. denied,* 533 U.S. 951 (2001). *Richey* v. *Tyson,* 120 F. Supp. 2d 1298 (S.D. Ala. 2000), summary judgment granted in part and denied in part; 2001 U.S. Dist. LEXIS 6542 (S.D. Ala. April 30, 2001), final opinion.

138. *Osterberg,* 12 S.W.3d at 42.

139. *Survival Education Fund,* 65 F.3d at 296.

140. *Richey,* 120 F. Supp. 2d at 1310.

141. *FEC* v. *Akins,* 524 U.S. 11 (1998).

142. Id. at 20, 21, 24–25.

143. *American Constitutional Law Foundation,* 525 U.S.

144. The majority consisted of Justices Ginsburg, Stevens, Kennedy, Souter, and Scalia.

145. *American Constitutional Law Foundation,* 525 U.S. at 203.

146. Id..

147. Notably, the Supreme Court has declined several opportunities to resolve the division among the lower courts on the express advocacy/issue advocacy question, in disclosure and other cases. See *FEC* v. *Colorado Republican Federal Campaign Committee,* 518 U.S. 604 (1996) (*Colorado I*).

148. In *Buckley,* the Court listed "'vote for,' 'elect,' 'support,' 'cast your ballot for,' 'Smith for Congress,' 'vote against,' 'defeat,' and 'reject'" as examples of "express words of advocacy of election or defeat." 424 U.S. at 43, n.52.

149. *FEC* v. *Central Long Island Tax Reform Immediately Committee,* 616 F.2d 45 (2d Cir. 1980). *Vermont Right to Life* v. *Sorrell,* 221 F.3d 376 (2002).

150. *North Carolina Right to Life, Inc., v. Bartlett,* 168 F.3d 705, 713 (4th Cir. 1999).

151. *Kansans for Life, Inc., v. Gaede,* 38 F. Supp. 2d 928, 936 (D. Kan. 1999).

152. *Iowa Right to Life* v. *Williams,* 187 F.3d 963, 969 (8th Cir. 1999).

153. *Chamber of Commerce* v. *Moore,* 288 F.3d 187, 199 (5th Cir. 2002). The Fifth Circuit Court noted that its decision may appear "counterintuitive" but added that it was constrained by Supreme Court precedent in *Buckley* and *MCFL*.

"To ensure that the mandatory disclosure provision in the federal statute did not encroach on protected political speech by individuals and groups, the Court held that the provision *must be narrowly construed* to be consistent with the First Amendment. Accordingly, the Court interpreted the provision to "apply only to expenditures for communications that in express terms advocate the election or defeat of a clearly identified candidate for Federal office." In a footnote, the Court then provided examples of terms of express advocacy: "'vote for,' 'elect,' 'support,' 'cast your ballot for,' 'Smith for Congress,' 'vote against,' 'defeat,' 'reject.'" Id. at 192 (citations omitted).

"We recognize that the result we reach in this case may be counterintuitive to a commonsense understanding of the message conveyed by the television political advertisements at issue. Nevertheless, the result is compelled by the First Amendment, as interpreted by the Supreme Court in its effort to balance the state's interest in regulating elections with the constitutional right of free speech." Id. at 198–99.

By contrast, the district court decision reversed by the Fifth Circuit Court characterized *Buckley* and *MCFL* as follows:

In *MCFL,* the Court seemingly moved away from a rigid, talismanic application of *Buckley's* footnote 52 to an "essential nature" inquiry, as the Court found express advocacy even though the communication at issue was "marginally less direct than 'Vote for Smith.'". . . The *MCFL* Court . . . determined that "express advocacy" was present . . . based on the timing of the election, the unusually large quantity of copies being disseminated, and the exhortations to vote for pro-life candidates, notwithstanding the absence of the magic words found in footnote 52 of the *Buckley* decision.

Chamber v. *Moore,* 191. F. Supp. 2d 747, 760 (S.D. Miss. 2000). The district court concluded: "In this court's view, a finding of any use of 'magic words' becomes unnecessary when an advertisement clearly champions the election of a particular candidate." The court then upheld the state injunctions requiring the Chamber of Commerce to abide by the disclosure requirements. Id. at 761.

154. Planned Parenthood Affiliates of Michigan v. Miller, 21 F. Supp. 2d 740, 745 (E.D. Mich. 1998).

155. Perry v. Bartlett, 231 F.3d 155, 161 (4th Cir. 2000).

156. *FEC* v. *Furgatch,* 807 F.2d 857 (9th Cir. 1987).

157. Id. at 864.

158. Id. at 862. Another disclosure case that adopted the *Furgatch* standard was *Krumpton* v. *Keisling,* 982 P.2d 3 (Or. Ct. App. 1999). The court indicated that its willingness to adopt the *Furgatch* standard was in part because "the issue in this case is simply the requirement to report expenditures." See id. at 11. Moreover, in *Elections Board* v. *Wisconsin Manufacturers and Commerce,* 597 N.W.2d 721 (Wis. 1999), the court indicated that the *Furgatch* standard was a permissible construction of express advocacy. In *Osterberg* v. *Peca,* the Texas Supreme Court applied threads of analysis from both *MCFL* and *Furgatch* in finding that an advertisement was subject to disclosure requirements. See Osterberg, 12 S.W. 3d at 52–53 : "In *Massachusetts Citizens for Life,* the Court clarified that a message can be 'marginally less direct' than the examples listed in *Buckley* so long as its essential nature 'goes beyond issue discussion to express electoral advocacy'" (internal citations omitted).

159. See *McConnell* v. *FEC,* Civ. No. 02-582 (D.D.C. May 1, 2003), Memorandum Opinion of Judge Kollar-Kotelly, pp. 370–82, joined here by Judge Leon.

160. See *Wisconsin Realtors* v. *Ponto,* 233 F. Supp. 2d 1078, 1086 (W.D. Wisc. 2002), quoting *Wisconsin Manufacturers and Commerce* v. *State of Wisconsin Election Board,* 978 F. Supp. 1200, 1205 (W.D. Wisc. 1997).

161. See *National Federation of Republican Assemblies* v. *United States,* 218 F.Supp.2d 1300, 1327 (S.D. Ala. 2002).

162. *RNC* v. *FEC,* 76 F.3d; *Survival Education Fund,* 65 F.3d.

163. *Terry,* 108 F.3d. *KVUE* v. *Moore,* 709 F.2d 922, 934 (5th Cir. 1983); but see *Doe* v. *State of Texas,* 2003 WL 21077961 (Tex.Crim.App.) (May 14, 2003), striking down a requirement in Texas law, as revised, that communications supporting or opposing candidates for public office identify the sponsor.

164. *Seymour,* 762 A.2d..

165. *Arkansas Right to Life* v. *Butler,* 29 F.Supp.2d 540 (W.D. Ark. 1998), finding that the statute was not sufficiently narrowly tailored to serve the state's interest and thus violated the First Amendment. *Stewart,* 953 F. Supp., finding that the statute was not narrowly tailored to meet a compelling state interest. *Yes for Life PAC* v. *Webster,* 74 F. Supp. 2d 37 (D. Me. 1999), preliminary injunction; 84 F. Supp. 2d, final opinion.

166. See *Arizona Right to Life Political Action Committee* v. *Bayless,* 320 F.3d 1002 (9th Cir. 2003).

167. See generally Lawrence Tribe, *American Constitutional Law* (1988), pp. 1039–61.

168. *Florida Right to Life* v. *Mortham,* 1998 U.S. Dist. LEXIS 16694 (M.D. Fla. 1998).

169. *North Carolina Right to Life* v. *Bartlett,* 3 F. Supp. 2d 675 (E.D.N.C. 1998), *aff'd* 168 F.3d 705 (4th Cir. 1999), *cert. denied,* 528 U.S. 1153 (2000).

170. Political fundraisers play a major role in the campaign finance system. Many fundraisers are also lobbyists, and many gain prominence and influence through their fundraising efforts. Because they deliver other people's money rather than contribute or spend their own, however, their campaign finance activities often go totally undisclosed. Fundraiser disclosure has been proposed to extend reporting requirements to cover this gap in the Federal Election Campaign Act's disclosure regime. Fundraiser disclosure proponents seek to require that reports by political committees list all persons who raise over a threshold amount, or indicate a range of fundraising amounts.

171. Union campaign spending is difficult to track because so much of it is made in the form of in-kind contributions of services, phone banks, and so forth. See "What If We Knew How Much Labor Really Spends on Elections?" *National Journal's* Cloakroom, December 10, 1997 (now called NationalJournal.com; a subscription service available at the website). Likewise, corporations often make in-kind contributions—such as the ready availability of corporate jet aircraft, use of corporate facilities for fundraising, and the like—which is undisclosed.

172. Implementing the Reform Act, FEC regulations now require that a disclaimer be included with phone bank calls by federal political committees or phone bank calls by others that expressly advocate the election or defeat of a federal candidate or solicit federal campaign contributions. See 11 C.F.R. sec. 110.11(a). Certain other proposals not yet enacted into federal law focus on so-called "push polling"—campaign communications designed to influence voters' perceptions of candidates under the guise of a standard opinion poll. See Push Poll Disclosure Act of 2003, H.R. 156, 108th Cong. (2003).

173. Cash payments made in the course of a campaign are one of the more contentious campaign spending issues. Cash transactions include "get-out-the-vote" activities or "walking around money" (also known as "street money") and honoraria or "tribute payments" paid to community leaders or religious organizations. See, for example, Larry Sabato and Glen Simpson, *Dirty Little Secrets: The Persistence of Corruption in American Politics* (Times Books, 1996), p. 187. Proposals have been made to ban cash payments (at least on Election Day), and instead require that such payments are to be made by check, credit card, or similar instrument.

174. Though committees must make "best efforts" to acquire contributors' employers and addresses, contributors are not required to actually provide this information. Candidate and political committees may nevertheless deposit contributions from these contributors. Proposals for so-called "no disclosure, no deposit" requirements would bar political committees from depositing contributions unless the donor has provided all required disclosure information.

175. Don Van Natta Jr., "Pressed, Bush Identifies Some of His Biggest Financial Backers," *New York Times,* July 21, 1999, p. A19.

176. See, for example, Susan B. Glasser, "Bush Piling up $50 Million," *Washington Post,* September 10, 1999, p. A4.

177. For instance, the Center for Responsive Politics website, www.opensecrets.org (last visited January 2005), categorizes donors by industry—and then aggregates spouses' contributions with the industry's donations, which in some cases may actually reflect judgments that would be problematic for a government agency to make. See also the Political Moneyline's website, www.tray.com (January 2005).

5

Party Finances

ANTHONY CORRADO

Political parties are a major source of funding in federal elections. Party committees provide resources to candidates, spend monies to support candidates, and finance a wide array of general party and election-related activities in pursuing their collective goals of winning elections and building partisan support in government. The role of parties in federal campaign financing has increased dramatically since the adoption of the 1974 Federal Election Campaign Act (FECA), with party monies rising from $58 million in 1976 to more than $1 billion in 2004.[1]

That growth was achieved in part through unregulated "nonfederal" or "soft money" contributions, which provided national and state parties with money from sources prohibited under federal law and in amounts that exceeded federal contribution limits. From 1988 through 2002, party soft money contributions rose from $45 million to $495 million, much of it coming from large corporate, labor union, and individual contributions of $100,000 or more. Such large gifts, often raised with the help of federal officeholders or national party officials, prompted concerns about corruption and highlighted the inefficacy of the contribution restrictions established by the FECA. As a result, party financing became a focal point of intense controversy and of proposals for reform.

One of the major objectives of the Bipartisan Campaign Reform Act of 2002 (BCRA) was to reform party funding by putting an end to the use of soft money in federal elections. Consequently, party committees were the political organizations most affected by the provisions of the new law. BCRA prohibited national party committees from raising or spending any monies that were not raised in accordance with federal contribution limits and source prohibitions. It also required all party committees, including state and local party organizations, to finance any federal election activities, as defined in the act, with federally regulated or "hard money" funds. The law also revised party contribution limits, codified provisions for party independent expenditures in federal elections, and established a new type of federally regulated state or local party funding known as "Levin money." In all, BCRA sought to restore the FECA's regulatory framework by making major changes both in the ways that party committees raise money and in the ways that they spend money to support federal candidates. This chapter reviews the rules governing party financing after the adoption of BCRA and the ways that parties have adapted to the requirements of the new law.

National Party Committee Fundraising

Federal law places restrictions on contributions to party committees. Under the original provisions of the FECA, national party organizations could receive annual contributions of no more than $20,000 from an individual and $15,000 from a PAC. Any contribution from an individual also was subject to the annual limit of $25,000 imposed on individuals' aggregate donations to federal candidates and political committees, which included the national party committees.[2] The statute specifically prohibited parties from receiving contributions from corporations or labor unions. The only statutory exception to the prohibition applied solely to contributions received for a special exempt category of funding known as a "building fund," which was an account established by a national party committee to receive monies to pay for the construction of party headquarters or office buildings. Apart from that "bricks-and-mortar" provision, parties were required to pay for all federal election–related expenses with monies raised through limited individual and PAC contributions.

The Rise of Soft Money

Soon after the FECA was implemented, state party organizations began to raise questions regarding the application of its contribution restrictions. The monies used by state parties to pay for federal election activities were subject to federal law, while the monies used for nonfederal election activities were governed by state law. In many states, state law was more permissive than federal law. For example, a number of states allowed party committees to accept corporate and labor union contributions or set no limits on the amount that a party could receive from an individual or a PAC. Given the role of state parties in nonfederal as well as federal elections, these organizations began to seek guidance from the FEC as to whether they could pay some portion of certain expenses with nonfederal funds and, if so, how to allocate those expenses between nonfederal and federally regulated funds.

Specifically, state parties asked whether nonfederal funds could be used to finance some of their general overhead and operating expenses, as well as the costs of voter registration and get-out-the-vote (GOTV) drives, which benefit both federal and nonfederal candidates. When the FEC first considered the issue in 1976, it ruled that a state party could use nonfederal funds, particularly corporate or labor union contributions when permitted by state law, to finance a portion of a party's overhead and administrative costs, but that those funds could not be used to finance a voter registration or GOTV drive that might influence the outcome of a federal election.[3] But the FEC reversed its position in 1978, declaring that a state party could use monies raised under state law, including corporate or labor union gifts, to finance a share of the costs of a voter registration or GOTV program, so long as the party allocated the costs to reflect the federal and nonfederal shares of any expenses incurred.[4]

In other words, the commission decided that the financing of such campaign activity had to be divided between federal and nonfederal funds to reflect the fact that it offered indirect benefits to both federal and nonfederal candidates. The federal portion had to be paid from monies raised under federal law, the nonfederal portion from a separate account containing monies raised under state law. That ruling, along with a number of subsequent FEC decisions issued in response to other state party queries, opened the door to the use of nonfederal, or soft money, on election-related activity conducted in connection with federal elections.

The FEC decisions spurred the national party committees to undertake soft money efforts of their own. Like state party committees, national party committees contended that they too were involved in both federal and nonfederal politics. National parties serve as umbrella organizations that work with party leaders and elected officials at all levels of government. They make contributions and provide campaign assistance to state and local candidates.

They work with state and local party organizations on a variety of party-building and political activities. National party leaders therefore argued that national committees also could allocate administrative costs and other generic party expenses between federal and nonfederal accounts, so long as they maintained separate accounts for depositing different types of money. The FEC accepted that view, allowing national parties to begin to raise and spend unlimited soft money.[5] A new era in party finance thus was born.

The parties quickly adapted to the relaxed regulatory environment and began to raise increasingly large sums of soft money. Because party committees were not required to disclose their soft money funds to the FEC until 1991, the available information on soft money fundraising in the 1980s is inexact, based on information culled from state disclosure reports and voluntary disclosures made by the national committees. The best available estimates indicate that the two major parties spent $19.1 million in the 1980 cycle, with the Republicans spending $15.1 million and the Democrats $4 million, and about $21.6 million in the 1984 cycle, with the Republicans again outspending the Democrats, $15.6 million to $6 million.[6] Thereafter, soft money contributions rose rapidly, growing from a combined $45 million in the 1988 cycle, with the Democrats taking in $23 million and the Republicans $22 million, to $496 million in 2002, with the Republicans outpacing the Democrats, $250 million to $246 million.[7]

As the amount of soft money grew, so did the controversy over this form of unregulated funding. By 1996, soft money fundraising activities were at the heart of a national scandal. That year, news reports disclosing private White House coffees and "sleepovers" in the Lincoln bedroom for large soft money donors and allegations that the Democratic National Committee had received illegal donations from foreign contributors made campaign finance a major issue in the final weeks of the presidential campaign. The revelations sparked a number of formal investigations, including a congressional inquiry into party fundraising practices, and spurred demand for reform. Consequently, the abolition of soft money became a top priority for advocates of campaign finance reform.

National Party Fundraising under BCRA

BCRA addressed the problem of soft money funding by requiring party committees to finance all of their political activities with hard money raised under federal contribution limits. The law prohibits national party committee officials and their agents as well as federal officeholders or candidates and their agents from soliciting, receiving, spending, directing, or transferring any funds that are not subject to federal contribution limits and disclosure requirements. Those restrictions also apply to any organization established, controlled, or maintained by a national party committee. Further, national party officials and their agents are not permitted to raise unregulated monies for nonparty political organizations that conduct activities related to federal elections. In that way, the law seeks to ensure that party leaders cannot circumvent the ban on soft money by creating subsidiary organizations or by raising soft money contributions for nonparty groups.

To acknowledge the essential role of parties in the electoral process and to help compensate for the anticipated loss of soft money, BCRA also raised the limit on individual contributions to party committees. The amount that an individual may give to a national party committee was increased from $20,000 to $25,000 a year, with the amount indexed for inflation. In 2005, the limit was adjusted to $26,700.[8]

Even more important, the law increased the ceiling on an individual's aggregate contributions and created sublimits for contributions to candidates and party committees to accommodate increased giving to parties. The law raised the aggregate amount that an individual may give to candidates, parties, and PACs to $95,000 per two-year election cycle (in contrast with $25,000 per year, or $50,000 every two years under the FECA) and indexed the ceiling to inflation. Under the aggregate ceiling, the statute provided a sublimit of $37,500 for contributions to candidates and a separate $57,500 sublimit for contributions to parties and other political committees. Of the latter amount, no more than $37,500 could be given to party or political committees other than national party committees. Thus, in order to reach the $57,500 maximum, an individual would have to give at least $20,000 to national party committees. With the adjustment for inflation, individuals may give an aggregate of $101,400 in the 2006 election cycle, including up to $40,000 to candidates and $61,400 to parties or PACs.[9] So an individual may give a total of up to $61,400 to national party committees in the 2006 cycle.

Party Adaptation and Response to BCRA

BCRA's ban on soft money compelled the national party organizations to alter their fundraising strategies. No longer able to rely on corporations, labor unions, and trade associations for a substantial share of their funding—those sources gave $280 million of soft money in 2000—both parties renewed their emphasis on soliciting individual donors.[10] While both parties revised their fundraising programs to take advantage of BCRA's more generous contribution limits, they invested especially heavily in small donor solicitation programs, because a substantial increase in the number of small donors was considered a key to replacing the sums of money lost as a result of the soft money ban.

The parties began to enhance their fundraising infrastructure even before BCRA took effect in November 2002. Anticipating the ban on soft money, both parties had used some of the soft money raised in the 2002 election cycle to improve their hard money fundraising capacity. Both Democrats and Republicans invested in technological improvements to build highly sophisticated, computerized direct mail, telemarketing, and Internet fundraising programs to target prospective contributors. Their efforts relied in part on complex "data mining" models that culled cultural and lifestyle information, which then was used to construct profiles of likely donors on the basis of personal information such as magazine subscriptions, personal vehicle ownership, and consumer buying habits.[11] In addition, the Democratic and the Republican National Committee (DNC and RNC) constructed e-mail lists of millions of party supporters who could be solicited for contributions. The DNC also built a modern national headquarters facility using soft money funds.

After BCRA was implemented, the parties also created programs designed to recruit $25,000 hard money donors and encourage the development of volunteer fundraising networks. The DNC, for example, formed a Presidential Trust Fund and pledged to deposit all $25,000 gifts into the trust and use the monies exclusively to support the party's 2004 presidential nominee.[12] The committee also established an elite Patriots program for volunteer fundraisers who each agreed to raise at least $100,000 for the party in 2004.[13] Similarly, the RNC revamped its long-standing Team100 program, which was used to solicit soft money gifts of up to $100,000, to recruit individuals willing to give the party $25,000 in each of the four years of a presidential election cycle.[14] The Republicans also sought to build on President Bush's strong personal fundraising base by creating a group of volunteer fundraisers known as Super Rangers. To become eligible for that status, an individual had to raise $300,000 for the party in addition to the $200,000 that he or she was required to raise for the Bush campaign in order to become a Ranger.[15]

Those changes occurred in the context of a political environment that was highly conducive to partisan fundraising. The tightly contested presidential race, deep partisan divisions within the electorate, and sharply contrasting partisan views on the key issues facing the nation motivated party supporters to participate financially in the campaign. Consequently, both parties were more successful than most observers predicted in adapting to the new regulatory regime.

The parties collected record sums of money in the 2004 election cycle. By the end of 2004, the national party committees had raised more money in hard dollars alone than they had raised in hard and soft dollars combined in any previous election cycle. The national party committees took in more than $1.2 billion, or about $144 million more than they received in the 2000 election cycle and $184 million more than in the 2002 cycle.

Both parties made up for the loss of soft money with new hard dollar contributions. As in the past, the Republican national committees surpassed their Democratic counterparts, but by a relatively small margin. In fact, the national parties were more financially competitive in 2004 than in any other recent election. The Republican national party committees took in $657 million, the Democratic committees $576 million. In the 2000 cycle, the Republican committees raised almost $620 million, while the Democrats raised about $470 million. In dollar terms, the gap between the Republicans and Democrats in the 2004 cycle was the smallest since the 1978 cycle, when the Republican national committees raised a total of $59 million and the Democrats raised $15 million. Moreover, for the first time since at least the adoption of the FECA and perhaps in the entire post–World War II era, the DNC led the RNC in fundraising, raising $394 million to the RNC's $392 million. In the 2000 cycle, the RNC had collected $89 million more than the DNC in hard money donations and $30 million more in soft money. In the 2002 cycle, the RNC had surpassed the DNC by more than $100 million in hard money and $20 million in soft dollars.

The parties' success in adapting to BCRA and increasing their hard money contributions was largely the result of an unprecedented surge in the number of party donors, particularly small donors. The RNC, benefiting from President Bush's strengthened support in the aftermath of 9/11 and building on the party's success in the 2002 elections, added more than 1 million new donors to its rolls by the beginning of the 2004 election year and continued to recruit large numbers of new contributors throughout 2004. That growth in the party's donor base was greater than the growth experienced during the eight years of the Reagan administration, the previous high-water mark with respect to new donors.[16] The Democrats, who began with a much smaller donor base than their Republican opponents, experienced an even greater surge in support. Beginning with only 400,000 direct mail donors after the 2000 election, the DNC completely revitalized its relatively moribund small donor fundraising program. By the end of the 2004 election, the DNC had recruited 2.3 million new direct mail donors. In addition, 4 million donors made contributions to the committee through the Internet.[17]

The growth in party donor rolls led to a significant increase in the sums raised through small contributions. One measure of the committees' success in attracting small donors is the amount raised in unitemized (less than $200) contributions. According to the parties' FEC disclosure reports, the RNC and DNC raised a total of at least $592 million in unitemized gifts.[18] The RNC reported $344 million in unitemized receipts by the end of the 2004 cycle, in contrast with $205 million in the 2000 cycle. That represents an increase of almost 75 percent in small donor contributions. The DNC reported more than $165 million in unitemized contributions, an extraordinary increase over the $35 million in unitemized donations that the party reported receiving in the 2000 cycle. The parties thus replaced more than half of the soft money collected in the 2000 cycle with an additional $270 million in small gifts.

The parties also capitalized on BCRA's higher contribution limits. According to a postelection analysis of party contributions conducted by the FEC, the RNC and DNC raised a total of $104 million in individual contributions of the maximum permissible amount ($25,000 per committee per year), with the RNC garnering almost $61 million from its large donors and the DNC more than $43 million. In the 2000 cycle, the two committees received less than $24 million of hard money from individual contributions of the maximum permissible amount (at the time, $20,000 per committee per year), with the RNC collecting less than $13 million and the DNC, $11 million.

Finally, national party committees can also garner funds through transfers from other party committees and from the campaign committees of candidates. For purposes of the law those committees are considered to be affiliated with the national committees; they can therefore transfer unlimited amounts of hard money to the national committees. Similarly, the national parties may transfer unlimited amounts of hard money to state or local party committees. They may not, however, transfer unlimited sums to candidate committees, since such transfers would be considered contributions to the candidates and thus are limited under the law.

In the 2004 cycle, the national party committees received substantial amounts from federal candidate committee transfers. In all, federal candidates gave $117.4 million to the national committees, almost four times the $31.4 million that was transferred to those committees in 2000. Almost half of the total, $54.6 million, came from leftover primary funds donated by the presidential nominees, with President Bush giving $26 million and John Kerry, $29.6 million. The remaining $62.8 million came from House and Senate candidates, who, for the most part, transferred sums to their respective congressional campaign committees. Democrats transferred a total of $33.1 million in 2004, compared with $13.6 million in 2000, while Republicans transferred $28.7 million, compared with $17.8 million four years earlier.[19]

National Party Committee Expenditures

The rules governing national party expenditures have changed significantly since the adoption of the FECA. Under the FECA's original provisions, national party committees were permitted to provide direct support to candidates in two basic ways, either by making direct contributions to candidates or by spending a limited amount of money in coordination with them on their behalf. In addition, as a result of an exemption in the act's definitions of "contribution" and "expenditure" adopted as part of the 1979 FECA amendments, party committees also were permitted to provide indirect support to candidates by spending unlimited sums of hard money on certain grassroots activities, including the production of campaign paraphernalia, sample ballots, and generic voter registration and turnout programs.[20] The Supreme Court's decision in *Colorado I* gave parties the added option of spending unlimited amounts of hard money on independent expenditures. But the 1979 amendments and *Colorado* decision had relatively little effect on party spending patterns, since both sides chose to focus expenditures on issue advocacy advertising and voter mobilization programs because those practices could be financed with a combination of hard and soft dollars.

With the adoption of BCRA, parties had to forsake the spending strategies that they had developed to take advantage of their ability to use soft money. In that regard, the law's most important consequence was to prevent the national parties from using soft money to partially fund "issue advocacy" advertisements (see chapter 8). Such advertising, because it could be partially financed with soft dollars, had become a primary means of party support in federal elections since the 1996 election cycle.[21] The law also prohibited other types of soft money spending, including the use of soft dollars to partially finance administrative costs and generic party activities such as voter registration and mobilization drives. Parties, of course, could still spend unlimited sums on advertising and other activities, but they had to use hard dollars.

Limited Candidate Support

As with other sources of campaign funding, federal law limits the amount that national party committees may contribute to candidates. Each national party committee may contribute $5,000 per election to a presidential candidate or a House candidate. Thus the maximum amount that typically can be given to a House candidate is $10,000, or $15,000 if a candidate is involved in a run-off election in addition to the primary and general elections. The maximum amount that can be given to a presidential candidate is $10,000, but only if the candidate does not accept public funding in the general election. Publicly funded presidential general election candidates are not permitted to raise additional contributions for their campaign committees. The parties' national and senatorial committees are allowed to give slightly more to a Senate candidate. Under the FECA, the national and senatorial committees were allowed to give a combined $17,500 to a Senate candidate in each six-year Senate election cycle. BCRA increased the limit to $35,000 per election cycle and indexed it for inflation. With the inflation adjustment, the committees will be allowed to contribute $37,300 to a candidate in the 2006 cycle.[22]

The national party committees also are allowed to spend money on behalf of candidates. Such outlays are known as "coordinated expenditures" because the monies may be spent in coordination with a candidate or a candidate's campaign; they also are known as 441a(d) monies, from the section of Title 2 of the *United States Code* that authorizes this form of spending. The candidate may work with the party committee to determine how best to make use of the funds; thus, although the expenditures are a direct form of candidate support, the funds differ from contributions in that both the party and the candidate share some control of them, giving the party some influence over how they are spent. Unlike contributions, which usually are in the form of monetary contributions to a candidate, coordinated expenditures generally take the form of some kind of campaign service paid for by the party. For example, the party may decide to pay for a poll, a television ad and broadcast time, a mailing to voters, or research on an issue. Coordinated expenditures also differ from direct party contributions in that such expenditures can be made only in connection with a general election campaign, whereas other party contributions may be made at each stage of a federal election.

The FECA limits the amount that a party committee may spend in coordination with a candidate, with the ceilings based on formulas set forth in the 1974 law. The amount depends on the type of election involved. Under the original provisions, national party committees could spend up to $10,000 per candidate in a House election, except in those states with a single congressional district, where the limit was $20,000. In Senate general elections, the limit was set at $20,000 per candidate or $0.02 multiplied by the state's voting-age population, whichever was greater. In presidential elections, the ceiling was simply $0.02 multiplied by the voting-age population, or approximately $2.9 million in 1974. Each of the limits was indexed for inflation, so they have increased with each new election cycle. By 2004, the ceilings were roughly four times the original amount. National party committees could spend more than $16.2 million on behalf of a presidential candidate, $37,310 on behalf of a House candidate (or $74,620 in a state with only one congressional district), and from $74,620 in the smallest states to $1.9 million in California on behalf of a Senate candidate.[23]

In House and Senate races, state and national party committees are allowed to spend the same amount in coordination with a federal candidate. State party committees, however, often lack the funds to use up their coordinated spending allowance, a problem that is commonly addressed through a practice known as an "agency agreement." In those states or districts where a state party lacks adequate funding to meet the coordinated spending limit, the state and national party committees form an agency agreement transferring the state party's spending quota to the national committee. Such agreements usually are made in instances in which a state party lacks the necessary resources and the national senatorial or congressional committee considers the relevant Senate or House race to be strategically important. In those instances, the national committee acts as the agent of the state committee; the national committee thus is allowed to double the amount of its permissible coordinated spending in that district or state, since it is essentially acting as both the national and the state committee.[24] Such agreements have become increasingly common in recent election cycles, thereby allowing national party organizations to maximize coordinated spending in crucial contests.

BCRA made one change in the limits on coordinated spending. As part of the "millionaire's amendment," the law identified a circumstance in which parties could spend unlimited amounts in coordination with a Senate or House candidate. If a candidate is facing a self-financed opponent and that opponent spends ten times more than a certain threshold amount and meets other conditions, then the cap on party coordinated spending is removed. That provision was not triggered in any of the 2004 races.

In the 2004 election cycle, the national party committees spent a total of more than $53 million on candidate contributions and coordinated expenditures. The national party committees contributed $2.8 million to candidates, with the Republican committees donating $1.6 million and the Democratic committees, $1.2 million. The national parties spent more than $50 million on coordinated expenditures. The Republican national committees spent almost $28 million in coordination with candidates, including more than $16 million in the presidential race. Their Democratic counterparts spent almost $23 million, including $16 million in the presidential race. In addition, Democratic state party committees devoted $10.2 million to coordinated spending, while Republican state parties spent $1.3 million on behalf of candidates.[25]

Unlimited Candidate Support

Before 1996, party committees were not allowed to make independent expenditures, nor were they permitted to spend unlimited amounts of money independent of candidates to expressly advocate their election or defeat. That restriction was predicated on the assumption that parties and their candidates are so closely linked that all expenditures should be assumed to be coordinated. The Supreme Court's 1996 decision in *Colorado I* questioned that presumption and determined that Congress could not bar party committees from making independent expenditures in support of candidates.[26] Consequently, the parties were freed to spend money independently in direct support of candidates, at least in the case of congressional candidates (see chapter 2).

The Court in *Colorado I* did not offer an explicit ruling on whether parties could make independent expenditures in support of a presidential candidate, particularly a publicly funded candidate. That issue was not before the Court, since the *Colorado* case concerned expenditures in a congressional race. However, after BCRA was adopted, the FEC addressed this open question by allowing parties to make independent expenditures in support of a presidential general election candidate, except in the case of a candidate who has designated the national committee to serve as his or her principal campaign committee.[27]

BCRA acknowledged the Supreme Court's ruling by codifying provisions for party independent expenditures in behalf of candidates. It thus allowed parties to spend money in coordination with or independent of candidates. In an effort to bring clarity to the party's relationships with its candidates, the law also attempted to force parties to declare how they would operate with individual candidates. As passed by Congress, BCRA included a provision that required a party committee to decide at the time of a candidate's nomination whether it would assist that candidate through limited coordinated expenditures or unlimited independent expenditures. Moreover, the act treated party committees at all levels as a single entity for that purpose, and the FEC interpreted the law to mean that a choice made by a party committee at any level within the party structure (for example, a state committee's decision to act in coordination with a candidate) would be binding on committees at all levels. But the Supreme Court struck down that provision (section 213 of the statute) in its *McConnell* decision.[28] The Court held that Congress could not place conditions or limits on a party's exercise of its right to make independent expenditures and expressed particular concern about the effect of a regulation that would restrict a national party's options on the basis of a decision made by another party committee, including a county or district organization. As a result, national party committees in the 2004 election cycle had the option of spending money in coordination with candidates or independent of them—or both, so long as they abided by the regulations and ensured that their independent expenditures were truly "independent."

Both national parties exercised both options in 2004. In addition to its coordinated expenditures, every national party committee made independent expenditures supporting federal candidates. In fact, in BCRA's new hard money world, independent advertising replaced issue advocacy advertising as the parties' principal means of candidate support. Overall, the party committees allocated more than $264 million to independent expenditures, or more than four times the amount spent in coordination with candidates. Almost all of that $264 million represented expenditures made by the national party committees ($3.6 million represented state and local party expenditures), with the majority of the sum, $176.5 million, spent by the Democrats. The DNC alone reported independent expenditures of $120 million in connection with the presidential race, while the RNC reported $18 million. The congressional campaign committees reported a combined $84 million in independent expenditures (compared with $5.6 million in coordinated spending), with the National Republican Congressional Committee spending $47.3 million independently and the Democratic Congressional Campaign Committee, $36.9 million. The senatorial campaign committees allocated a combined $39 million to independent expenditures (compared with about $13 million in coordinated spending), with the National Republican Senatorial Committee disbursing $19.4 million in this manner and the Democratic Senatorial Campaign Committee, $18.7 million.[29]

Allocated Hybrid Expenditures

As the figures given indicate, the RNC spent significantly less than the DNC on independent expenditures in the presidential race. That disparity was due in part to the RNC's use of an innovative funding strategy that was not antic-ipated by the provisions of current law. The new form of financing consisted of campaign advertisements jointly funded by the presidential campaign and the RNC in an "allocated" or "hybrid" manner. The Republicans produced advertisements that combined a message of support for the president with a generic party message and divided the costs of the ads between the presiden-tial campaign and the party. The party operated on the assumption that FEC allocation rules, still in place after the adoption of BCRA, would allow cost sharing for ads that included a generic party message. They further reasoned that such allocated expenditures would not count against the party's coordi-nated spending limit or constitute a contribution to the publicly funded presidential nominee. Whether the FEC accepted that interpretation of the law was not made clear at the time, since neither the party nor the presiden-tial campaign committee requested a formal opinion from the FEC at the time the practice was initiated.

The Republicans chose the hybrid spending approach over the alterna-tive—independent expenditures—because it allowed the presidential cam-paign to exercise more control over the content of the advertising message, since the party did not have to act independently of the presidential cam-paign in this instance. It also was a highly creative way of reducing the sever-ity of the spending caps imposed on both a publicly funded presidential nominee and party coordinated expenses. In effect, the tactic allowed the presidential campaign to stretch its limited public resources by enabling the party to spend more in coordination with its presidential candidate than the amount permitted under the coordinated spending limit.

The initial advertisements financed in this way were broadcast in Septem-ber; they featured President Bush and included a mention of the Republican "leaders in Congress" with a generic message about the Republican Party's agenda. Once the practice became evident, the DNC soon followed suit, pro-ducing a number of jointly financed hybrid advertisements with the Kerry campaign.[30] By the end of the general election campaign, the RNC reported $45.8 million in generic hybrid expenditures to the FEC. The DNC did not specify the amount that it spent on hybrid ads, but postelection analyses estimate that it spent at least $18.6 million.[31] Party funds were thus used to augment an estimated $64 million in expenditures by the presidential campaigns, for a total of $128 million in paid media advertising.

State and Local Party Funding

In addition to reforming national party funding, BCRA established new rules for state and local party activity conducted in connection with federal elections. The regulations were adopted to ensure that the ban on soft money at the national level was not undermined by the use of soft money at the state or local level. Specifically, the law identified the types of activity that had to be financed solely with hard money, while establishing a new category of funding for generic voter registration and mobilization efforts.

BCRA sets forth a statutory definition of "federal election activities" and requires that they be paid for with monies subject to federal contribution limits and source prohibitions. The definition includes

—any voter registration activity beginning 120 days before a regularly scheduled federal election and ending on the date of the election,

—any get-out-the-vote activity, generic campaign activity, and voter identification activity conducted in connection with an election in which one or more federal candidates appear on the ballot,

—any public communications, including television or radio ads, mass mailings, telephone calling programs, or general public advertising, that promote, support, attack, or oppose a clearly identified federal candidate, and

—salaries of any state or local party employee who devotes more than 25 percent of his or her paid time in a month to federal election activities.[32]
State and local party activities that do not fall into one of those categories are not subject to BCRA's hard money restriction. Instead, they generally are subject to the rules established before the adoption of BCRA or to state law. Thus any contributions made by a state or local party to state or local candidates or any public communications that refer solely to state or local candidates are not affected by the new rules. Similarly, state parties can continue to finance administrative expenses or voter registration activities conducted more than 120 days before a federal election with a combination of federal and nonfederal funds based on the FEC's allocation rules.

When BCRA was being considered in Congress, some members expressed concern about the effects of a ban on soft money, noting that such a prohibition might reduce the resources available to state and local party committees to finance voter registration and turnout programs. To address that concern, the law includes a provision written by Senator Carl Levin (D-Mich.) that allows state and local committees to use a combination of federal and nonfederal funds to pay for some voter registration, identification, and turnout efforts, as well as some generic party activities. That provision, known as the "Levin amendment," operates as a narrow exception to the general rule that federal election–related activity must be financed with hard money.

Under the terms of the Levin amendment, state or local parties may receive contributions of up to $10,000 per donor, if allowed by state law. That is, if state laws allow contributions of $10,000 or more to a party committee, as most do, then any donor allowed to contribute under state law may contribute up to $10,000 per calendar year in Levin money. Otherwise, the amount a donor may give in Levin funds is limited to a state's ceiling on the amount of a permissible contribution to a party committee. Levin funds can be used in conjunction with federal funds to pay for generic voter registration drives conducted more than 120 days before an election and for generic voter identification and turnout efforts that do not mention a federal candidate. Allocation formulas established by the FEC determine the mix of hard and Levin money that a state or local committee must use in paying for such types of activity.

Congress placed a number of additional restrictions on Levin funding to guard against the possibility of the exception becoming a major loophole in the soft money prohibition. All monies used to pay for activities that qualify under the Levin exception must be raised by the state or local committee making the expenditures: that includes both the federally regulated funds and the Levin funds. No federal funds transferred from the national committees to state committees may be used to pay for the federal portion of Levin expenditures. Further, no Levin funds may be used for any registration, identification, or turnout efforts that mention federal candidates, nor may they be used to pay for broadcast, cable, or satellite communications, even when the communications are made in connection with a voter registration or turnout effort. The Levin exception is designed to provide state or local parties with resources for generic grassroots voter mobilization; therefore the funds are not to be used to finance broadcast advertising.

The Levin amendment was designed to provide state and local party organizations with an additional means of generating resources for activities conducted in connection with election campaigns. In 2004, however, few state or local committees took advantage of the option, and Levin funding did not play a major role in party financial strategies. Nonetheless, state and local committees spent substantial amounts of money in connection with the

2004 federal contests. Overall, excluding transfers from the national committees, the state parties reported $237.5 million in federal receipts to the FEC in the 2004 election cycle, with Republican committees reporting $132.4 million and Democratic committees, $105.1 million. The total was slightly less than the $244.7 million, excluding national committee transfers, reported in the 2000 cycle. In addition, state and local committees reported $66.5 million in soft money expenditures, which represented the nonfederal share of joint federal and nonfederal expenditures made in the 2004 cycle. Democratic state and local organizations disbursed $34.9 million in soft money funds on joint activities, while Republican committees reported $31.6 million in soft money spending.[33]

Conclusion

BCRA required party committees to make major changes in the way that they raised and spent money in connection with federal elections. The parties' response to the challenge was more effective and vigorous than many observers expected. Once again, the parties demonstrated their resiliency and efficacy in adapting to changes in the regulatory environment, just as they did after the adoption of the FECA. Consequently, the national party committees look to future elections with reinvigorated donor bases that are the largest in their history. That development, combined with the variety of means now available to party organizations to assist their candidates, suggests that parties will continue to play a vital and dynamic role in the financing of campaigns in the years ahead.

Notes

1. Figures based on Federal Election Commission data.

2. Both of the major parties have a national, senatorial, and congressional committee, so there are six national party committees in all. They include the Democratic National Committee (DNC), Democratic Senatorial Campaign Committee (DSCC), Democratic Congressional Campaign Committee (DCCC), Republican National Committee (RNC), National Republican Senatorial Committee (NRSC), and the National Republican Congressional Committee (NRCC).

3. FEC Advisory Opinions 1976-72 and 1976-83.

4. FEC Advisory Opinion 1978-10. See also Advisory Opinion 1978-46 and FEC, "800 Line: Allocation of Party Expenses," *Record* 4 (November 1978): 5.

5. FEC Advisory Opinions 1979-17 and 1982-5. For a more detailed discussion of the origins and development of soft money, see Anthony Corrado, "Party Soft Money," in

Campaign Finance Reform: A Sourcebook, Anthony Corrado and others (Brookings, 1997), pp. 167–77.

6. Corrado, "Party Soft Money," p. 173.

7. Figures based on data reported by the FEC.

8. FEC, "New Federal Contribution Limits Announced," press release, February 3, 2005.

9. Ibid.

10. David Rogers, "'Soft Money' Study Shows Concentration of Donations by Wealthy Contributors," *Wall Street Journal*, March 16, 2001, p. A16.

11. Paul Fahri, "Parties Square Off in a Database Duel," *Washington Post*, July 20, 2004, p. A1.

12. "Democrats Start Presidential Fund," Associated Press news release, January 31, 2003; and Thomas B. Edsall and David VonDrehle, "Republicans Have Huge Edge in Campaign Cash," *Washington Post*, February 14, 2003, p. A1.

13. Democratic National Committee, "DNC Finance: Patriots 2003–2004" (www.democrats.orgt/pdfs/patriots/pdf [January 7, 2005]).

14. Glen Justice, "The 2004 Campaign: Campaign Finance; Republicans Rush to Form New Finance Groups," *New York Times*, May 29, 2004.

15. Jonathan Kaplan, "RNC Offers 'Super-Ranger' Status," *The Hill*, May 18, 2004.

16. "GOP Has Gained 1M Donors since 2001," *USA Today*, October 3, 2003.

17. Democratic National Committee, "Democratic News: 2004 Progress Report," electronic newsletter, December 10, 2004; and Terence McAuliffe, chairman of the Democratic National Committee, telephone interview with the author, December 16, 2004.

18. A summary of the unitemized and itemized receipts of national party committees in 2004 is found in FEC, "Party Financial Activity Summarized for the 2004 Election Cycle," press release, March 2, 2005.

19. Ibid. See also Robin Kolodny and Diana Dwyre, "The Parties' Congressional Campaign Committees in 2004," in *The Election after Reform*, edited by Michael J. Malbin (Lanham, Md.: Rowman and Littlefield, 2005).

20. For a discussion of the 1979 amendment, see Corrado, "Party Soft Money," pp. 170–71.

21. On the role of issue advocacy in federal elections, see Anthony Corrado, "Financing the 1996 Elections," in *The Election of 1996*, edited by Gerald Pomper (Chatham, N.J.: Chatham House Publishers, 1997); and Diana Dwyre and Robin Kolodny, "Throwing Out the Rule Book: Party Financing of the 2000 Elections," in *Financing the 2000 Election*, edited by David B. Magleby (Brookings, 2002).

22. FEC, "New Federal Contribution Limits Announced."

23. FEC, "2004 Coordinated Party Expenditure Limits," *Record* 30 (March 2004): 15–16.

24. 11 C.F.R. sec. 109.33.

25. FEC, "Party Financial Activity Summarized for the 2004 Election Cycle."

26. *Colorado Republican Federal Campaign Committee* v. *FEC*, 518 U.S. 604 (1996).

27. 11 C.F.R. sec. 109.36.

28. *McConnell* v. *FEC*, 124 S. Ct. 619 (2003).

29. FEC, "Party Financial Activity Summarized for the 2004 Election Cycle."

30. Liz Sidoti, "Bush Team Orchestrates Larger Ad Campaign," Associated Press news release, September 22, 2004; "Kerry Campaign, DNC to Run Joint Ads," Associated Press news release, September 24, 2004; and, "Campaign Briefing: The Advertising Campaign," *New York Times*, September 25, 2004.

31. Thomas A. Devine, senior strategist, Kerry for President, telephone interview with author, January 11, 2005. See also FEC, "Party Financial Activity Summarized for the 2004 Election Cycle," which notes that the DNC spent $24 million during the general election period for media production and consulting that was not included in the independent expenditure totals reported by the committee.

32. 11 C.F.R. sec. 100.24.

33. FEC, "Party Financial Activity Summarized for the 2004 Election Cycle," and FEC, "Party Committees Raise More than $1 Billion in 2001–2002," press release, March 20, 2003.

6

Public Funding of Presidential Campaigns

Anthony Corrado

I n 1974, as part of the Federal Election Campaign Act (FECA), Congress created a voluntary system of public funding for presidential campaigns. This system, adopted in response to the Watergate scandal, was designed to reduce the risk of corruption in the political process by offering candidates public funding as an alternative to private contributions and providing national party committees with public funds to finance presidential nominating conventions. The law sought to reduce the role of money in presidential politics by linking public subsidies to caps on campaign spending. It also sought to expand the participation of small donors in the financing of presidential campaigns by offering matching funds to enhance the value of small contributions. At the time of its adoption, public funding was heralded as the most innovative change in federal campaign finance law in American history. It remains so to this day.

The public funding system provides taxpayer-funded support to candidates or national party committees at each stage of the presidential selection process. In the prenomination or primary period, a candidate can qualify for public matching funds on a dollar-for-dollar basis for the first $250 contributed by an individual donor. A national party committee can receive a publicly funded grant that provides a specified sum of money to be used to pay the costs of a national nominating convention. In the general election, presidential nominees of the major parties can receive a publicly funded grant that provides full funding equal to the amount that a candidate is permitted to spend under the law's expenditure ceiling. Non–major party nominees or independent candidates may qualify for a prorated convention or general election grant based on their share of the presidential general election vote.

Public funding has been widely accepted by presidential candidates since its implementation in 1976. Almost all of the major contenders who have sought the Oval Office, whether Democrat or Republican, have used public funds to help finance their campaigns. Every major party presidential nominee has chosen public funding in the general election, and both major parties have used public resources to help pay for their national nominating conventions. However, a growing number of candidates in recent elections have begun to question the benefits of public funding, particularly in the primaries. The Bipartisan Campaign Reform Act of 2002 (BCRA) made no changes in the public funding program, so the law has not been revised in more than thirty years. It has not been amended to accommodate changes that have taken place in the nomination process and the rapidly growing financial demands associated with the front-loading of the presidential primary calendar.[1] Consequently, candidates have found it increasingly difficult to conform to the public funding rules—particularly the now outdated caps on spending attached to the acceptance of public funds—and still meet the financial and strategic imperatives of a presidential campaign.

The strategic problems created by the current rules are encouraging candidates, especially those most likely to win their party's nomination, to rethink the value of public funding. In 2000, then-Governor George W. Bush became the first major party candidate to win the presidential nomination without accepting public funds during the primaries. In 2004, both of the major party nominees, President George W. Bush and Senator John Kerry, opted out of public funding during the primaries, as did former Governor Howard Dean, the putative Democratic frontrunner prior to the voting in Iowa. Their decisions suggest that candidates no longer regard the basic trade-off at the core of the current system—public money in exchange for spending limits—to be a desirable or worthwhile exchange. They highlight the challenges facing the system and the need for major reform.

Although no significant statutory changes have been adopted since 1974, the regulations governing public financing have been modified in a variety of ways, often with major effects. The regulations are complex, due in part to the tripartite nature of the public funding program, which establishes different types of subsidies for primary and general elections and separate rules for party conventions. This chapter reviews the diverse provisions of the presidential campaign public funding program and discusses related aspects of presidential campaign finance.

Financing Public Financing

In the eight presidential elections from 1976 through 2004, presidential candidates and party committees received more than $1.3 billion in public funds.[2] Candidates seeking their party's nomination received about $342 million; national party committees, $152 million; and general election contenders, $839 million. Republicans and Democrats alike have participated in the program, with a greater number of Democrats qualifying for public funds largely because of the greater number of contested Democratic nominations during that period. In total, Democratic candidates and their national party committee received $646 million in public support, while Republican candidates and their national party committee received $628 million. Relatively few of the non–major party challengers qualified for public funds. Those who did qualify received a total of only $60 million. More than $42 million of that total consists of the subsidies given to the Reform Party and its nominee in 1996 and 2000 as a result of the support garnered by Ross Perot in the 1992 and 1996 elections. When the Reform Party is excluded, non–major party candidates received only about 1 percent of the total public monies distributed.

The financing for the public funding program comes from a voluntary check-off option on the individual federal income tax form. The check-off allows taxpayers to designate a deposit to the Presidential Election Campaign Fund (PECF), a separate account administered by the Department of the Treasury, from which all public funding disbursements are made. Under the original terms of the program, an individual tax filer was allowed to designate $1 to the PECF, or $2 if filing jointly. In 1993, in response to concerns about the financial solvency of the PECF, Congress increased the amount to account for inflation, setting it at $3 for an individual and $6 for a joint filer.[3] Designating the allowed amount does not affect the amount of an individual's tax liability or tax refund; it simply directs the Treasury Department to allocate a specific amount from general revenues to the PECF. However, the Treasury Department deposits only funds from tax filers with a tax liability. If a tax filer designates a contribution on his or her tax form but does not have a tax liability, a deposit is not made into the PECF.

Funds deposited into the PECF are used to pay for all three components of the presidential public funding system: primary matching funds, party nominating convention subsidies, and presidential general election grants. No general treasury funds other than those designated through the check-off may be used to cover the costs of these benefits. If the available funding is insufficient to meet the costs, the law requires the Department of the Treasury to allocate funds in a particular order, with first priority given to the conventions, second priority to the general election, and third priority to the primaries. In 1991, the Treasury Department, anticipating a shortfall in the monies needed to finance the costs of the 1992 election, adopted revised rules that specify how the priorities are to be met, even if there is no projected shortfall in the PECF.[4] Under those regulations, Treasury sets aside the amount of money needed for the conventions and general election grants by January 1 of the election year. The remaining balance in the PECF and any additional deposits received during the election year are then made available for matching fund payments to primary candidates. If the funds available in the PECF are inadequate to cover the matching subsidies accrued by the candidates, then each candidate receives a partial payment, and the balance owed a candidate is paid when sufficient funding becomes available. The amount of the partial payment is based on a percentage determined by the FEC by dividing the total amount of money available in the PECF at the end of each month by the total amount of matching funds requested by all qualified candidates. The difference between the amount a candidate has earned in matching funds and the amount a candidate is actually paid is then carried over to the next month and paid as funding becomes available.[5]

The tax form check-off has always provided enough money to meet the needs of the public funding program. But in recent elections the system barely managed to remain solvent and often failed to meet all obligations on a timely basis. That financial strain is the result of a combination of declining check-off revenues and rising costs. Check-off participation rates and revenues have experienced a steady decline since reaching a peak in 1981. From 1981 to 1993, the percentage of individual tax returns that designated a check-off contribution fell from 28.7 percent to 18.9 percent, while annual revenues declined from $41 million to $28 million. After the adoption of the $3 check-off, the participation rate dropped to 14.5 percent; it continued to slide to about 11 percent in 2002, with annual deposits falling from $71 million to about $62 million.[6]

Consequently, since 1992, PECF deposits have barely kept pace with the rising costs of public funding (payments generally increase in each election

cycle, since the convention and general election grants are indexed for inflation). In 1996, there was not enough money in the PECF to cover the January matching fund payments, so each candidate received 60 percent of the
amount due.[7] In 2000, candidates did not receive the full amount of matching money they had accrued until the end of the primary process.[8] In 2004,
even though the demand for public funds was down sharply because the
leading candidates did not accept matching funds, those who did participate
received only 46 cents on the dollar in the February payment.[9] In those
instances, however, candidates did not have to continue campaigning without access to the monies they were owed; instead, they typically pledged the
public monies still due as collateral to secure bank loans for equivalent sums,
a practice allowed by the FEC. Even so, the fact that candidates had to resort
to loans to gain access to the public money that they earned indicates the
financial problems inherent in the current check-off system. Had all of the
candidates chosen to accept public funds in the 2004 election cycle, the
PECF might not have been able to make full payment until well after the end
of the presidential nomination contests.

Financing Primary Campaigns

Candidates who accept public funds are subject to the same financial disclosure requirements and contribution limits that apply to other federal candidates. A candidate must disclose all receipts and expenditures of $200 or
more and file reports electronically with the FEC. In the elections prior to
2004, a candidate could accept $1,000 per election from an individual and
$5,000 per election from a PAC. BCRA increased the individual limit to
$2,000 per election and indexed it for inflation; thus the 2004 election was
the first presidential campaign conducted under the new limit. In 2004, a
candidate could also receive a contribution of up to $1,000 per election from
the campaign committee of another federal candidate. After the election, a
provision included in an omnibus appropriations bill increased the limit to
$2,000.[10] The higher limit will be operative in the 2008 presidential election.

Eligibility for Funding

To be eligible to receive public funds, a candidate must accept a number of
financial restrictions in addition to those imposed on all federal candidates. A
candidate must agree to limit personal contributions to his or her own campaign to a maximum of $50,000. (A candidate who does not accept public

funds may give any amount of money to his or her own campaign, so long as it comes from his or her personal resources or share of assets held jointly with a spouse.) Candidates also must raise $5,000 in contributions of $250 or less in twenty states, for a total of at least $100,000, to qualify for funding, and they must agree to abide by spending limits. Finally, all publicly funded candidates must agree to a postcampaign financial audit conducted by the FEC.

Once the eligibility requirements are met, a candidate may receive public funds on a one-for-one basis on the first $250 contributed by an individual donor. Only individual contributions received after January 1 of the year before the election are eligible for matching; donations from PACs or other political committees are not. Prior to the 2000 election cycle, contributions had to be made by check or money order to be matched. In 1999, the FEC modified that rule to allow public matching of qualified contributions made by credit or debit card, including those made over the Internet.[11]

The first matching fund payments are made on January 1 of the election year and monthly thereafter.[12] The law caps the total amount of public money that a candidate may receive to a sum equal to one-half of the law's base primary spending limit. In the 2004 election, the maximum amount of public matching money that a candidate could receive was $18.7 million.[13] Since 1976, the only candidate to have drawn the maximum was President Ronald Reagan in 1984.

To ensure that the availability of public money does not serve to prolong the candidacy of challengers who are unlikely to win, the law sets forth thresholds for continued eligibility. The 1976 FECA amendments included a provision that calls for terminating a candidate's eligibility within thirty days of failure to receive at least 10 percent of the vote in two consecutive primaries.[14] This rule only applies to a candidate's performance in a primary election; states that hold caucuses to select nominees are not included. A candidate whose public funding has been terminated may regain eligibility by winning 20 percent of the vote in a subsequent primary.[15]

The 10 percent rule does not affect a candidate's initial qualification for public funding once the voting in state primaries has begun. A candidate may fulfill the eligibility requirements—specifically the fundraising requirement of at least $5,000 from small contributions in at least twenty states—after failing to receive 10 percent of the vote in consecutive primaries and still be certified to receive public funds. In 1992, Larry Agran, a candidate for the Democratic nomination, did not qualify for public funding until mid-May of the election year, yet he still was able to receive some matching funds.[16]

The FEC has interpreted this rule to refer to two consecutive primaries in which a candidate is entered on the ballot, rather than two consecutive primaries as determined by the delegate selection calendar. A candidate therefore can exclude particular primaries from the requirement and continue to be eligible for funding despite poor showings in a number of primaries.[17] For example, in 1992, Lenora Fulani, a New Alliance Party candidate, informed the FEC that she would seek the presidential nomination under the banner of a number of different parties in selected states. She thereby retained eligibility for matching funds despite failing to capture 10 percent of the vote in the early primaries and failing to appear on the ballot in a number of states.[18] Similarly, in 2004, Ralph Nader, who ran as an independent candidate in the general election, informed the FEC that he was seeking the presidential nomination of the Populist Party and other third-party nominations, and he was able to receive matching payments after initially qualifying for public funding at the end of May.[19]

The FEC has also established rules for candidates who compete in parties, such as the Natural Law Party or Green Party, that do not hold state primaries or caucuses as part of their selection process. As with all presidential hopefuls, their aspirants must fulfill the basic eligibility requirements of the matching funds program. They also must be seeking the nomination of a party that is qualified as a "political party" under FEC regulations, which generally means that the party has some record of political activity and has a procedure for holding an election to nominate a candidate to the office of president or vice president.[20] However, because these non–major party contenders do not compete in primaries and are typically unopposed for their respective party's nomination, they are not subject to the 10 percent eligibility rule; they therefore may continue to accrue matching funds throughout their formal prenomination campaign period. In 1992, John Hagelin, who sought the Natural Law Party's presidential nomination, did not fulfill the eligibility requirements for matching fund certification until October, but the FEC approved a matching fund payment to his campaign since the party's national nominating convention was not held until early October.[21] In the case of a candidate who seeks the nomination of a party that does not use a national nominating convention to make its choice or one who seeks the nomination of a number of parties, one or more of which may use a convention, the FEC has ruled that the eligibility period for accruing matching funds ends on whichever date is earlier: the date that a candidate is nominated by a party convention or the last day of the last national convention held by a major party during the election year.[22]

After a candidate has stopped actively campaigning for a party's nomination, he or she may continue to accrue a limited amount of public funding to retire campaign debts or pay the costs incurred in "winding down" a campaign.[23] The combined total of public money and private donations received to pay off such expenses may not exceed the amount of campaign debt or obligations. For this purpose, a candidate may submit qualified contributions for public matching funds until late February or early March of the year following the election. But only contributions deposited into a campaign's account by December 31 of the election year are eligible for matching.[24]

Spending Limits

In the primaries, publicly funded candidates must agree to abide by aggregate and state-by-state ceilings. The aggregate ceiling, which determines the total amount a candidate may spend, was set in 1974 at a "base limit" of $10 million, plus an additional 20 percent for fundraising costs, with an adjustment for inflation. The fundraising "exemption" from the base limit was adopted to recognize the higher costs incurred in raising funds from small contributions, as required by the contribution limits established by the FECA. In 1976, the base limit was $10.9 million, plus $2.2 million for fundraising costs, for a total aggregate limit of $13.1 million. By 2004, the base limit had grown to $37.3 million, plus $7.4 million for fundraising costs, for a total of $44.7 million.

Any monies spent to pay legal and accounting costs incurred to comply with the law are exempt from expenditure limits. Under the FEC's initial interpretation of the law, there was no specific limit on the amount that a publicly funded candidate could spend on compliance. In 2000, the commission modified the rules, limiting compliance funding to 15 percent of the base spending limit while a candidate is actively campaigning. Once a campaign is over and the candidate's operation is closing down and going through the audit process, all salary and overhead costs may be considered exempt compliance spending, which does not count against any spending ceiling.[25] In 2004, that guideline allowed a publicly funded candidate to spend an additional $5.6 million on compliance, bringing the effective aggregate ceiling to $50.3 million.

The law also limits the amount a publicly funded primary candidate may spend in each state. These ceilings were established to level the playing field among candidates in particular state contests. The amount that may be spent in each state is based on a formula in the 1974 FECA that allows a candidate to spend $0.16 multiplied by a state's voting-age-population, plus adjustments for inflation, or a minimum of $200,000, adjusted for inflation, whichever is higher. In 2004, the state limits ranged from a minimum of $746,200 in low-population states, including New Hampshire, to $15.6 million in California.[26]

In practice, the state limits have had relatively little effect on campaign spending. They have been a factor in candidate spending decisions primarily in the key early contests in Iowa, New Hampshire, and South Carolina.[27] Almost since the time of the law's adoption, candidates have sought to circumvent the limits or reduce their effect by taking advantage of technical provisions in the law or FEC administrative rulings that permit campaigns to exempt certain expenditures. For example, throughout the 1980s, candidates often established precandidacy PACs or other political organizations to facilitate early campaigning without having to allocate expenses against state spending limits. Campaigns also developed complicated accounting mechanisms for allocating expenditures in Iowa or New Hampshire to neighboring states or the national headquarters, as permitted by FEC rules. Those allocations exempted substantial amounts of money from the state limits, including fundraising, media, personnel, and overhead expenses.[28]

Following the 1988 election, the FEC noted that the state limits had had little effect on campaign spending and recommended that Congress abolish the ceilings because they had proven to be "a significant accounting burden for campaigns and an equally difficult audit and enforcement task."[29] But Congress took no action on the recommendation. In 1991, the FEC revised its regulations to liberalize and streamline the state limits, minimizing their importance.[30] Under the new rules, a candidate's expenses are subject to a state limit only if they fall within one of five specific categories: media expenses, mass mailings conducted within twenty-eight days of an election, overhead expenses, special telephone programs, and public opinion polls. The rules also allow a campaign to treat up to 50 percent of the expenses allocable to a state as exempt fundraising costs, thereby excluding them from a state's ceiling.[31] The rules thus permit a candidate to spend substantially more in a state than the amount suggested by the state limit.

Unlike the state limits, the aggregate expenditure ceiling has had a major effect on the conduct of primary campaigns. Because the ceiling is adjusted only for inflation rather than the changing costs and dynamics of the presidential selection process, it has proven to be increasingly inadequate. Consequently, it has become a major strategic concern of presidential hopefuls. Since 1980, most of the prospective nominees of the major parties have had to cut back significantly on anticipated expenditures or otherwise restrict campaigning in an effort to adhere to the requirements of the aggregate limit. Moreover, the point in the selection process at which the spending limit becomes a major concern for candidates has been arriving earlier and earlier in the process. In the late 1980s, prospective nominees tended to come within reach of the limit (factoring in forward costs to get through the nominating convention) by early June or late May. By 1996 and 2000, candidates were constrained by mid-April or late March. In 2000, defeated Democrat Bill Bradley and defeated Republican John McCain essentially reached the spending limit before the end of March.

The aggregate ceiling has been particularly problematic for a challenger who wins a hard-fought nomination contest and faces a prospective general election opponent who captured his party's nomination without opposition or with relative ease. In this scenario, the nominee who ran in a competitive race faces a prospective opponent who still has a substantial amount of money left to spend before the conventions. For example, in 1996, Republican Robert Dole captured the presidential nomination, but he did so in a tough race in which he faced, among others, Steve Forbes, who did not accept public funds and spent tens of millions of his own money on his campaign. Dole essentially reached the spending cap by the end of April. His prospective general election opponent, President Bill Clinton, who was renominated without challenge, had $20 million left to spend under the cap.[32] Dole thus faced a significant strategic disadvantage, and his predicament was one of the principal reasons that Republican George W. Bush chose to forgo public funding and spending limits in the 2000 Republican primary campaign. Thus, in 2000, then-Vice President Al Gore won the Democratic nomination, but his position was similar to that of Dole four years earlier. By the time Gore had emerged as the Democratic nominee, he had relatively little money left to spend under the cap throughout the summer months. Bush, however, faced no spending limit and raised an additional $20 million to spend against Gore after he wrapped up the nomination.[33] Gore's predicament was a factor in leading Howard Dean and John Kerry to forgo public funding in the primaries in 2004.

In advance of the 2000 primaries, the FEC took some steps to address the financial problem created by the inadequate spending ceiling and the widening gap between the effective end of the nominating process and the party conventions. The commission eased some of the restrictions on certain types of spending to give candidates and party committees more financial flexibility between June 1 of the election year and the date of a party's convention. During that period, a candidate who accepts public funding may allocate salary and overhead expenditures equal to no more than 15 percent of the base primary spending limit against the general election spending ceiling. In that way a prospective general election challenger may begin spending money to prepare for the general election without having to count those disbursements against the primary expenditure cap. But the disbursements are counted against the general election cap if the candidate accepts public funding in the general election.[34] The commission also revised its rules on party coordinated expenditures, expressly granting party committees the option of making coordinated expenditures on behalf of a presidential candidate before that candidate is formally nominated. Any amounts spent in that manner are subject to the party's coordinated spending limit, whether or not the candidate with whom they are coordinated receives the party's nomination.[35]

These regulatory changes had no significant effect on the financial activity in primary campaigns. Instead of starting to spend money against general election limits, candidates in 2000 relied on party soft money expenditures—specifically candidate-specific issue advertisements that were exempt from limits—to carry their campaign. Now, following the adoption of BCRA, party committees are no longer allowed to use soft money to support their presidential standard-bearer, but they can rely on party independent expenditures, which can be made without limit (see chapter 6). Yet that option leaves the decisionmaking regarding expenditures and strategies in the hands of the party rather than the candidate, since the party is not allowed to coordinate with a candidate when spending money independently on his or her behalf. Consequently, candidates prefer to refuse matching funds and thereby avoid primary spending ceilings. They are likely to continue to prefer that option until the public funding statute is revised to establish a more realistic aggregate spending limit.

Financing Presidential Nominating Conventions

As part of the presidential campaign public funding program, national party committees have the option of accepting a publicly funded grant to pay the costs of their nominating conventions. A party that accepts the grant may not spend more than the amount provided. The amount was originally set in 1974 at $2 million, plus adjustments for inflation, with the base amount subsequently increased to $3 million in 1979 and $4 million in 1984. With adjustments for inflation, the amount available in 2004 to each of the major parties (defined in the law as a party whose presidential nominee received at least 25 percent of the vote in the previous presidential election, which means, in practical terms, the Democrats and the Republicans) was $14.9 million.[36]

A non–major party, defined as a party whose presidential nominee received at least 5 percent but not more than 25 percent of the presidential vote in the previous election, may qualify for a proportional share of the total convention grant. The proportion is based on the proportion of the major parties' average vote share represented by the non–major party's or candidate's share. In 2004, only the Democrats and Republicans qualified for convention funding. In 2000, however, the Reform Party received a convention grant of $2.5 million based on Ross Perot's performance in the 1996 presidential race.[37] The major parties each received a convention grant of $13.5 million that year.[38] A non–major party that receives a partial convention subsidy may raise additional funds up to the total amount of the public grant awarded to each major party committee, so long as the contributions received are allowed under federal contribution limits.

The public grant was intended to cover all of a party's costs in connection with a national nominating convention. But soon after the public financing system was put into place, the FEC allowed cities hosting presidential conventions to establish nonprofit convention "host committees" or "municipal funds" that could raise and spend money to finance activities associated with a presidential convention. These committees were treated as separate from the party convention committees. Specifically, the FEC ruled that payments made by state or local governments to provide facilities and services to the national committee of a political party in connection with a party's national nominating convention do not constitute prohibited contributions to the national party, so long as the payments to any vendors represent fair market value.[39] The commission further permitted separate "host committees" to raise and spend funds, including contributions from businesses and other donors with a commercial interest in convention activities, for use in "promoting the convention city and its commerce."[40] However, according to a 1980 FEC administrative ruling, those contributions could come only from local retail businesses within a convention city and were to be limited to an amount "proportionate to the commercial return reasonably expected by the business, corporation or agency during the life of the convention."[41]

The commission allowed host committees to finance a wide array of convention-related projects that might otherwise have been the responsibility of the party convention committee, such as the redesign and construction of convention hall facilities, lighting and electrical work, communications and audio systems, convention transportation services, and security services.[42] The commission also allowed businesses to discount the sale or lease of products to national party convention committees so long as the discounts or price reductions constituted a transaction that would occur in "the ordinary course of business" and would be offered at nonpolitical events, not just national party conventions.[43]

Originally, only local businesses, unions, organizations, and individuals were permitted to make contributions to convention host committees. But in 1994 and 2003, the FEC revised its regulations, eventually permitting companies to provide goods or services to a party convention committee in exchange for promotional consideration, provided that the company does so in the ordinary course of business.[44] In recognition of the complex structure of many business and labor organizations, the FEC in 1994 loosened the definition of "local businesses" allowed to contribute to host committees to include branch offices, local dealers, and affiliates of state or national business or labor organizations. In 2003, the FEC did away with the local retail proviso on contributions altogether, noting that the "restriction no longer served a meaningful purpose because the disbursements that host committees and municipal funds are permitted to make are consistent with the narrow purpose of promoting commerce in the convention city."[45] So contributors to host committees are no longer required to have a local presence and the amounts donated are no longer tied to a business's expectation of an economic return from convention activity. The 2003 regulations further noted that while BCRA's provisions, particularly the ban on soft money, applies to national party convention committees, the law does not "significantly alter current rules governing the financing of national conventions."[46] Accordingly, convention committees may still receive in-kind donations of goods and services from host committees and municipal funds to cover certain convention expenses as specified in the regulations.

Since 1992, the role of host committees and municipal funds in financing nominating conventions has grown dramatically, reaching the point where the private donations raised by these entities greatly exceed the amount provided to the national party committees by the public grant. In 2004, for example, the convention host committees established in New York City for the Republican National Convention and in Boston for the Democratic National Convention raised a combined $138 million in private contributions, more than four times the amount of public money given to the two party convention committees.[47] Host committee funding thus has become a matter of significant controversy, particularly because the committees may accept contributions from corporations or other donors that would be considered illegal soft money donations if given to the party committees. Some observers therefore contend that host committees facilitate circumvention of BCRA's ban on soft money and argue that the rules should be reformed to impose more stringent limits on host committee finances.[48]

Financing the General Election

Presidential general election candidates can choose to receive a public grant that provides full funding for a campaign. The amount of the grant is based on a formula established in the 1974 FECA that sets the general election spending limit at $20 million, plus adjustments for inflation. By 2004, the amount of the grant had grown to $74.6 million. A candidate who does not accept public financing in the primaries may choose public financing in the general election, so long as that candidate meets the qualifying requirements and conditions. To be eligible, a candidate must be the presidential nominee of a major party or non–major party that qualifies for funding under the terms set out in the law. A candidate also must agree to raise no additional private contributions for general election campaigning (with the exception of monies to finance general election legal and accounting compliance costs); abide by the general election spending limit; spend no more than $50,000 from personal funds (including any expenditures by either the presidential or vice presidential nominee); and permit an audit after the election.

The limits established by the public funding program apply jointly to the presidential and vice presidential nominees on a party ticket. The nominees run in a unified campaign, which is subject to a single spending limit, and both are prohibited from raising private contributions for their campaign committee in the general election. Thus, a vice presidential candidate is generally not allowed to raise monies separately from the presidential candidate. Prior to the 2000 election cycle, a person selected by a presidential nominee-apparent to serve as a vice presidential running mate could raise funds prior to the nominating convention to finance convention expenses. However, after the 1996 conventions, the FEC changed its regulations to limit such activity.[49]

A major party nominee, defined in the law as the nominee of a party that received at least 25 percent of the vote in the previous presidential election, is eligible to receive the full amount provided by the public funding grant. A non–major party nominee or independent candidate is eligible for a proportionate share of the grant, if the party or candidate received at least 5 percent of the presidential vote in the previous election. The amount of funding provided by the proportionate subsidy is based on the proportion of the major parties' average vote share represented by the non–major party's or candidate's share. Thus in 1996 Reform Party nominee Ross Perot received $29.1 million in general election public funding, slightly less than half the amount given to each of the major party nominees that year ($68.1 million), based on the share of the vote that he received in the 1992 presidential race, which was slightly less than half of the average share received by the Democratic and Republican nominees. Similarly, in 2000, Reform Party nominee Patrick Buchanan received $12.6 million in public funding, based on the share of the vote received by Perot in 1996. A non–major party candidate who receives a proportionate subsidy is not limited to spending the amount provided by the grant. A candidate also may raise private contributions, subject to federal contribution limits, to make up the difference between the amount of the public subsidy and the overall general election spending limit applied to publicly funded major party candidates.

The rules also allow new parties or candidates who did not compete in the previous presidential election to qualify for postelection funding. As in the case of other non–major party candidates, such contenders may receive a proportionate share of the general election grant, so long as the presidential nominee receives at least 5 percent of the national vote. In 1980, John Anderson, a candidate in the Republican primaries who ran in the general election as the nominee of the National Unity Party, garnered more than 5 percent of the vote in the presidential race and, after the election, was given $4.2 million in public money (the total grant that year was $29.4 million) to help defray the costs incurred by his campaign. If the National Unity Party had remained active and selected a nominee in 1984, it would have been eligible for a proportionate public grant in advance of the election.

To qualify for public funding, a non–major party candidate must, in addition to meeting the general requirements imposed on all candidates, be certified to appear on the general election ballot as a party's presidential nominee in ten or more states. That provision was important in resolving competing claims to the public entitlement available to the Reform Party nominee in 2000. Ross Perot, whose 8.4 percent of the vote in the 1996 presidential race had earned the Reform Party the opportunity to receive $12.6 million in general election public funding, did not run again in 2000. Patrick Buchanan, a former Republican, and John Hagelin, the Natural Law Party's presidential nominee in 1992 and 1996, sought the Reform Party mantle and continued to vie for the nomination after a factious Reform Party convention failed to produce a nominee. Buchanan and Hagelin each submitted formal requests to the FEC asking to be certified as the Reform Party nominee eligible for the public subsidy, and each submitted a list of certified ballot positions in more than ten states.[50]

While the rules require a candidate to be on the ballot in at least ten states, they do not specify the action to be taken when two candidates meet that qualification and claim to be the nominee of the same party. The FEC therefore had to resolve the competing claims. The commission's task was complicated by the complexities arising from ballot access laws, since Buchanan was listed as the Reform Party nominee in some states, Hagelin in other states, and in yet others, state officials were awaiting the FEC's ruling to complete the Reform Party ballot line. Hagelin also was listed on the ballot in some states as an independent. The FEC ultimately determined that Buchanan had met the law's eligibility requirements, since he was officially listed as the Reform Party candidate in twelve states, while Hagelin was listed that way in only three states. The commission thus awarded the grant to Buchanan without resolving the issue of which of the two was the "legitimate" party nominee and without establishing guidelines to resolve the issue if two candidates meet the minimum qualification requirement again.[51]

GELAC Funds

Publicly funded candidates are allowed to raise private contributions exempt from the fundraising prohibition and expenditure limits to finance general election legal and accounting compliance costs (GELAC). To do so, a candidate must establish a separate GELAC fund, a special account maintained exclusively to pay for compliance costs. All donations to a GELAC fund are governed by federal contribution limits and prohibitions (for example, an individual may give no more than $2,000, adjusted for inflation).

The law allows candidates to establish a GELAC fund in order to facilitate compliance with the law and ensure that regulatory requirements do not impose an undue burden on the use of limited public campaign funds. The basic purpose of a GELAC fund is to finance legal and accounting expenses, pay the costs of raising GELAC monies, cover winding-down expenses (such as maintaining a campaign office and small staff to handle such postelection tasks as filing disclosure reports and managing the audit process), and provide for any repayments of public funds imposed by the FEC for violations of the public funding regulations.

Over time, the FEC has adopted regulations that have expanded the definition of compliance activity and the purposes for which GELAC funds may be used.[52] For example, the regulations permit a campaign to pay 10 percent of payroll expenses, including payroll taxes, as well as 10 percent of the overhead for national and state campaign headquarters from GELAC monies on the assumption that that portion of salary and overhead are related to compliance activities. The overhead expenses that qualify under this provision include rent, utilities, office equipment, furniture, supplies, and all telephone charges except for those related to special uses such as voter registration and get-out-the-vote efforts. A candidate also may use GELAC funds to reimburse up to 50 percent of the costs associated with computer services, including rental and maintenance of computer equipment, nonstaff data entry services, and related supplies.

A candidate may set up a GELAC fund before becoming the official party nominee. Some candidates have established GELAC funds early in the selection process, at times as early as a year before the general election.[53] This practice allows a campaign to raise GELAC funds throughout the primary process, coterminous with other fundraising activity. More important, it provides a campaign with the opportunity to redesignate excess contributions (amounts above an individual donor's contribution limit) or excess monies not needed for primary campaigning (such as monies remaining after the spending limit is reached) to the GELAC fund for use in the general election.[54] Such early fundraising raises a number of potential problems. The raising and spending of GELAC funds prior to the convention increases the difficulty of ensuring that GELAC monies are not being improperly used to finance primary campaign expenditures or facilitate spending beyond the amount specified by the expenditure limit. In addition, if a candidate loses the primary race and does not become the party's presidential nominee, the regulations require all monies in the GELAC account to be refunded to donors within sixty days. However, the amounts needed to meet that requirement are not always readily available, since some have already been spent for fundraising and other costs.

In recent election cycles, the FEC modified its regulations to address the problems posed by GELAC funding. The commission continued to allow a primary contender to establish a GELAC fund but imposed new restrictions on GELAC fundraising. In advance of the 2000 election, the FEC established June 1 of the election year as the threshold date for GELAC fundraising.[55] Before that date, a GELAC account may be established, but a candidate may deposit only primary election contributions that exceed the amount a donor is allowed to give and that have been properly redesignated to the

GELAC fund. A candidate may not begin to solicit contributions for a GELAC account prior to June 1. After that date, general GELAC fundraising may commence. In advance of the 2004 election, the FEC altered the timetable slightly, pushing the fundraising threshold date back to April 1 of the election year, in recognition of the earlier start of the presidential selection process (that is, the earlier scheduling of a number of state primaries).[56] The new fundraising timetable was based on the notion that, in usual circumstances, a party's prospective nominee will have been determined by that date, so it is unlikely that a candidate will have to refund the GELAC monies raised. At the same time, the date was assumed to give a prospective nominee the time needed to raise the sums required to cover compliance expenses. The new rules also permit a candidate to use any GELAC funds not needed for general election–related expenses to pay a primary committee's winding-down costs and to make any required repayments to the U.S. Treasury for violations of the law committed during the primary campaign.[57]

Party Support

Party committees are an important source of funding in presidential elections. Under the provisions of the FECA and FEC regulations, party committees may spend funds in coordination with a presidential candidate or independent of a candidate, provided that the monies are raised in accordance with federal contribution limits and source prohibitions.

A national party committee may spend a limited amount of money in coordination with its presidential nominee; the amount is based on a formula established by the FECA that permits a total equal to $0.02 multiplied by the national voting-age-population, with adjustments for inflation. In 2004, the Democratic National Committee and Republican National Committee each could spend up to $16.2 million on behalf of their presidential candidate.[58] Prior to the 2000 election, party committees were permitted to make coordinated expenditures only in connection with the general election after the party had formally chosen a presidential nominee. In 1999, the FEC revised that rule to allow a party committee to make coordinated expenditures on behalf of a candidate before he or she was nominated, with the proviso that all such prenomination expenditures would be subject to the coordinated spending limit, even if made on behalf of a candidate who did not receive the party's nomination.[59]

Party committees also may spend unlimited amounts of money independently to support a presidential candidate. Such expenditures were specifically prohibited before the 2004 election cycle.[60] Even after the Supreme Court's ruling in *Colorado I*, which recognized the right of parties to make independent expenditures, the law was not clear as to whether independent expenditures were permissible in the case of publicly funded presidential candidates.[61] BCRA recognized the right of parties to make independent expenditures, and the regulations adopted by the FEC in implementing BCRA clarified the law and permitted party independent expenditures in presidential races (see chapter 6). Consequently, the 2004 election was the first presidential contest since the adoption of the FECA in which parties spent money independently to *expressly* advocate the election of their candidates. (In 1996 and 2000, the parties supported their candidates by sponsoring soft money–funded "issue ads" to promote their candidates.) In all, the national party committees reported independent expenditures totaling more than $138 million in the presidential general election, with the Democrats reporting $120 million and the Republicans, $18 million.[62]

Independent spending was not the only new form of direct party support in the 2004 presidential race. In addition to coordinated and independent expenditures, the party committees also engaged in another, much more innovative form of spending. Undertaken first by the Republicans, this new form of financing involved campaign advertisements jointly funded by the presidential campaign and national party committee in an "allocated" or "hybrid" manner. The initial advertisements financed in this way featured President Bush and included generic party messages discussing the party's agenda or message, as well as mention of the Republican "leaders in Congress."[63] The Republicans contended that such ads, which combined a message of support for the president with a generic party message, could be partly allocated to generic party spending that did not count against the party's coordinated spending limit or constitute a contribution to the publicly funded presidential nominee. The party therefore chose to emphasize hybrid expenditures over independent expenditures.

At the time those ads were produced, neither the party nor the candidate submitted a request to the FEC for an advisory opinion on whether the practice was permissible. Not to be outdone, the Democrats and John Kerry soon followed suit, broadcasting hybrid advertisements of their own financed jointly by the candidate and the Democratic Party.[64] The hybrid financing approach allowed the presidential campaigns to exercise more control over the content of an ad than did the party independent expenditure approach. It allowed the presidential campaigns to stretch their limited public funding and, in effect, spend significantly more than they could have in public funds and coordinated expenditures alone. Whether the FEC will respond to the practice by adopting regulations to restrict it or at least by setting guidelines for financing such communications is one of the key questions to emerge from the financing of the 2004 general election campaign.

Recount Funding

The 2000 Florida recount controversy raised the issue of recount funding for the first time in a presidential race. The issue, however, was not new; the FEC had previously considered the rules for recount funding in federal elections in contested congressional races and approved regulations for financing recounts and election challenges.[65]

A federal candidate may use campaign funds to finance a recount. A candidate also may establish a separate bank account or separate "recount fund" for that purpose. Such a fund is legally separate from a candidate's authorized campaign committee and is used solely for financing costs incurred in connection with a recount or another election challenges. The rules do not define a recount as an attempt to "influence" a federal election, so the monies raised and spent on a recount are considered exempt from certain federal campaign finance restrictions. Any money spent by a publicly funded presidential candidate on a recount or legal challenge does not count against the general election expenditure limit, and any monies raised for a recount do not constitute a violation of the prohibition on general election fundraising.

Contributions made to recount funds are not included in the legal definition of "contributions" under current FEC regulations, so they are not subject to federal contribution limits. An individual or PAC may make unlimited recount contributions. The regulations do, however, prohibit corporate or labor union contributions, as well as gifts from foreign nationals.[66] In 2000, the Bush campaign established a separate account to finance recount activities and imposed a voluntary limit on contributions of no more than $5,000 per donor. The Gore campaign established a separate recount fund, the Gore/Lieberman Recount Committee, under section 527 of the Internal Revenue Code, placing no limit on contributions. The Bush campaign raised approximately $14 million, while the Gore committee raised $3.7 million.[67]

In 2004, with the possibility of a recount or legal challenge to the election results looming, the FEC was again asked to issue guidance on recount funding. In responding to a request from the Kerry campaign for an advisory opinion on whether GELAC funds could be used to pay for any recount expenses that might arise, the FEC determined that GELAC funds could be used for that purpose.[68] The commission's opinion did not have to address the issue of whether, in the aftermath of BCRA, unlimited individual or PAC contributions still could be used to finance recount activities. That issue came to the fore as a result of separate advisory opinion requests submitted in October by the U.S. Senate campaign of Representative George Nethercutt (R-Wash.) and the Washington State Republican Party.[69] In response to their requests, the congressional sponsors of BCRA and other campaign finance reform advocates filed comments contending that recounts should be seen as connected to a federal election and thus subject to BCRA's ban on the use of soft money. Others noted that recounts are not elections under federal campaign finance law, so any funds received and spent in connection with a recount are not funds received or spent in connection with the election. They further noted that the FEC did not revise its rule permitting unlimited recount contributions by individuals or PACs when it revised its regulations to implement BCRA.[70] The two pending requests were withdrawn before the commission issued a ruling on the matter; thus the regulations still permit unlimited contributions for that purpose. It is likely, however, that the FEC will be asked to revisit the issue in a future election cycle.

Conclusion

Public financing has been a major source of campaign monies in every presidential election since the program was first implemented in the 1976 campaign. The basic framework of the public funding system has not been revised since then, and the system is in dire jeopardy. In 2004, public funding played a smaller role in the financing of the presidential campaign than in any previous election cycle since 1976. Public funding now constitutes a small share of the monies spent to stage a national convention. The law's primary expenditure limits can no longer accommodate the level of spending required of presidential candidates to meet the financial demands of the nominating process. As a result, the leading candidates are deciding to opt out of the system. At the same time, candidates and parties are continuing to find new ways to circumvent the general election spending limits. Such practices, combined with the questionable sustainability of the funding provided by the tax check-off mechanism, raise serious questions about the future integrity and efficacy of the program. The presidential public funding system thus has become a focal point for future campaign finance reform efforts (see chapter 11).

Notes

1. For a discussion of front-loading and its effects on the presidential nomination process, see William G. Mayer and Andrew E. Busch, *The Front-Loading Problem in Presidential Nominations* (Brookings, 2004).

2. The dollar amounts in this paragraph are based on the author's calculations based on data reported by the FEC for each election cycle.

3. The increase in the amount of the check-off was passed as a provision in the Omnibus Budget Reconciliation Act (Pub. L. 103-66).

4. The Department of the Treasury adopted these regulations on May 10, 1991, and the FEC passed conforming regulations on July 18, 1991; see 56 *Federal Register* 91 (May 10, 1991), pp. 21596–600. For a discussion of the rules, see FEC, *Record* 17 (July 1991): 1–3.

5. For example, if on January 1 of an election year only $10 million is available in the PECF after setting aside the monies needed to finance the party convention subsidies and the general election grants and the candidates have been certified to receive matching fund payments totaling $20 million, each candidate would receive 50 percent of the amount of matching funds requested, or fifty cents on the dollar. If a candidate had been certified to receive $3 million in matching payments, that candidate would receive $1.5 million. The remaining obligation would carry over to the next month. So in February, the candidates would be eligible to receive the $10 million owed from the previous month, plus any additional matching funds that they had earned in the month of January. If the new deposits received by the PECF from tax forms being filed in the election year provided enough money to cover the total cost of the obligation and new submissions, the candidates would then be paid in full. If not, the payments would again be prorated and the carryover procedure repeated.

6. Congressional Research Service, *The Presidential Election Campaign Fund and Tax Checkoff: Background and Current Issues*, March 2000. Updated by author with data from the FEC for 2000 and 2002.

7. FEC, "Insufficient Public Funds Still Predicted for 2000 Election," *Record* 24 (July 1998): 5.

8. FEC, "FEC Approves Matching Funds for 2000 Presidential Candidates," press release, December 22, 1999. The release noted that there were "insufficient funds" to pay the amounts requested and stated that "Treasury will calculate a reduced amount for each campaign." That statement was included on every monthly FEC press release on matching funds until July 31, 2000.

9. FEC, "FEC Approves Matching Funds for 2004 Presidential Candidates," press release, January 30, 2004.

10. This change to 2 U.S.C. sec. 439(a) was included in Division H, Title V, section 532 of the Consolidated Appropriations Act of 2005 (H.R. 4818), which was passed by Congress in November 2004. See Kenneth P. Doyle, "Officials Can Give Federal Campaign Funds to State, Local Race under New Measure," *BNA Money and Politics Report*, November 23, 2004; and Paul Kane, "Change Restores Federal Money for State Bids," *Roll Call*, November 29, 2004.

11. The FEC first decided to permit credit card contributions in response to an advisory opinion request from the Bradley for President Committee in 1999. See FEC

Advisory Opinion 1999-9. The FEC then approved new rules on July 30, 1999, that were applied retroactively to contributions made on or before January 1, 1999. FEC, *Record* 25 (July 1991): 4.

12. Matching fund payments were made twice a month during the election year until 1992, when the payment schedule was changed to once a month in regulations adopted by the Treasury Department and FEC to address concerns about a potential revenue shortfall. See note 4 above.

13. FEC, "Background: Presidential Election Campaign Fund" (www.fec.gov/press/bkgnd/fund.shtml [December 23, 2004]).

14. 26 U.S.C. sec. 9033(c) and 11 C.F.R. sec. 9033.5.

15. 11 C.F.R. sec. 9033.8.

16. Anthony Corrado, *Paying for Presidents* (New York: Twentieth Century Fund Press, 1993), pp. 46–47.

17. 11 C.F.R. sec. 9033.5(b).

18. Letter to John McGarry, chair, FEC, from Gary Sinewski, general counsel, Fulani for President, December 12, 1991. A copy of the letter is on file at the FEC.

19. FEC, "Nader Ninth Presidential Candidate Declared Eligible for Primary Matching Funds in 2004 Race," press release, May 28, 2004. By November 30, 2004, Nader had received $865,424 in matching funds. FEC, "FEC Approves Matching Funds for 2004 Presidential Candidates," press release, December 1, 2004.

20. 11 C.F.R. sec. 9033.2(b)(1).

21. Corrado, *Paying for Presidents*, p. 47.

22. FEC Advisory Opinion 2000-18.

23. 26 U.S.C. sec. 9033(c) and 11 C.F.R. sec. 9033.5.

24. FEC, *Public Funding of Presidential Elections*, August 1996 (www.fec.gov/pages/brochures/pubfund.shtml [December 23, 2004]).

25. These rules on compliance funding were approved by the FEC on September 2, 1999. See FEC, *Record* 25 (October 1999): 3.

26. The state primary spending limits are available at www.fec.gov/pages/brochures/pubfund_limits_2004.shtml [December 23, 2004]).

27. Corrado, *Paying for Presidents*, pp. 55–57.

28. Ibid., pp. 53–54.

29. FEC, *Annual Report 1992*, p. 51.

30. 56 *Federal Register* 91 (July 29, 1991), pp. 35896–35950, and FEC, *Record* 17 (September 1991): 2–5.

31. FEC, *The Presidential Public Funding Program*, April 1993, p. 14.

32. For a discussion of the financing of the 1996 presidential nomination campaign, see Anthony Corrado, "Financing the 1996 Elections," in Gerald M. Pomper and others, *The Election of 1996* (Chatham, N.J.: Chatham House Publishers, 1997), pp. 136–50: and Wesley Joe and Clyde Wilcox, "Financing the 1996 Presidential Nominations: The Last Regulated Campaign?" in *Financing the 1996 Election*, edited by John C. Green (Armonk, N.Y.: M. E. Sharpe, 1999), pp. 37–61.

33. Anthony Corrado, "Financing the 2000 Elections," in Gerald M. Pomper and others, *The Election of 2000* (New York : Chatham House Publishers, 2001), pp. 97–105.

34. FEC, *Financial Control and Compliance Manual for Presidential Primary Candidates Receiving Public Financing* (Washington, July 1979), revised April 2000, pp. iv–v.

35. This revision was adopted by the FEC on July 29, 1999. See FEC, *Record* 25 (September 1999): 12; and 11 C.F.R. sec. 110.7(d).

36. FEC, "FEC Approves Matching Funds for 2004 Presidential Candidates," press release, March 31, 2004. The FEC initially certified convention payments of $14.6 million to each party, which was increased to $14.9 million when the cost-of-living adjustment for 2004 was added.

37. FEC, "Reform Party to Receive Additional Funds for Nominating Convention," press release, May 25, 2000.

38. FEC, "Republican and Democratic Parties to Receive Additional Funds for Party Nominating Conventions," press release, March 28, 2000.

39. FEC Advisory Opinion 1975-1.

40. FEC Advisory Opinion 1980-120.

41. Ibid.

42. FEC Advisory Opinions 1982-27 and 1983-29.

43. FEC Advisory Opinion 1988-25.

44. 59 *Federal Register* 124 (June 29, 1994), p. 33616; and FEC, Advisory Opinion 1996-17.

45. FEC, *Record* 29 (September 2003): 2.

46. Ibid.

47. Figure is based on the sums reported by the convention host committees in their public disclosure reports.

48. See, among others, Campaign Finance Institute, *The $100 Million Exemption: Soft Money and the 2004 National Party Conventions* (Washington, July 2004).

49. 11 C.F.R. sec. 9035.3. A vice presidential candidate may raise funds to pay the costs of attending the convention, including costs incurred by family members and staff; legal and accounting costs associated with the background checks required in the selection process; and fundraising expenses.

50. Kenneth P. Doyle, "Buchanan, Hagelin Submit Rival Requests to FEC for $12.6 Million in Federal Funding," *BNA Money and Politics Report*, August 16, 2000, p. 1.

51. Kenneth P. Doyle, "FEC Staff Says Buchanan's Ballot Status Entitles Him to Reform Party's $12.6 Million," *BNA Money and Politics Report*, September 11, 2000, p. 1; and FEC, "FEC Certifies General Election Public Funds for Buchanan-Foster Ticket," press release, September 14, 2000.

52. 11 C.F.R. sec. 9003.3(a)(2).

53. For example, in the 1992 election cycle, President George Bush established a GELAC account for his reelection campaign in October of 1991.

54. The regulations include procedures that allow candidates to redesignate contributions from one account to another or for one election (for example, a primary) to another (for example, a general election). A contribution may be redesignated, for example, if the amount exceeds the applicable contribution limit or if the contributor approves the transfer from one election account to another in writing. See 11 C.F.R. sec. 110.1.

55. 64 *Federal Register* 176 (September 13, 1999), pp. 49355–65; and 64 *Federal Register* 218 (November 12, 1999), p. 61475.

56. FEC, *Record* 29 (September 2003): 2–3.

57. Ibid., p. 3.

58. FEC, *Record* 30 (March 2004): 15. The coordinated expenditures made by a party

in support of a presidential ticket do not have to be made by the national party committee. The national party committee can make such expenditures through a designated agent, such as a state or local party committee; 11 C.F.R. sec. 110.7(a)(4). In practice, the coordinated expenditures in presidential races have usually been made by the national party committees, specifically the Democratic National Committee and the Republican National Committee.

59. FEC, *Record* 25 (September 1999): 12; and 11 C.F.R. sec. 110.7(d).

60. See 11 C.F.R. sec. 110.7(a)(5), 2000 edition.

61. *Colorado Republican Federal Campaign Committee* v. *FEC*, 518 U.S. 604 (1996); Michael J. Malbin, "Political Parties under the Post-*McConnell* Bipartisan Campaign Reform Act," *Election Law Journal* 3, no. 2 (2004): 185.

62. Based on FEC data as of December 7, 2004.

63. Liz Sidoti, "Bush Team Orchestrates Larger Ad Campaign," Associated Press news release, September 22, 2004.

64. "Campaign Briefing: The Advertising Campaign," *New York Times*, September 25, 2004, p. A7; and Liz Sidoti, "Kerry Campaign, DNC to Run Joint Ads," Associated Press news release, September 24, 2004.

65. FEC Advisory Opinions 1978-92 and 1998-26.

66. 11 C.F.R. sec. 100.91.

67. Anthony Corrado, "Financing the 2000 Presidential General Election," in *Financing the 2000 Election*, edited by David B. Magleby (Brookings, 2002), pp. 100–01; and Sharon Theimer, "FEC OKs Unlimited Donations for Recounts," Associated Press news release, October 28, 2004.

68. FEC Advisory Opinion 2004-35.

69. FEC Advisory Opinion Requests 2004-38 and 2004-39. See also Kenneth P. Doyle, "FEC to Take Up GOP Request to Rule Whether Soft Money Can Fund Recount," *BNA Money and Politics Report*, October 19, 2004.

70. Kenneth P. Doyle, "FEC Commissioners Eye Competing Rulings on Whether Soft Money Allowed in Recount," *BNA Money and Politics Report*, October 27, 2004.

7

Speech Governed by Federal Election Laws

TREVOR POTTER AND KIRK L. JOWERS

Congress has for the last four decades attempted to limit the sources and amounts of monies that enter into the federal election process. The Federal Election Campaign Act (FECA) of 1971, as amended, sought to regulate independent communications seeking to influence federal elections, but the scope of the act was significantly reduced by the Supreme Court in *Buckley* v. *Valeo*.[1] The Court created a system that essentially divided political speech into two categories: issue advocacy (unregulated) and express advocacy (regulated). That division was largely unchallenged by political actors until the early 1990s, but it quickly eroded thereafter to the point that candidate-focused "issue" ads, with no intent other than to influence the election, proliferated in the weeks leading up to election day. Those ads were not, however, governed by the federal campaign finance laws. As Chris Cox, chairperson of the National Rifle Association's PAC, observed prior to the passage of the Bipartisan Campaign Reform Act of 2002 (BCRA):

> Today, there is erected a legal . . . wall between issue advocacy and political advocacy. And the wall is built of the same sturdy material as the emperor's clothing. Everyone sees it. No one believes it.[2]

Campaign finance reformers were concerned that the distinction between "issue advocacy and political advocacy" had become "a line in the sand drawn on a windy day."[3] The result was that corporate and labor funds not permitted in federal elections were in fact spent in abundance in those elections. Further, the source of the funding of often-vicious last-minute election advertising was hidden from public disclosure because of the claim that it did not qualify as "express advocacy" and therefore was not within the scope of the disclosure requirements. The efforts of congressional reformers to remedy these problems culminated with the enactment of BCRA (the Reform Act), which, among other things, widened the definition of election-related communications. It did so by creating a new category, "electioneering communications": broadcast advertisements that refer to federal candidates in the sixty-day period before a general election and the thirty-day period before a primary election and that target the relevant electorate. Unions and corporations may not fund electioneering communications. They retain, however, the right to spend unlimited funds on true issue advocacy, including ads just days before an election, so long as the communications within the preelection periods do not specifically mention the names or show the likeness of federal candidates. Furthermore, by BCRA's terms, these restrictions do not even apply to candidate-specific advertising *outside* the designated preelection period or to direct mailings, telephone banks, or other forms of communication.

BCRA's electioneering communication provisions were attacked, as were almost all of its other provisions, as unconstitutional infringements of the First Amendment. Ultimately, on December 10, 2003, the Supreme Court issued its opinion in *McConnell* v. *Federal Election Commission.*[4] *McConnell* upheld virtually the entire Reform Act, including the electioneering communication provisions. It also made clear that *Buckley* did not require the use of "magic words" in order to regulate election-related speech, observing that

> *Buckley* and *MCFL* . . . in no way drew a constitutional boundary that forever fixed the permissible scope of provisions regulating campaign-related speech. . . . [t]he notion that the First Amendment erects a rigid barrier between express and issue advocacy . . . cannot be squared with this Court's longstanding recognition that the presence or absence of magic words cannot meaningfully distinguish electioneering speech from a true issue ad.[5]

This chapter begins by defining express and issue advocacy and related terms and concepts. It then traces the evolution of campaign finance law from the Supreme Court's seminal *Buckley* decision through the ensuing Supreme Court and lower federal court decisions to *McConnell*—and the responses of the Federal Election Commission (FEC) to those court rulings. Finally, it analyzes the post-BCRA era.

The Supreme Court Establishes an Express Advocacy Test: *Buckley* v. *Valeo*

In *Buckley* v. *Valeo*, the Supreme Court reviewed a challenge to the constitutionality of the FECA. The case was a "facial challenge" to the statute, meaning that the courts had no specific case of political spending before them but were judging the overall constitutional validity of the act as drafted by Congress. As a result, the courts were declaring general principles of constitutional law disconnected from any practical application in specific election contests.

The first decision in *Buckley* came from the Court of Appeals for the D.C. Circuit, which largely upheld the law as passed by Congress. The D.C. Circuit did, however, strike down the act's broadly drafted issue advocacy provision, which would have required disclosure of all contributions of over $10 received by any organization that publicly referred to any federal candidate; to any such candidate's voting record or positions; or to official acts of such candidates who were federal officeholders.[6]

The Supreme Court confronted in *Buckley* a wide array of congressionally enacted prohibitions and restrictions on contributions and expenditures in connection with federal elections. Congress had written the act broadly, regulating all spending "in connection with" or "for the purpose of influencing" a federal election or "relative to" a federal candidate. One of the questions the Court faced was whether these statutory phrases were so vague and overbroad as to provide an unconstitutional lack of notice to persons potentially affected by the act. The Court stressed that vagueness concerns are especially acute where, as here, "the legislation imposes criminal penalties in an area permeated by First Amendment interests."[7] "The test is whether the language . . . affords the [p]recision of regulation [that] must be the touchstone in an area so closely touching our most precious freedoms."[8] The Court noted that Congress had failed to define "in connection with" an election or "relative to a candidate."

The Supreme Court held that greater precision and clarity were required to avoid vagueness and that specific words were acceptable constructions for narrowing candidate-related speech within the act's provisions.[9] The Court gave examples of such terms: "'vote for,' 'elect,' 'support,' 'cast your ballot for,' 'Smith for Congress,' 'vote against,' 'defeat,' 'reject.'"[10] The Court explained that such a clear test was useful because *the distinction between discussion of issues and candidates and advocacy of election or defeat of candidates may often dissolve in practical application* [emphasis added]. Candidates, especially incumbents, are intimately tied to public issues involving legislative proposals and governmental actions. Not only do candidates campaign on the basis of their positions on various public issues, but campaigns themselves generate issues of public interest.[11]

Buckley cautioned that a standard that turned on the speaker's purpose or the listener's understanding would have a chilling effect on political speech.[12]

In narrowing the reach of the act to avoid declaring it vague, the Court in *Buckley* significantly restricted the reach of the federal election laws. Instead of Congress's intended broad coverage of "all spending" to "influence" federal elections (phrases presumably to be defined with greater specificity over time by the courts and the FEC), the law as interpreted by the Supreme Court was narrowed (at least for noncandidate and nonpolitical committee purposes) to speech that constituted "express advocacy." While that new term was not yet defined in practice, it prospectively meant that much of the political speech that Congress intended to regulate and disclose might instead be beyond the reach of the campaign finance laws.

FEC *v.* Massachusetts Citizens for Life, Inc.

Although the Supreme Court enunciated the express advocacy test in *Buckley* in 1976, it was not until ten years later, in *FEC* v. *Massachusetts Citizens for Life, Inc.* (*MCFL*), that the Supreme Court had occasion to apply the test to an actual communication.[13] MCFL was a nonprofit, non-stock corporation organized to advance antiabortion goals. In 1972, MCFL began publishing a newsletter that typically contained information on the organization's activities, including the status of various proposed bills and constitutional amendments. In September 1978—just weeks before the primary elections— MCFL published a special edition of the newsletter. While previous newsletters had been sent to 2,000 to 3,000 people, MCFL published more than 100,000 copies of the special edition. The front page of the publication was headlined "EVERYTHING YOU NEED TO KNOW TO VOTE PRO-LIFE" and readers were reminded that "[n]o pro-life candidate can win in November without your vote in September." "VOTE PRO-LIFE" appeared in large black letters on the back page, and a list of the names of the pro-life candidates was available for voters to cut out and take to the polls as a reminder. Next to the list was the following disclaimer: "This special election edition does not represent an endorsement of any particular candidate." An accompanying flyer placed a "Y" next to the names of candidates who supported the MCFL's view on a particular issue; an "N" indicated that a candidate opposed MCFL's position.

Section 441b of the FECA prohibits any corporation from using treasury funds "in connection with" a federal election and requires that any such expenditure be financed by voluntary contributions to a PAC. The FEC alleged that MCFL's expenditures in financing the special election newsletter constituted an illegal corporate contribution to the candidates named in the newsletter. As in *Buckley*, the Court ruled that an expenditure "must constitute 'express advocacy' in order to be subject to the prohibition of § 441b."[14]

The Court, however, went on to hold that the MCFL newsletter constituted express advocacy because it urged readers "to vote for 'pro-life' candidates" and provided the names and photographs of candidates meeting that description. Said the Court:

> The Edition cannot be regarded as a mere discussion of public issues that by their nature raise the names of certain politicians. Rather, it provides in effect an explicit directive: vote for these (named) candidates. *The fact that this message is marginally less direct than "Vote for Smith" does not change its essential nature* [emphasis added]. The Edition goes beyond issue discussion to express electoral advocacy. The disclaimer of endorsement cannot negate this fact.[15]

The Court's application of the express advocacy test in *MCFL* is noteworthy in two respects. First, in determining whether the MCFL newsletter was express advocacy, the Court did not appear to consider any factual circumstances outside the communication itself. While the Court noted external circumstances such as proximity of the publication to the election, the number of copies published (which was well in excess of the newsletter's normal distribution), and the intent of the speakers in their recitation of facts, it did not appear to rely on any of those factual circumstances in its finding of express advocacy. In that regard *MCFL* is consistent with *Buckley*: the express advocacy test turns on the communication itself. Second, the Court clarified the *Buckley* definition of express advocacy to include words that are "in effect" an explicit directive "marginally less direct" than the *Buckley* language.[16] As a result, *MCFL* has been used by the FEC in court pleadings to justify a definition of express advocacy based on implied or nonverbal electoral messages or both.

FEC v. *Furgatch* and *Faucher* v. *FEC:* Competing Approaches

Using *Buckley* (and later *MCFL*), the federal courts initially struggled to apply the express advocacy test. The courts disagreed over the evidentiary threshold for ascertaining whether a given communication contains specific terms of advocacy. Some courts looked at external evidence to help illuminate the meaning of the terms contained within a given communication; others limited their inquiries solely to the text of the communication in question. The two contrasting approaches led the courts to apply the express advocacy standard with what appeared to be inconsistent results.

The Ninth Circuit Court's ruling in *FEC* v. *Furgatch,* which was the first major decision to follow *MCFL*, is perhaps the most pro-regulation decision.[17] *Furgatch* focused on the purpose of the FECA and sought to reconcile the *Buckley* standard to the practical issues of regulating spending on candidate-specific communications. In *Furgatch*, an individual had published a full-page advertisement in the *New York Times* one week before the 1980 presidential election. The advertisement read:

Don't Let Him Do It

The president of the United States continues degrading the electoral process and lessening the prestige of the office.

It was evident months ago when his running mate outrageously suggested Ted Kennedy was unpatriotic. The President remained silent.

And we let him.

It continued when the President himself accused Ronald Reagan of being unpatriotic.

And we let him do it again.

In recent weeks, Carter has tried to buy entire cities, the steel industry, the auto industry, and others with public funds.

We are letting him do it.

He continues to cultivate the fears, not the hopes of the voting public by suggesting the choice is between "peace and war," "black or white," "north or south," and "Jew vs. Christian." His meanness of spirit is divisive and reckless McCarthyism at its worst. And from a man who once asked, "Why not the best?"

It is an attempt to hide his own record, or lack of it. If he succeeds the country will be burdened with four more years of incoherencies, ineptness and illusion, as he leaves a legacy of low-level campaigning.

DON'T LET HIM DO IT.[18]

The Ninth Circuit Court ruled that the advertisement was express advocacy and therefore could be regulated under the act. The court began its analysis by contending that the *Buckley* express advocacy test "does not draw a bright and unambiguous line . . . [W]here First Amendment concerns are present, we must construe the words of the regulatory statute precisely and narrowly, *only as far as is necessary to further the purposes of the Act* [emphasis added]."[19] Because of these important regulatory concerns, the court concluded in *Furgatch* that the court must

> prevent speech that is clearly intended to affect the outcome of a federal election from escaping, either fortuitously or by design, the coverage of the Act. This concern leads us to fashion a more comprehensive approach to the delimitation of "express advocacy," and to reject some of the overly constrictive rules of interpretation.[20]

In *Furgatch* the Ninth Circuit Court rejected the notion that express advocacy is limited to the list of specific terms identified by the Supreme Court in *Buckley*. Instead, the court ruled that when evaluating whether a communication constitutes express advocacy, a reviewing court must take into account the context in which the communication is made. The court established a standard that, to be express advocacy, speech "must, when read as a whole, and with limited reference to external events, be susceptible of no other reasonable interpretation but as an exhortation to vote for or against a specific candidate."[21] The court left no mistake, however, that it believed implied meanings can form the basis for a finding of express advocacy: "A consideration of the context in which speech is uttered may clarify ideas that are not perfectly articulated, or supply necessary premises that are unexpressed but widely understood by readers or viewers."[22]

In applying its analysis, the Ninth Circuit Court ruled that the *Furgatch* advertisement expressly advocated the defeat of President Carter.[23] In making that determination, the court focused on the words "'don't let him.' They are simple and direct. 'Don't let him' is a command. The words 'expressly advocate' action of some kind."[24] The court acknowledged that there was no express indication in the advertisement of what kind of action the reader should take. However, it ruled "that this failure to state with specificity the action required does not remove political speech from [the Act] . . . *[r]easonable minds* could not dispute that Furgatch's advertisement urged readers to vote against Jimmy Carter [emphasis added]."[25] *Furgatch* remains the most pro-regulation and increasingly isolated decision on what constitutes express advocacy.[26]

At the other end of the spectrum is the First Circuit Court's ruling in *Faucher* v. *FEC*.[27] In that case, the Maine Right to Life Committee (MRLC) published a voting guide surveying the positions of federal and state candidates on pro-life issues and distributed it widely immediately prior to election day. Using its general corporate monies, MRLC produced a 1988 voting guide titled "November Election Issue 1988" and subtitled "Federal & State Candidate Surveys Enclosed—Take-Along Issue for Election Day!" It included candidate and party positions on pro-life issues and stated: "PLEASE NOTE: A 'yes' response indicates agreement with the National Right to Life position on each question."[28] The guide also carried the following disclaimer: "The publication of the MRLC [November Election Issue 1988] does not represent an endorsement of any candidate(s) by MRLC."[29]

The First Circuit Court, citing *Buckley* and *MCFL*, hewed to a strict definition of express advocacy requiring explicit "vote for, support/oppose" language in the communication. The court stressed that:

> [d]iscussion of public issues and debate on the qualifications of candidates are integral to the operation of the system of government established by our Constitution. The FEC nevertheless has sought to restrain the very same activity which the [Supreme] Court in *Buckley* sought to protect. This we cannot allow.[30]

The court ruled that the MRLC voting guide was not express advocacy, concluding that "trying to discern when issue advocacy in a voter guide crosses the threshold and becomes express advocacy invites just the sort of constitutional questions the [Supreme] Court sought to avoid in adopting the bright-line express advocacy test in *Buckley*."[31] The implication of the court's ruling is that a voting guide that contains a discussion of public policy issues and does not include "elect" or "defeat" or any of the other magic words identified in *Buckley* and *MCFL* is per se issue advocacy and cannot be regulated—even if candidates are the focus of the guide and the manner in which the issues are discussed is clearly favorable or unfavorable to particular candidates. At the very least, *Faucher* can be read as rejecting any consideration of implied meanings in determining whether a communication contains express advocacy.

The FEC Responds

In the wake of the Supreme Court and lower federal court rulings, the FEC promulgated new regulations in 1995 regarding what kinds of communications constitute express advocacy. The regulation states:

Expressly advocating means any communication that—

(a) uses phrases such as "vote for the President," "re-elect your congressman," "support the Democratic nominee," "cast your ballot for the Republican challenger for U.S. Senate in Georgia," "Smith for Congress," "Bill McKay in '94," "vote Pro-Life," or "vote Pro-Choice" accompanied by a listing of clearly identified candidates described as Pro-Life or Pro-Choice, "vote against Old Hickory," "defeat" accompanied by a picture of one or more candidate(s), "reject the incumbent," or communications of campaign slogan(s) or individual word(s), which in context can have no other reasonable meaning than to urge the election or defeat of one or more clearly identified candidate(s), such as posters, bumper stickers, advertisements, etc., which say "Nixon's the One," "Carter '76," "Reagan/Bush," or "Mondale!"; *or*

(b) When taken as a whole and with limited reference to external events, such as the proximity to the election, could only be interpreted by a reasonable person as containing advocacy of the election or defeat of one or more clearly identified candidate(s) because—

(1) The electoral portion of the communication is unmistakable, unambiguous, and suggestive of only one meaning; and

(2) Reasonable minds could not differ as to whether it encourages actions to elect or defeat one or more clearly identified candidate(s) or encourages some other kind of action.[32]

Two aspects of the FEC's express advocacy regulation bear comment. First, subpart (a) of the regulation includes all of the express advocacy terms that the Supreme Court identified in *Buckley* and thereby incorporates and broadens the Court's decision into the commission's regulations. In subpart (b) of the regulation, however, the FEC clearly attempted to incorporate the more flexible *Furgatch* express advocacy standard of the Ninth Circuit Court. But in 1999, a successful challenge to the FEC's new express advocacy regulations resulted from the First Circuit Court's ruling in *Maine Right to Life Committee, Inc., v. FEC (MRLC)*. The First Circuit Court affirmed the Maine district court's finding that subpart (b) of the commission's new regulations was unconstitutional on its face, regardless of how it might be applied.[33] The court stressed that a Supreme Court precedent bound its decision, even if the ruling served to restrict the scope of the federal election laws and leave much election-related speech unregulated:

> If the Supreme Court had not decided *Buckley* and [*MCFL*] and if the First Circuit had not decided *Faucher*, I might well uphold the FEC's subpart (b) definition of what should be covered.
>
> But there is another policy at issue here. . . . Specifically, the Supreme Court has been most concerned not to permit intrusion upon "issue" advocacy—discussion of the issues on the public's mind from time to time or of the candidate's positions on such issues—that the Supreme Court has considered a special concern of the First Amendment. . . . *FEC restriction of election activities was not to be permitted to intrude in any way upon the public discussion of issues* [emphasis added].[34]

The court also highlighted the tensions between the purposes of the election laws (as upheld by the Supreme Court) and the Court's strict express advocacy test:

> The advantage of this . . . [strict] approach, from a First Amendment point of view, is that it permits a speaker or writer to know from the outset exactly what is permitted and what is prohibited. . . . The result is not very satisfying from a realistic communications point of view and does not give much recognition to the policy of the election statute to keep corporate money from influencing elections in this way, but it does recognize the First Amendment interest as the Court has defined it.[35]

Since the First Circuit Court's affirmation of the district court's decision on appeal,[36] the FEC has been enjoined from enforcing this part of its regulations in the First Circuit,[37] and the Second and Fourth Circuit Courts' precedents before the *McConnell* decision indicate that they would have taken the same view of the unconstitutionality of the express advocacy regulations in subpart (b).[38] The FEC did not withdraw its "reasonable person" express advocacy definition despite those court decisions.[39] However, it became extremely passive in its defense in the years prior to the Supreme Court's *McConnell* decision.[40]

Other Circuit Court Rulings

Several other circuit courts adopted the strict approach to express advocacy exemplified by *Faucher*. For example, in *FEC* v. *Central Long Island Tax Reform Immediately Committee* (*CLITRIM*), the Second Circuit Court considered whether a bulletin published by a nonprofit association prior to a general election was express advocacy.[41]

The bulletin detailed the voting record of a local congressman but did not refer to any federal election or to the congressman's party affiliation, nor did it identify the congressman's electoral opponent. The FEC concluded that the bulletin was express advocacy. The Second Circuit court rejected that conclusion, reaffirming that the federal election laws do not

> reach all partisan discussion . . . [but only] those expenditures that expressly advocate a particular election result. . . . This is consistent with the firmly established principle that the right to speak out at election time is one of the most zealously protected under the Constitution.[42]

The court stressed that

> contrary to the position of the FEC, the words "expressly advocating" mean exactly what they say. . . . [T]he FEC would apparently have us read "expressly advocating the election or defeat" to mean for the purpose, express or *implied*, of encouraging election or defeat. This would, by statutory interpretation, nullify the change in the statute ordered in *Buckley v. Valeo* and adopted by Congress in the 1976 amendments. This position is totally meritless.[43]

Similarly, in *FEC* v. *Christian Action Network*, a district court adopted this strict view toward defining "express advocacy," and the Fourth Circuit Court summarily affirmed its ruling.[44] The Christian Action Network (CAN) described itself as a grassroots organization that seeks to inform the public about "traditional family values." During the weeks immediately prior to the 1992 presidential election, CAN aired television advertisements criticizing the alleged "militant homosexual agenda" of the Clinton/Gore ticket. The district court's opinion describes the advertisement as opening with a full-color picture of candidate Bill Clinton's face superimposed upon an American flag, which is blowing in the wind. Clinton is shown smiling and the ad appears to be complimentary. However, as the narrator begins to describe Clinton's alleged support for "radical" homosexual causes, Clinton's image dissolves into a black and white photographic negative. The negative darkens Clinton's eyes and mouth, giving the candidate a sinister and threatening appearance. Simultaneously, the music accompanying the commercial changes from a single high pitched tone to a lower octave. The commercial then presents a series of pictures depicting advocates of homosexual rights, apparently gay men and lesbians, demonstrating at a political march.

As the scenes from the march continue, the narrator asks in rhetorical fashion, "Is this your vision for a better America?" Thereafter, the image of the American flag reappears on the screen, but without the superimposed image of candidate Clinton. At the same time, the music changes back to the single high pitched tone. The narrator then states, "[f]or more information on traditional family values, contact the Christian Action Network."[45]

The FEC argued that any viewer would understand the advertisement to advocate Clinton's defeat. Specifically, it contended that the way the American flag was used in the commercial sent an explicit anti-Clinton message: "By graphically removing Clinton's superimposed image from the presidential setting of the American flag, the advertisement visually conveys the message that Clinton should not become President. [It] is a powerful visual image telling voters to defeat Clinton."[46] The FEC also noted:

(1) the visual degrading of candidate Clinton's picture into a black and white negative; (2) the use of the visual text and audio voice-overs; (3) ominous music; (4) unfavorable coloring; (5) codewords such as "vision" and "quota"; (6) issues raised that are relevant only if candidate Clinton became president; (7) the airing of the commercial in close proximity to the national election; and (8) abrupt editing linking Clinton to the images of the gay rights marchers.[47]

Nevertheless, the court ruled that the Christian Action Network's advertisement was constitutionally protected issue advocacy that could not be regulated:

Concededly, the advertisements "clearly identified" the 1992 Democratic presidential and vice presidential candidates. . . . Similarly, it is beyond dispute that the advertisements were openly hostile to the proposals believed to have been endorsed by the two candidates. Nevertheless, the advertisements were devoid of any language that directly exhorted the public to vote. Without a frank admonition to take electoral action, even admittedly negative advertisements such as these, do not constitute "express advocacy" as that term is defined in *Buckley* and its progeny. . . . It is clear from the cases that expressions of hostility to the positions of an official, implying that [the] official should not be reelected—even when that implication is quite clear—do not constitute express advocacy.[48]

After summarily affirming the district court's ruling, the Fourth Circuit Court later awarded the Christian Action Network attorneys' fees and costs under the Equal Access to Justice Act.[49] In a blistering opinion highly critical of the FEC's legal arguments, the court found that the commission's legal position "if not assumed in bad faith, was at least not 'substantially justified.'" The court held that there was no legal basis for the FEC's contention that the Christian Action Network's advertisement could ever be express advocacy without the required magic words.[50]

In *Kansans for Life, Inc.,* v. *Gaede,* a federal district court held that a television ad that "contrasts the positions of two candidates on the issue of abortion and asserts that one candidate is honestly stating his position on the issue while the other candidate is not" was issue advocacy, rather than express advocacy of a candidate's defeat or election, and may be not be held subject to a disclosure requirement.[51] The court wrote that although the ordinary, reasonable person would understand that the ad was *intended* to—and *did*—favor one candidate over the other, the ad did not *expressly* advocate the election or defeat of a candidate because it did not use the magic words set forth in *Buckley* and therefore could not be regulated.[52]

What Is Broadcast Issue Advocacy and Where Did It Come From?

Issue advocacy, with respect to influencing the federal electoral process, became a topic of serious national debate and interest in the mid-1990s. In 1994, the Clinton administration's health care reform package was, in part, killed by the "Harry and Louise" issue ads produced by the Health Insurance Association of America, in a serious blow to the president's legislative agenda and political fortunes. Political parties and interest groups took note, and issue advocacy communications exploded during the 1996 congressional and presidential elections, continuing unabated through the 2002 elections. Political parties and private groups saturated radio and television airwaves across the country with issue-oriented advertisements that typically praised or disparaged a candidate but stayed outside the disclosure and funding requirements of the federal election laws.[53]

Critics—and often even candidates—found many of these issue advertisements to be clearly designed to influence the outcome of selected races.[54] Indeed, the sponsors and beneficiaries of many of the advertisements often proudly proclaimed that the advertisements achieved the goal of influencing an election.[55] There are many examples, but one ad captures the essence of "sham issue advocacy": often-vicious descriptions of a federal candidate that look like every other negative political ad in the middle of an election campaign but that simply omit the tag line of "Vote for" or "Vote against." The following advertisement was broadcast in Montana a few days before a federal election by an out-of-state not-for-profit corporation that appeared to be a shell entity used to funnel funds anonymously into the election campaign in its closing days. The ad, about a congressional candidate named Bill Yellowtail, said in its entirety:

> Who is Bill Yellowtail? He preaches family values, but he took a swing at his wife. And Yellowtail's response? He only slapped her. But "her nose was broken." He talks law and order . . . but is himself a convicted felon. And though he talks about protecting children, Yellowtail failed to make his own child support payments—then voted against child support enforcement. Call Bill Yellowtail. Tell him to support family values.[56]

Ads such as this became increasingly prominent in the run-up to federal elections, often playing a dominant role. Although clearly written to persuade voters to vote for or against a federal candidate, such ads were labeled issue ads rather than express advocacy and therefore were unregulated.

A short summation of the current legal definitions governing express and issue advocacy may be helpful. First, if a communication contains *express advocacy* of the election or defeat of a clearly identified federal candidate, the communication is regulated under federal law. Thus express advocacy is a political communication that includes specific language advocating election or defeat of a candidate or its functional equivalent—terms such as "vote for," "Smith 2004," or "defeat" (the so-called "magic words"). Some courts have held that it also includes language that could be interpreted by a reasonable person only as containing advocacy of the election or defeat of a candidate—but that nevertheless does not necessarily contain the magic words, such as "vote for" or "defeat."

Second, an *electioneering communication* is a broadcast, cable, or satellite television ad that refers to a clearly identified federal candidate and that targets the candidate's state or district within specific preelection time periods. (A corporate or trade association or union PAC may still run or finance such ads because its funds are, by definition, hard money). Those provisions also require noncorporate or non-union persons or entities that spend in excess of $10,000 on electioneering communications during a calendar year to file disclosure reports listing the persons making or controlling the disbursements and the custodian of the records, all contributors who gave more than $1,000 to finance the communications, and those to whom disbursements of more than $200 have been made.

Third, if a communication does not contain express advocacy and is not an electioneering communication, it is not deemed to be made in connection with a federal election (unless it raises coordination issues noted below) and is therefore outside the scope of federal law. Thus, a sponsor may run an unlimited number of such *issue advocacy* communications and may pay for the communication however it chooses, including from sources (such as corporations and unions) and in amounts otherwise prohibited by federal election laws.

Fourth, if a communication containing issue advocacy has been made in consultation with a candidate, it may be considered *coordinated* and result in an in-kind contribution by the speaker to the candidate. The definition of "coordination" depends on the outcome of current and future legal battles.

Fifth, *independent expenditures* refer to yet another variation of regulated, election-related speech: communications that expressly advocate the election or defeat of a clearly identified federal candidate, that are financed with federal hard money, and that are publicly disclosed. They may not be coordinated with any candidate or campaign committee. Individuals and organizations, including political action committees (PACs) and parties, may make independent expenditures, but they must report them to the FEC. Generally, organizations that are not registered with the FEC and do not have PACs may engage in issue advocacy, but they may *not* run independent expenditure campaigns.[57]

In summary, issue advocacy is best understood by what it does *not* do—it is a communication that does not expressly advocate the election or defeat of a clearly identified federal candidate, and it is not an "electioneering communication."

The Bipartisan Campaign Reform Act

On March 27, 2002, President Bush signed BCRA into law. BCRA represents the most significant changes to campaign finance laws since those enacted after the Watergate scandal more than twenty-five years ago. Most of BCRA's provisions went into effect immediately following the 2002 election, and the 2004 federal elections were conducted under the provisions of the new law.

McConnell *v.* FEC

Almost immediately after President Bush signed BCRA into law, plaintiffs began filing lawsuits seeking to strike it down on constitutional grounds. On the final day for filing complaints, more than eighty plaintiffs were challenging nearly every provision of the act.

The plaintiffs in these suits—consolidated into *McConnell* v. *FEC*—mirrored the political coalition that fought reform in Congress. They spanned the political spectrum from the Republican National Committee and the Christian Coalition to the California Democratic Party and the U.S. Public Interest Research Group. BCRA was defended in this case by the FEC, the Department of Justice, and the act's principal congressional sponsors.

Because a provision in the bill called for expedited judicial review, the suit followed an unusual litigation process. An extensive discovery process was conducted, oral arguments heard, and a decision issued by a special three-judge panel of the U.S. District Court for the District of Columbia within twelve months. The panel consisted of Circuit Court Judge Karen LeCraft Henderson, a George H. W. Bush appointee, who presided; District Court Judge Colleen Kollar-Kotelly, a Clinton appointee; and District Court Judge Richard J. Leon, a George W. Bush appointee. The opinion itself was complex and fractured, and at 1,638 pages, it was the longest decision in the court's history.[58] It upheld major provisions of BCRA while striking down or modifying key provisions involving soft money and issue advertising.

With regard to issue advocacy, the court acknowledged that the problem of "sham" issue advocacy was real and a threat to the integrity of the federal election process.[59] Nevertheless, citing First Amendment concerns, the court struck down the act's primary restriction on independent corporate or labor spending, which forbade the use of treasury funds to finance broadcast, cable, or satellite communications that mentioned a clearly identified federal candidate within thirty days of a primary or sixty days of a general election and that targeted the candidate's electorate.[60] The court upheld, however, part of the act's "backup" restriction on independent corporate or labor spending.[61] The backup restriction targets any political ad that supports or attacks a federal candidate "regardless of whether the communication expressly advocates a vote for or against a candidate."[62] But to prevent the backup from being unconstitutionally vague, the court excised the restriction's final clause, which also required the message to be "suggestive of no plausible meaning other than an exhortation to vote."[63]

The practical effect of that decision, the majority held, was still to prohibit the use of corporate or labor-union treasury funds to finance broadcast, cable, or satellite communications that promote, support, attack, or oppose a federal candidate at any time. Likewise, the District Court upheld the FEC disclosure requirements for spending by individuals and organizations on such advertisements. The District Court concluded, however, that despite its decision to allow Congress to broaden the definition of express advocacy, such groups would be able to seek advisory opinions from the FEC to determine whether their communications were in fact regulated by BCRA. These two results, taken together, suggest that the district court was ultimately urging the development over time of a narrow, case-by-case approach to sham issue advocacy to be handled by the FEC.[64]

On the very same day that the court issued the decision, parties on both sides began filing notices of appeal with the U.S. Supreme Court. Under the provision in the act regarding expedited judicial review, the cases bypassed the normal circuit court review process and proceeded directly to the High Court. The late date of the district court's decision made when the Supreme Court would hear the case uncertain. The Court's term ended, unofficially, on July 5, and the next term began on October 1. However, pending Supreme Court review, a number of litigants asked the district court to "stay" all or part of its judgment from taking effect. The district court ultimately decided to stay the entirety of its judgment.

On September 8, a historic four-hour oral argument on the constitutionality of BCRA was held in the Supreme Court. On December 10, 2003, the Supreme Court issued its opinion in *McConnell*, in which it upheld virtually the entire act.[65]

McConnell *Confirms that Magic Words Are Unnecessary*

"The major premise of plaintiffs' challenge . . . [wa]s that *Buckley* drew a constitutionally mandated line between express advocacy and so-called issue advocacy, and that speakers possess an inviolable First Amendment right to engage in the latter category of speech."[66] The Supreme Court flatly rejected that argument:

That position misapprehends our prior decisions, for the express advocacy restriction was an endpoint of statutory interpretation, not a first principle of constitutional law. In *Buckley* we . . . provided examples of words of express advocacy, such as "vote for," "elect," "support," . . . "defeat," [and] "reject," and those examples eventually gave rise to what is now known as the "magic words" requirement. . . . [But] our decisions in *Buckley* and *MCFL* were specific to the statutory language before us; they in no way drew a constitutional boundary that forever fixed the permissible scope of provisions regulating campaign-related speech.

Nor are we persuaded, independent of our precedents, that the First Amendment erects a rigid barrier between express advocacy and so-called issue advocacy. That notion cannot be squared with our long-standing recognition that the presence or absence of magic words cannot meaningfully distinguish electioneering speech from a true issue ad. *See Buckley*, [424 U.S.] *at 45*. Indeed, the unmistakable lesson from the record in this litigation . . . is that *Buckley*'s magic-words requirement is functionally meaningless. Not only can advertisers easily evade the line by eschewing the use of magic words, but they would seldom choose to use such words even if permitted. And although the resulting advertisements do not urge the viewer to vote for or against a candidate in so many words, they are no less clearly intended to influence the election.[67]

Broad Definition of Campaign Speech Vindicated

Prior to the passage of BCRA and the *McConnell* ruling, a clear pattern emerged from the foregoing rulings on issue and express advocacy in the circuit courts. Other than the Ninth Circuit Court in *Furgatch*, every other federal appeals court that had considered the question—including the First, Second, Fourth, Eighth, Tenth and Eleventh Circuit Courts—adopted a narrow interpretation of the express advocacy test set out in *Buckley*, as further clarified in *MCFL*.[68] Thus, those courts concluded that only communications containing *explicit* and unambiguous words urging readers (or viewers) to elect or defeat a clearly identified candidate would meet the express advocacy test, on the erroneous basis that it was required by the Supreme Court in *Buckley* and by the Constitution. This bright-line approach "may err on the side of permitting things that affect the election process, but at all costs avoids restricting, in any way, discussion of public issues, as a federal District Court said."[69]

These circuit court decisions rejected attempts to find express advocacy based on implied electoral messages, even if the electoral message was clear and arguably unmistakable. However, with the *McConnell* ruling and the removal of the magic words requirement, a broader reading of the definition of campaign speech was vindicated. That includes, of course, the "bright line" electioneering communication standard in BCRA, but it may also include communications that have the "clear purpose" of supporting or opposing a candidate.

Several recent court filings have tested or will test the parameters of the new regulatory standard. In *Wisconsin Right to Life, Inc.,* v. *Federal Election Commission,* the Supreme Court denied a motion for an injunction barring the enforcement of section 203 of BCRA, which bans corporations and unions from using general treasury funds to finance electioneering communications, in further support of express advocacy as explained in *Faucher.*[70] More recently, in *Kean for Congress* v. *FEC,* Kean filed suit against the FEC for failure to apply the law against a section 527 group located in Virginia that funded a mailing campaign against Kean with unregulated funds one month prior to the primary election.[71] One ad included a photograph of Mr. Kean wearing a "Tom Kean Jr. for Congress" campaign button with the following statement superimposed:

TOM KEAN JR.

No experience. Hasn't lived in New Jersey for 10 years.

It takes more than a name to get things done.

The back page explained in more detail why voters should reject Mr. Kean, concluding: "We can't afford on-the-job training. Tell Tom Kean Jr. . . . New Jersey needs New Jersey leaders." Another ad restated the same warning. None of the ads discussed any issue, other than that the Council for Responsible Government deemed Mr. Kean unfit for office. This case is currently before a district court in the District of Columbia.

The Sixth Circuit Court of Appeals in *Anderson* v. *Spear* narrowly construed a state law prohibiting "electioneering" within 500 feet of a polling place to restrict only express advocacy related to a clearly identified candidate or ballot measure.[72] The court reasoned that, unlike the BCRA electioneering communication restrictions upheld in *McConnell,* the state ban on electioneering was both vague and overbroad. The state had interpreted the prohibition to include activities such as the distribution of instructions on how to cast a write-in ballot. The Sixth Circuit Court found that, despite the

Supreme Court's disavowal of the distinction between express advocacy and issue advocacy in *McConnell*, the *McConnell* Court "left intact the ability of courts to make distinctions between express advocacy and issue advocacy, where such distinctions are necessary to cure vagueness and overbreadth in statutes."[73]

Conclusion

During the 2002 election cycle, interest groups, individuals, and political parties continued to communicate through "issue advertisements" that undoubtedly had an (intended) impact on federal elections. In some U.S. House races, more money was spent on issue advocacy than was spent by the two major party candidates combined.

In the 2004 election cycle, the first presidential election cycle governed by BCRA, several developments occurred. First, soft money contributions from corporations and union treasury funds to national party committees were eliminated and the use of such funds for issue advertising was substantially curtailed by the electioneering communication provision. Second was the dispute over section 527 groups. The FEC failed to write regulations defining which 527 groups meet the standard for federal political committee status, leaving 527s able to raise and spend money on ads promoting or attacking federal candidates without registering as political committees and without complying with the federal campaign finance rules that apply to political committees.

The question of how the states, the FEC, and the federal courts will attempt to apply the now discredited "express advocacy" test is likely to remain unresolved for several years. The Supreme Court's *McConnell* decision says that the "magic words" test is neither constitutionally required nor effective—but that does not prevent state legislatures from attempting to use it. Nor does *McConnell* resolve disputes over how broadly the FEC should interpret *express advocacy* when that phrase is used in its regulations.[74]

Notes

1. The FECA was codified at 2 U.S.C. secs. 431–55; *Buckley* v. *Valeo*, 424 U.S. 1 (1976).

2. Defendants' Congressional Sponsors' Redacted Supreme Court brief, p. 42 (www.campaignlegalcenter.org/McConnell-101.html [June 30, 2005]).

3. Ibid., p. 53.

4. *McConnell* v. *FEC,* 124 S.Ct. 619 (2003).

5. Id. at 687.

6. *Buckley* v. *Valeo*, 519 F.2d 821, 869–78 (D.C. Cir. 1975). The D.C. Circuit held that this language, which used a "for the purpose of influencing the outcome of an election" standard to regulate even nonpartisan communications by groups that were not political committees, was unconstitutional. The D.C. Circuit Court cited two reasons: the provision was too vague (providing no real guidance as to regulated or unregulated speech) and too inclusive (requiring disclosure by groups not overtly involved in political activity). The provision, intended to provide disclosure of all donors to "many groups, including liberal, labor, environmental, business and conservative organizations," was declared unconstitutional in its entirety by the D.C. Circuit Court, and that holding was the only part of the D.C. court's decision not appealed to the Supreme Court.

The D.C. Circuit Court cited with approval another issue advocacy case decided in 1972 by the Second Circuit Court, *United States* v. *National Committee for Impeachment*, 469 F.2d 1135, 1142 (2d Cir. 1972). There, the Department of Justice had prosecuted a group that took out newspaper advertisements urging the impeachment of President Nixon for failure to register as a political committee under the disclosure provisions of the 1971 act. The Second Circuit Court held that communications primarily directed toward advocacy of a position on a public issue, rather than urging a vote for or against a candidate, did not qualify as an election expenditure and thus political committee status was not triggered.

7. *Buckley,* 424 U.S. at 41.

8. Id., internal quotation omitted.

9. Id. at 43.

10. Id. at 44, n. 52, describing the list of terms as "express words of advocacy of election or defeat, *such as* 'vote for', 'elect'" (emphasis added). These have become known as the "magic words," although *Buckley* and subsequent cases indicate that they do not constitute an exhaustive list of phrases meeting the "express advocacy" definition. Id.; see also *FEC* v. *Massachusetts Citizens for Life, Inc.,* 479 U.S. 238, 249 (1986) ("*MCFL*"): "The fact that this message is marginally less direct than 'Vote for Smith' does not change its essential nature. The Edition goes beyond issue discussion to express electoral advocacy"; *FEC* v. *Furgatch*, 807 F.2d 857 (9th Cir.), *cert. denied*, 484 U.S. 850, 861 (1987), concluding that the *Buckley* express advocacy test "does not draw a bright and unambiguous line."

11. *Buckley,* 424 U.S. at 42.

12. Id. at 43.

13. *MCFL,* 479 U.S.

14. Id. at 249.

15. Id. Because the Court found the MCFL newsletter to be express advocacy, it ruled that MCFL's expenditures violated the act. The Court then ruled that the ban on federal election expenditures by incorporated entities was unconstitutional as applied to issue-oriented organizations such as MCFL and other 501(c)(4)–type organizations that are not themselves funded by for-profit corporations. In reaching that conclusion, the Court first noted that the expenditures were made independently of any candidate. Id. at 251, "independent expenditures 'produce speech at the core of the First Amendment,'" quoting *FEC* v. *National Conservative Political Action Commission*, 470 U.S. 480, 493 (1985); *Buckley*, 424 U.S. at 39, invalidating a $1,000 limit on independent individual expenditures.

Second, the Court relied on several institutional aspects of MCFL that differentiated the organization from most corporations, including the facts that MCFL

—"was formed for the express purpose of promoting political ideas, and cannot engage in business activities"

—"has no shareholders or other persons affiliated so as to have a claim on its assets or earnings"

—"was not established by a business corporation or a labor union, and [has a] policy not to accept contributions from such entities." *MCFL*, 479 U.S. at 264.

16. See id. at 249 (concluding that the MCFL publication provides "*in effect* an explicit directive: vote for these (named) candidates"; see also id., acknowledging that the electoral message in *MCFL* is "marginally less direct than 'Vote for Smith' [and other terms identified in *Buckley*]."

17. *Furgatch*, 807 F.2d.

18. Id. at 858, emphasis in original.

19. Id. at 861.

20. Id. at 862.

21. Id. at 864.

22. Id. at 863–64.

23. Id. at 864–65.

24. Id. at 864.

25. Id. at 865.

26. *FEC* v. *National Organization for Women*, 713 F. Supp. 428 (D.D.C. 1989) *(NOW)* applied *Furgatch*'s express advocacy test to evaluate speech allegedly calling for the election or defeat of particular persons seeking federal office. The FEC argued that three mailings contained express advocacy and therefore contended that NOW had violated the FECA. The court held that the letters did not contain express advocacy, *despite* their use of magic words, identification of specific candidates, and direct references to upcoming elections. It explained:

> Under *Furgatch*'s broad test of whether speech constitutes express advocacy, the central message of all three letters was to expand the organization. . . .
>
> Further implementation of *Furgatch* necessarily involves the "reasonable minds could differ" test. Reasonable minds could certainly dispute what NOW's letters urged the readers to do. The letters make numerous appeals: . . . raise the nation's consciousness, . . . speak out, . . . and put pressure on the Senate and the President. *The letters call for action, but they fail to expressly tell the reader to go to the polls and vote against particular candidates in the 1984 election. Because the letters are suggestive of several plausible meanings, because there are numerous pleas for action, and because the types of action are varied and not entirely clear, NOW's letters fail the express advocacy test proposed by the Ninth Circuit in* Furgatch [emphasis added].

NOW, 713 F. Supp. at 434–35, citations omitted.

27. *Faucher* v. *FEC*, 928 F.2d 468 (1st Cir.), *cert. denied*, 502 U.S. 820 (1991).

28. Id. at 469.

29. Id.

30. Id. at 471, internal citations and quotations omitted.

31. Id. at 472.

32. 11 C.F.R. sec. 100.22.

33. *Maine Right to Life Committee, Inc.,* v. *FEC,* 914 F. Supp. 8, 12 (D. Me.), *aff'd,* 98 F.3d 1 (1st Cir. 1996), *cert. denied,* 118 S. Ct. 52 (1997) ("*MRLC*").

34. *MRLC,* 914 F. Supp. at 11–12.

35. Id. at 12.

36. *MRLC,* 98 F.3d 1 (1st Cir. 1996).

37. Subsection (b) was enjoined in *Right to Life of Dutchess County, Inc.,* v. *FEC,* 6 F. Supp. 2d 248 (S.D.N.Y. 1998) and enjoined nationwide in *Virginia Society for Human Life, Inc.,* v. *FEC,* 83 F. Supp. 2d 668 (E.D. Va. 2000). The Fourth Circuit Court recently overturned the district court's nationwide injunction on the FEC's express advocacy rule, however, finding that the district court had abused its authority by issuing a nationwide injunction and noting that such an "injunction . . . encroaches on the ability of other circuits to consider the constitutionality of" the FEC's express advocacy regulations. The court upheld the injunction, however, as applied to the pro-life organization that brought the lawsuit, concluding that the regulation violated the First Amendment "because it is not limited to communications that contain express words of advocacy as required by *Buckley* v. *Valeo.*" The court explained that the regulation violates *Buckley's* and *MCFL's* prohibition that the government may not define "express advocacy with reference to the reasonable listener's or reader's overall impression of the communication." Thus "the regulation goes too far because it shifts the determination of what is 'express advocacy' away from the words 'in and of themselves' to 'the unpredictability of audience interpretation.'" *Virginia Society for Human Life* v. *FEC,* Nos 00-1252 and 00-1332 (4th Cir. Sept. 17, 2001).

38. *FEC* v. *Christian Action Network,* 92 F.3d 1178 (4th Cir. 1996); *FEC* v. *Central Long Island Tax Reform Immediately Committee* (*CLITRIM*), 616 F.2d 45 (2d Cir. 1980).

39. In 1998, the FEC declined a petition to initiate a rulemaking to rescind its definition. 63 *Federal Register* 8363 (February 19, 1998), citing Supreme Court cases such as *United States* v. *Mendoza,* 464 U.S. 154 (1984), which states approval of a standard agency practice of seeking review in several circuits in order to facilitate Supreme Court resolution of difficult issues.

40. For example, the FEC decided not to appeal the *Right to Life of Dutchess County,,* 6 F. Supp. 2d at 250, which found that the FEC's definition of express advocacy was impermissible.

41. *CLITRIM,* 616 F.2d.

42. Id. at 53, internal quotations and citations omitted.

43. Id.

44. *Christian Action Network,* 894 F. Supp., *aff'd* 92 F.3d 1178 (4th Cir. 1996).

45. *Christian Action Network,* 894 F. Supp. at 948–49, internal citations omitted.

46. Id. at 956, internal quotations and citations omitted.

47. Id.

48. Id. at 953, internal quotations and citations omitted.

49. 28 U.S.C. sec. 2412(d)(1)(A).

50. *FEC* v. *Christian Action Network,* 110 F.3d 1049, 1050 (4th Cir. 1997). The court stated:

In the face of unequivocal Supreme Court and other authority discussed, an argument such as that made by the FEC in this case, that "no words of advocacy are necessary to expressly advocate the election of a candidate," simply cannot be advanced in good faith . . . much less with "substantial justification." . . . It may be that "[i]mages and symbols without words can also convey unequivocal meaning synonymous with literal text." [FEC Brief at 28] It may well be that "[m]etaphorical and figurative speech can be more pointed and compelling, and can thus more successfully express advocacy, than a plain, literal recommendation to "vote" for a particular person[,]" and that "it would indeed be perverse to require FECA regulation to turn on the degree to which speech is literal or figurative, rather than on the clarity of the message," "[g]iven that banal, literal language often carries less force." [FEC Brief at 25–26] It may even be, as the FEC contends in this particular case, that "the combined message of words and dramatic moving images, sounds, and other non-verbal cues such as film editing, photographic techniques, and music, involving highly charged rhetoric and provocative images . . . taken as a whole sent an unmistakable message to oppose [Governor Clinton]." [FEC Memorandum at 8] But the Supreme Court has unambiguously held that the First Amendment forbids the regulation of our political speech under such indeterminate standards. "Explicit words of advocacy of election or defeat of a candidate," "express words of advocacy," the Court has held, are the constitutional minima. To allow the government's power to be brought to bear on less, would effectively be to dispossess corporate citizens of their fundamental right to engage in the very kind of political issue advocacy the First Amendment was intended to protect—as this case well confirms.

Id. at 1064.

51. *Kansans for Life, Inc.,* v. *Gaede,* 38 F. Supp. 2d 928, 936 (D. Kan. 1999).

52. Id. at 936.

53. According to a study conducted by the Annenberg Public Policy Center, "more than two dozen organizations engaged in issue advocacy during the 1995–1996 election cycle, at an estimated total expense of $135 million to $150 million." Deborah Beck and others, *Issue Advocacy Advertising during the 1996 Campaign* (Washington: Annenberg Public Policy Center,1997). A study of the 1999–2000 election cycle by the Annenberg Public Policy Center estimates that more than $509 million was spent on issue advocacy. Kathleen Hall Jamison and others, *Issue Advocacy Advertising in the 1999–2000 Election Cycle* (Washington: Annenberg Public Policy Center, 2001). "The Republican and Democratic parties accounted for almost $162 million (32%) of this spending."

While some of the ads and mailings appeared to be designed to achieve their stated purpose of shaping public opinion on selected policy matters, most were aimed primarily at decreasing (or occasionally increasing) support for the featured candidate. David B. Magleby studied the scope and impact of outside issue advocacy efforts in the 2000 presidential primaries. He summarized his research as follows:

The idea that most issue advocacy is not election-related is disproved by the data we collected. Less than one-tenth (8.9 percent) of all communications we intercepted were pure issue advocacy (had no reference to a candidate or the election). Rather issue advocacy provides a powerful tool for agenda setting and candidate definition. . . .

[W]hen issues are discussed in the context of an election and candidates' positions are presented, compared, and judged, much of this communication is intended to influence a vote. Although some groups legitimately present nonpartisan information about candidates up for reelection, usually these communications are thinly veiled advocacy.

David B. Magleby, *Getting Inside the Outside Campaign* (Brigham Young University, Center for the Study of Elections and Democracy, July 2000), pp. 4, 26.

54. FEC General Counsel Lawrence M. Noble stated, "It is very easy to write these ads and do these commercials without using those magic words, but they are very clearly campaign ads." David L. Hunter, campaign manager to Senator Max Baucus (D-Mont.), commenting on the National Right to Work Committee's issues ads criticizing Senator Baucus and more than a half dozen other senators, complained that "[t]his is totally about influencing the outcome of the election." Eliza Newlin Carney, "Air Strikes," *National Journal,* June 6, 1996, p. 1313.

55. President Bill Clinton discussed the effectiveness of the issue ads that he and his reelection staff ran through the Democratic National Committee at a fundraising event: "I cannot overstate to you the impact that these [ads] have had in the areas where they have run. . . . [I]n the areas where we have shown these ads we are basically doing 10 to 15 points better." Jill Abramson, "Political Parties Channel Millions to 'Issue' Attacks," *New York Times,* October 26, 1998, p. A1. Likewise, Senator Bob Dole, in commenting on a sixty-second Republican National Committee issue ad titled "The Story" that never mentioned the presidential election but devoted fifty-six seconds to a biography of candidate Dole, quipped that the ad "never says that I'm running for President," but "hope[d] that's fairly obvious, since I'm the only one in the picture." Adam Clymer, "System Governing Election Spending Found in Shambles," *New York Times,* June 16, 1996, p. A1.

In the 2000 presidential campaign, the poster child organization of section 527 infamy was Republicans for Clean Air. This group, led by George W. Bush supporter Sam Wyly, launched a $2.5 million issue ad campaign against GOP presidential candidate John McCain that took the form of criticism of Senator McCain's environmental record. "Mr. Wyly said that 'of course' he hoped the commercials would benefit Mr. Bush." Richard W. Stevenson and Richard Perez-Pena, "The 2000 Campaign: The Tactics; Wealthy Texan Says He Bought Anti-McCain Ads," *New York Times,* March 4, 2000, p. A1.

56. U.S. Senate, Committee on Governmental Affairs, *Investigation of Illegal or Improper Activities in Connection with the 1996 Federal Election Campaigns,* S. Rep. 105-167 (1998), pp. 6304–05.

57. 11 C.F.R. sec. 114.2. Nonprofits that do not accept corporate or labor funds and otherwise meet the terms of the FEC regulation adopted after the Supreme Court's decision in *FEC v. Massachusetts Citizens for Life, Inc.,* 479 U.S. 238 (1986), are the exception. See 11 C.F.R. sec. 114.10.

58. See *McConnell v. FEC,* Civ. No. 02-0582 (D.D.C. May 2, 2003).

59. See id., Judge Leon's memorandum opinion, p. 89: "[T]he factual record unequivocally establishes that ['sham' issue ads] have not only been crafted for the specific purpose of directly affecting federal elections, but have been very successful in doing just that"; and Judge Kollar-Kotelly's memorandum opinion, p. 388: "The Findings of Fact with regard to the evisceration of Section 441b resemble a mosaic with each piece of evidence building on the next, and when viewed as a whole, present a damaging portrait of

corporations and labor unions using their general treasury funds to directly influence federal elections."

60. See BCRA sec. 203.

61. The "backup" restriction was included by Congress in the event that a reviewing court found Congress's primary definition of electioneering communication to be unconstitutional—as it was here. See BCRA sec. 201(a).

62. Id.

63. Id. That phrase closely tracked the Ninth Circuit Court's definition of when advocacy becomes express even though it does not contain the "magic words." See discussion of *Furgatch*, 807 F.2d at 857.

64. See *McConnell*, Judge Leon's memorandum opinion, p. 95.

65. *McConnell*, 124 S. Ct.

66. Id. at 687.

67. Id. at 687–89 (footnotes, citations, and quotations omitted).

68. *McConnell* at 249 (citing *Buckley*, 424 U.S. at 44, n.52); see, for example, *Florida Right to Life* v. *Lamar*, 238 F.3d 1288 (11th Cir. 2001), striking down Florida's definition of "political committee" as unconstitutionally overbroad, because it swept within its regulatory ambit groups whose primary purpose is to engage in issue advocacy; *Citizens for Responsible Government* v. *Davidson*, 236 F.3d 1174 (10th Cir. 2000), applying a bright-line view of what constitutes express advocacy and then finding the Colorado law's definitions of "independent expenditure," "political committee," and "political message" to be unconstitutional because they extended the reach of the act's "substantive provisions 'to advocacy with respect to public issues, which is a violation of the rule enunciated in *Buckley* and its progeny'"; *Perry* v. *Bartlett*, 231 F.3d 155 (4th Cir. 2000), *cert. denied*, 532 U.S. 905 (2001), in which the circuit court found a disclosure statute requiring the sponsors of political advertisements that "intended" to advocate the election or defeat of a candidate to be unconstitutionally overbroad because the statute would allow regulation beyond the bright-line rule of express advocacy established by *Buckley*; *Vermont Right to Life, Inc.,* v. *Sorrell*, 221 F.3d 376 (2d Cir. 2000), reversing a lower-court decision that had upheld a Vermont law that required individuals and organizations who run advertisements "expressly or implicitly advocat[ing] the success or defeat of a candidate" to identify the name and address of the buyer of the advertisement because it unconstitutionally limited issue advocacy, in violation of *Buckley's* bright-line test; *Iowa Right to Life Committee* v. *Williams*, 187 F.3d 963 (8th Cir. 1999), finding a state disclosure statute modeled on the *Furgatch* standard to be in violation of the *Buckley* bright-line test; *North Carolina Right to Life, Inc.* v. *Bartlett*, 168 F.3d 705, 713, 718 (4th Cir. 1999), *cert. denied* 528 U.S. 1153 (2000), in which the circuit court found a statute unconstitutionally vague and overbroad because it encompassed entities engaging in issue advocacy and did not limit its coverage to entities engaging in express advocacy; *Christian Action Network*, 110 F.3d; *Faucher*, 928 F.2d; see also *CLITRIM*, 616 F.2d at 52–53, stating that section 441d of the FECA "clearly establish[es] that, contrary to the position of the FEC, the words 'expressly advocating' mean exactly what they say"; *Right to Life of Dutchess County*, 6 F. Supp. 2d at 250, citing with approval the approach of the First and Fourth Circuit Courts in ruling that the FEC's definition of express advocacy was impermissible; *MRLC*, 914 F. Supp. at 12. But see *Furgatch*, 807 F.2d, permitting some reference to outside circumstances in evaluating whether words constitute express advocacy.

69. *MRLC*, 914 F. Supp. at 12.

70. *Faucher*, 928 F.2d 468 (1st Cir.).

71. *Kean for Congress* v. *FEC*, no. 04-0007 (JDB) (D.D.C. 2005).

72. *Anderson* v. *Spear*, 356 F.3d 651, 665 (6th Cir. 2004), *cert. denied, Stumbo* v. *Anderson*, 125 S. Ct. 453 (2004).

73. *Anderson*, 356 F.3d at 664–65.

74. 11 C.F.R. sec. 100.22.

8

The FEC: Administering and Enforcing Campaign Finance Law

Thomas E. Mann

The absence of effective enforcement machinery has plagued campaign finance law from the outset. Compliance with the Federal Corrupt Practices Act of 1925 was notoriously weak, at least in part because no public agency was given the authority, resources, and incentives to administer it. In line with that practice, the Federal Election Campaign Act (FECA) of 1971 dispersed authority for compliance and enforcement among the clerk of the House, the secretary of the Senate, the General Accounting Office, and the secretary of state for the state where campaign activities took place. After the Watergate hearings uncovered serious campaign abuses in both parties, Congress passed amendments to the FECA that for the first time created an agency, the Federal Election Commission (FEC), mandated to enforce the law. But Congress had no interest in an independent, powerful FEC. As chronicled by Brooks Jackson in *Broken Promise: Why the Federal Election Commission Failed*, lawmakers designed the agency carefully to ensure that they would be able to keep it on a tight leash.[1]

Although ostensibly modeled on traditional independent regulatory agencies such as the Federal Trade Commission (FTC), the Federal Communications Commission (FCC), and the Securities and Exchange Commission (SEC), the Federal Election Commission was distinct in at least one crucial respect: only two of its six voting members were to be appointed by the president, the others by leaders of the House and Senate. (The commission also was to include two nonvoting, ex officio members: the secretary of the Senate and the clerk of the House.) The six voting members were to include no more than three from the same political party; in practice, that has meant three Democrats and three Republicans. The FEC was given no authority to sanction violators of the FECA. For criminal prosecutions, it had to refer cases to the Justice Department; for civil cases, its only recourse was to ask a federal court to impose penalties. Congress also gave itself veto power over FEC rules and regulations, although it lost that power when the Supreme Court declared all legislative vetoes unconstitutional in 1983.[2]

In *Buckley* v. *Valeo,* the Supreme Court upset those arrangements by ruling unconstitutional the role that Congress played in appointing four of the six members of the FEC.[3] The Court held that the statute violated the Constitution's appointments clause by encroaching on the president's authority to appoint the "Officers of the United States" with the advice and consent of the Senate. (Seventeen years later, the D.C. appeals court in *Federal Election Commission* v. *NRA Political Victory Fund* took the additional step of declaring that the presence of the two ex officio members violated the Constitution's separation of powers.)[4] Thus, in the middle of the 1976 presidential nominating season, with responsibility for administering the new system for publicly financing presidential elections, the FEC was effectively out of business.

In May 1976 Congress resurrected the FEC's legal authority and broad responsibilities by giving the president the power to appoint the six voting members of the commission, but it moved in other ways to tighten its hold on the agency. Lawmakers added to the FECA a new provision requiring that at least four of the six commissioners vote for any action to be taken. Another provision forbade the commission from investigating anonymous complaints, however well-founded they might appear. Yet another required the FEC to seek negotiated agreements with violators before taking them to court for civil action. Perhaps most important, as Jackson points out, was the fact that Congress retained enormous influence over the selection of commissioners despite its loss of legal authority. Presidents were "persuaded" to select appointees from lists prepared by congressional leaders. In most cases, the original provision calling for two nominations by House leaders and two by Senate leaders has been informally maintained. It was not uncommon to appoint commissioners who were openly hostile to the FECA or to reappoint longterm commissioners who were considered safe by the politicians whose campaign finance practices they were charged with overseeing. For example, in 2000 Senate Republicans threatened reprisals against a series of presidential nominations to executive and judicial positions to pressure President Clinton to appoint Bradley Smith, an outspoken opponent of campaign finance regulation, to the commission.

In the early years of the FEC, Congress took other actions to ensure that delay and timidity would become the watchwords of the agency. It denied the commission the multiyear budgeting authority that other independent agencies enjoyed and skeptically viewed requests for real budget increases to help the FEC cope with a rapidly expanding workload. Congress banned random audits of candidates. It insisted on procedural requirements that were incredibly time-consuming and often made it impossible for the commission to take timely action against abuses. And it kept up a barrage of criticism that weakened the FEC's legitimacy and reinforced the contempt with which political operatives came to view the commission.

FEC Responsibilities and Activities

The statutory responsibilities of the FEC are to disclose campaign finance information, ensure compliance with the FECA, administer the public funding of presidential campaigns and conventions, and serve as a clearinghouse for information on election administration. The first three responsibilities are major components of an effective campaign finance enforcement regime; the last is a minor part of the FEC's charter and budget and unrelated to campaign finance.

Disclosure

The FEC's most visible and arguably its most important duty involves disclosing the sources and amounts of funds used to finance federal elections. The United States provides more extensive and timely disclosure of political contributions and expenditures than any other democracy in the world. The commission receives reports filed by political committees, reviews them for accuracy and completeness, makes the reports available to the public within forty-eight hours of receipt, and enters the financial information into its database. Public access to digital images of the reports and to the disclosure database is provided at the FEC's public records office and through the Internet.

The FEC has recently moved to cope with its growing workload by making more extensive and sophisticated use of information technology. A voluntary electronic filing program was launched for the 2000 election cycle, and more than 1,000 committees took advantage of this new opportunity to submit their reports by diskette, by modem, or through the Internet. In 1999 Congress mandated electronic filing with the FEC for committees that exceeded a certain threshold of financial activity ($50,000) in the 2002 election cycle. Senate candidates and Senate party campaign committees were exempted, because the law provides that they file their reports with the secretary of the Senate. Efforts are under way to optically scan reports provided to the secretary so that those reports and their data also can be made available on a timely basis (requiring Senate candidates to file with the FEC like everyone else is apparently beyond the pale). For affected committees, early experience indicates a high degree of compliance with mandatory electronic filing and a substantial reduction in the time taken to process the itemized data.

The commission's responsibilities also include compiling and releasing analytic summaries of campaign finance data and arranging a series of educational outreach activities to promote voluntary compliance with the disclosure requirements. Outreach activities include making information and advice available through the commission's website and offering a toll-free telephone hotline, an automated faxline, roundtables, conferences, and publications.

The commission's impressive and improving performance in receiving and disclosing financial reports was frustrated in one important respect. As discussed in chapter 4, a large and growing share of campaign activity—election-oriented issue advocacy by outside groups—was exempted from federal disclosure requirements. National party committees disclosed their soft money donors and expenditures, but the specific uses of funds transferred to state parties was difficult to track. Expenditures by unions and corporations for internal communications with their restricted classes and by nonprofit groups organized under sections 527 and 501(c) of the Internal Revenue Code are not reported to the FEC. By banning national party soft money and regulating electioneering communications by outside groups, the Bipartisan Campaign Reform Act of 2002 (BCRA) aspires to reduce this disclosure deficit. BCRA critics assert that just the opposite might occur as unrestricted funds are shifted from political parties to independent groups.

Compliance

The FEC discharges its responsibility for ensuring that candidates and political committees comply with the limitations, prohibitions, and disclosure requirements of federal election law primarily by promoting voluntary compliance. Initially, that involves the educational outreach activities discussed above. It also entails a formal rulemaking process, in which regulations are promulgated to explain and interpret federal election law, and the issuance of advisory opinions, which clarify how the statute and regulations apply to specific situations. The latter are issued within sixty days of a request (or twenty days if submitted by a candidate's committee just before an election). Advisory opinions, which now number well in excess of 1,000, serve both as guidance to a particular committee and as precedent for others in similar situations.

Information and advice go only so far in achieving compliance with federal election law. Those who might violate the law must face the possibility of sanctions sufficient to make the potential costs outweigh the benefits. And that, of course, requires an enforcement process in which violators are identified and punished in a timely fashion. The FEC was given exclusive jurisdiction for civil enforcement of the FECA (criminal enforcement authority, now even more important under BCRA, was retained by the Justice Department) and the authority to conduct investigations, authorize subpoenas, receive evidence, administer oaths, and initiate civil actions to enforce the act. At the same time, Congress saddled the commission with detailed procedural requirements that have made it "virtually impossible for the Commission to resolve a complaint during the same election cycle in which it is filed. Indeed, a factually complex case with extensive discovery and investigation may take three or four years."[5]

Possible violations of the law may come to the commission's attention from FEC staff reviews or audits of financial reports, from formal complaints, and from referrals by other government agencies. Once a potential violation is opened as a "matter under review," a process is triggered that requires at least four commissioners to find "reason to believe" that a violation has occurred, a step that opens an investigation. At the end of the investigation, the commission similarly must muster four votes to find "probable cause to believe" the same. At that point the agency attempts to resolve the matter by entering into a conciliation agreement with the respondent. If the conciliation attempt fails, the commission (again with four affirmative votes) may file a civil suit to enforce the law in federal court.

This time-consuming process—often lengthened by insufficient staff resources, the need for extensive investigations and audits, and judicial intervention to help enforce subpoenas when respondents fail to comply voluntarily—has led to an extensive backlog involving thousands of cases. In response, the commission has attempted to manage its heavy caseload through an enforcement priority system (EPS). In describing the system in its annual report, the agency states that it "uses formal criteria to decide which cases to pursue. Among those criteria are: the intrinsic seriousness of the alleged violation, the apparent impact the alleged violation had on the electoral process, the topicality of the activity and the development of the law and the subject matter."[6] Under EPS the agency has dismissed hundreds of cases that were deemed stale or of relatively low priority. More recently, it has implemented an administrative fine program mandated by Congress for assessing civil money penalties for violations of reporting requirements and created an alternative dispute resolution program to promote compliance by encouraging settlement outside the agency's regular enforcement process.

These administrative strategies have succeeded in reducing the commission's enforcement caseload and improving its productivity. The question is whether they have strengthened or weakened the commission's record in punishing serious violations of the law and deterring potential violations. The administrative initiatives are directed only at relatively straightforward and uncontroversial cases. Critics argue, however, that it is the commission's action or inaction on major questions of campaign finance law and practice—party soft money, electioneering issue advocacy, coordination, national party convention funding—and its ability and willingness to impose serious sanctions on high-stakes violations that determine the credibility of the enforcement process. By those standards its record is abysmal. It is no wonder that candidates, parties, and groups have little fear of pushing the boundaries of the law.

Public Financing

The FEC administers public funding of the presidential election system, including programs for matching funds of qualified candidates for primary elections, subsidies to parties for their presidential nominating conventions, and grants to presidential nominees for their general election campaigns. Most of the work entails certifying that candidates have met the eligibility requirements, authorizing payments to candidates and parties, and auditing the accounts of publicly funded candidates. The commission also is called on to issue regulations clarifying the requirements and procedures for public funding and to initiate enforcement cases that arise from audits, referrals, or complaints.

As discussed in chapter 6, threats to the system for publicly funding presidential elections have emerged in recent years. The fund from which public payments are made, financed by a voluntary $3 tax form check-off, has suffered serious shortfalls. Problems experienced in making timely payments to eligible candidates in 2000 would have been magnified in 2004 had three major candidates—George W. Bush, Howard Dean, and John Kerry—not opted out of the program. In 2000, George W. Bush became the first success-ful candidate to be nominated for president by a major party who declined to participate in the prenomination public matching program. With both Bush and Kerry following that route in 2004, the exception may well become the norm, barring a major restructuring of the program.

Private funding of national party conventions now overwhelms what was intended to be full public funding of official costs. Similarly, the full public financing of the general election presidential campaigns was eclipsed by the rise of party soft money and electioneering issue advocacy. While BCRA has abolished soft money and regulated electioneering communications, another of its provisions increased individual contribution limits from $1,000 to $2,000 (indexed for inflation), thus raising the possibility that some major party candidates in future presidential elections will decline public funding in the general election as well as in the primaries. All of these issues raise important questions about the viability of the public funding system, yet the commission has been notably ineffective in persuading Congress to grapple with them. Congress must change the law governing the public funding of presidential elections if the commission is to have any chance of administer-ing the system effectively.

Resources

FEC resources have not kept pace with the agency's expanding workload. As reported in the FEC's fiscal year 2003 budget submission to Congress, total disbursements in federal elections increased more than 1,000 percent between the 1976 and 2000 elections (from $300 million to $3.7 billion), yet Con-gress has made only very modest increases in the commission's budget and staff. The number of full-time FEC employees increased from 200 to only 350 over that period. Funds are available for only forty-five audits per elec-tion cycle, which represents barely 0.6 percent of the 8,000 committees filing reports each cycle. And that modest effort is accomplished by using only two full-time staffers and eight part-time student interns. Prior to that, the com-mittee averaged barely twenty audits per year.[7]

Resource constraints also limit the activity of the enforcement process. Less than half of the complaints received by the FEC are activated. Congress has long labored to keep the compliance staff from growing by limiting the agency's overall budget and by earmarking funds for other purposes. In recent years roughly 110 full-time employees were assigned to compliance activities at the commission, less than the number of staff that the Department of

Justice assigned as part of its investigation of possible criminal violations arising out of the 1996 election.[8]

The commission's workload increased substantially as a consequence of BCRA. Regulations had to be promulgated, advisory opinions proffered, filing forms revised, information about the new law disseminated to the regulated community, Internet disclosure enhanced, and a defense mounted in federal courts against a constitutional challenge to the new law. Adequate funding for those activities has not been requested by the president or appropriated by Congress.

Reform

The FEC has no shortage of critics and none more hostile than some of its congressional overseers. That is unsurprising given politicians' natural fear that charges of financial impropriety, if legitimated by an official investigation, will be used against them by their opponents. Many in Congress worry that a strengthened commission will intervene directly in campaigns, harass candidates and parties, and threaten political freedom. As recounted earlier in this chapter, Congress has long sought to maintain some degree of control over the commission and to limit its effectiveness. In recent years criticism has taken on a more partisan and ideological tone, with (the mainly Republican) opponents of the McCain-Feingold reform legislation arguing that the commission has been too independent and aggressive in trying to enforce its own definition of express advocacy. Senator Mitch McConnell (R-Ky.) has referred to the commission as the "speech police." At times members of Congress have charged the FEC with overly zealous and partisan enforcement of the law. Yet a major independent audit in 1998–99 by PricewaterhouseCoopers, undertaken in response to congressional criticism, concluded that the "agency operates in a fair, impartial manner, maintaining strict confidentiality and a low tolerance for errors."[9]

One important congressional school of reform, therefore, would weaken rather than strengthen the independence and capacity of the commission.[10] Most reform proposals, however, are predicated on the assumption that the agency needs to be empowered to do a more effective job of administering and enforcing the law. Some reformers suggest making incremental changes in the law, enforcement procedures, resources, and number and status of commissioners. Others propose the wholesale restructuring or replacement of the agency.

One source of ideas for incremental change is the commission itself. As part of its annual report to Congress, it is required to submit legislative recommendations covering a range of topics, from technical adjustments to substantive changes in law and procedure. Perusing the recommendations made over time provides a fascinating window on the market for change in the commission and Congress. Those who believe that the commission's present structure and limited authority have rendered it fully submissive may be surprised by some of its legislative recommendations. In recent years the commission has proposed restoring its authority to conduct random audits; ensuring its authority to initiate and conduct its own Supreme Court litigation; giving itself explicit authority to refer appropriate matters to the Justice Department for criminal prosecution at any stage of its proceedings; providing a statutory definition of express advocacy; stipulating that issue advocacy communications may not be coordinated with a candidate or campaign; effectively eliminating leadership political action committees (PACs); requiring Senate candidates and Senate party campaign committees to file reports with the commission instead of the secretary of the Senate; and providing for expedited enforcement (including injunctive relief) of complaints filed shortly before an election. Of course, many of the commission's proposals are perennials, dutifully served up each year by the FEC and ignored by Congress, which has had little appetite for strengthening the commission or imposing new limits on candidates. And on many controversial matters, the commission studiously avoids making substantive recommendations.

Other middle-range reform proposals suggested by analysts of the commission include establishing a multiyear budget cycle, an independent funding source, a private right of legal action, a single eight-year term for commissioners, a permanent nonvoting chairman, the use of adjudicatory proceedings conducted by administrative law judges, and more extensive use of criminal law in enforcing campaign finance law.[11] However constructive such changes might be, some critics argue that more radical surgery is required to invigorate the agency. Brooks Jackson provides one such blueprint, which calls for replacing the current commissioners with a five-member panel, including one public commissioner who is not strongly aligned with either major party. The commission would be headed by a strong chairperson and empowered by new rules and procedures and adequate budgetary resources.[12]

The most ambitious plan to restructure the agency is outlined in "No Bark, No Bite, No Point," a report of the Project FEC Task Force sponsored by the Democracy 21 Education Fund (full disclosure: I was a member of the task force).[13] Concluding that the FEC must be replaced by a new agency that can act decisively and provide real enforcement, the task force identified five principles for establishing such a new agency:

—making a single prominent and publicly credible administrator (instead of a multimember body) responsible for civil enforcement of federal campaign finance laws

—ensuring the agency's independence

—giving the new agency the authority to find violations, act in a timely and effective manner, and impose appropriate penalties by incorporating into it a system of adjudication before administrative law judges

—establishing a means to ensure adequate resources for the agency

—strengthening the enforcement process by providing stiffer penalties for major criminal violations and establishing a limited private right of action when the agency chooses not to act.

Getting Congress and the political class more broadly to accept an agency as independent and powerful as the one envisioned by the Project FEC Task Force would be very difficult. While such election agencies are commonplace in other democracies, Americans traditionally have been reluctant to delegate to nonpartisan officials responsibility for overseeing the conduct of elections and the financing of campaigns. Yet Senators John McCain and Russell Feingold have forged ahead by introducing a bill that incorporates many of the task force recommendations.[14] Moreover, there is some encouraging evidence from around the country, including from New York City and Los Angeles, that suggests that an effective campaign finance enforcement regime in Washington is not impossible.

Notes

1. Brooks Jackson, *Broken Promise: Why the Federal Election Commission Failed*, a Twentieth Century Fund Paper (New York: Priority Press, 1990): 23–37, 59–73.

2. *Immigration and Naturalization Service* v. *Chadha*, 462 U.S. 919 (1983).

3. *Buckley* v. *Valeo*, 424 U.S. 1 (1976).

4. *FEC* v. *NRA Political Victory Fund*, 6 F.3d 821 (1993).

5. Scott E. Thomas and Jeffrey H. Bowman, "Obstacles to Effective Enforcement of the Federal Election Campaign Act," *Administrative Law Review* 52, no. 2 (2000): 575–608.

6. FEC, *Annual Report 2000* (June 2001).

7. FEC, "Budget Request Justification for FY 2003," presented to Congress pursuant to GPRA and OMB A-11, February 25, 2002.

8. FEC, *Annual Report 2000*; FEC, *Annual Report 2002* (June 2003).

9. FEC, "Technology and Performance Audit and Management Review of the Federal Election Commission," prepared by PricewaterhouseCoopers (January 1999).

10. Bradley A. Smith and Stephen M. Hoersting, "Toothless Anaconda: Innovation, Impotence, and Overenforcement at the Federal Election Commission," *Election Law Journal* 1, no. 2 (2002): 145–72.

11. Kenneth A. Gross, "The Enforcement of Campaign Finance Laws: A System in Search of Reform," *Yale Law and Policy Review* 9, no. 2 (1991): 279–300.

12. Jackson, *Broken Promise.*

13. Project FEC Task Force, "No Bark, No Bite, No Point: The Case for Closing the Federal Election Commission and Establishing a New System for Enforcing the Nation's Campaign Finance Laws"(Washington: Democracy 21 Education Fund, April 2002).

14. McCain and Feingold introduced their bill, S. 1388, in the 108th Congress as the "Federal Election Administration Act of 2003."

9

Election Law and the Internet

TREVOR POTTER AND KIRK L. JOWERS

The Internet today is having a greater effect than ever before on the American electoral process, dramatically reshaping the way that candidates run for office, even at the highest levels—from grassroots organizing to get-out-the-vote activities, from advertising to fundraising, and from webcasts to virtual town hall meetings. Consider Howard Dean, who began his 2004 presidential election campaign as an obscure former governor of Vermont but was briefly the front-runner of the Democratic Party. Much of his short-lived success could be attributed to a groundswell of support organized through the use of new tools such as Internet "meet-ups"; more than 150,000 people participated in 900 meet-ups in 265 different cities in February 2004 alone.[1] Or take Wesley Clark, whose supporters launched a Draft Clark campaign, collecting signatures and raising millions of dollars in campaign pledges, in part over the Internet—an effort the retired general said was "pivotal in persuading him to jump into the race."[2]

The eventual major party nominees reaped benefits from the technology as well. The Kerry and Bush campaigns together raised an estimated $100 million in contributions (most of it in donations of less than $200) over the Internet in the time leading up to the conventions.[3] President George W.

The authors gratefully acknowledge the invaluable assistance of Trevor Dryer and Paul Ryan.

243

Bush's campaign developed a database of more than 6 million e-mail addresses that allowed it to reach organizers and supporters around the country instantly.[4] In addition, roughly 1.5 million unique users per month visited each campaign's website in the months leading up to the 2004 conventions.[5] These are just a few examples of how the Internet has emerged as not just another communications tool but as a force that has and continues to reshape the campaign process.

Not just candidates turned to the Internet; nonprofit organizations and political action committees increasingly tapped its resources. MTV and MoveOn.org held the first-ever online primaries in 2004, attracting hundreds of thousands of online "voters."[6] And thousands of websites built by both individuals and organizations cropped up—replete with video, photographs, blogs, online chatrooms, and links to resources—as thousands of Americans used the Internet both to gather information and to express their political views.

Part of the explanation for the Internet's rising importance is its pervasiveness. At the beginning of 2004, approximately 75 percent of the adult population of the United States had home Internet access (not to mention access at work)—up from 66 percent at the same time in 2003.[7] Moreover, American Internet users spend more time online than users in any other country.[8] Recognizing those trends, campaigns are devoting more resources to the Internet; some observers estimated that campaigns would spend more than $25 million—an amount previously unheard of—on online ads during the 2004 presidential election cycle.[9]

The accessibility and relatively low cost of the Internet provide hope that it will become the "greatest tool for political change since the Guttenberg press."[10] It already has become a "democratizing force" in connecting millions of Americans with the political process. Before the birth of the Internet, for example, in order to give money to a campaign, supporters typically had to know someone who could tell them how to make their check out and where to send it. Since the average American was not plugged into the major party fundraising system, most did not have an opportunity to donate. The Internet has changed that, as virtually all federal candidates now allow individuals to make contributions through their campaign websites. The Internet, for example, is largely credited for the dramatic increase in smaller donations to both parties during the 2004 election cycle. As of July 2004, the Bush and Kerry campaigns each had raised roughly $60 million in donations of less than $200, which represented a 460 percent increase over the 2000 levels for the Republicans and a 570 percent climb for the Democrats.[11] Similarly, the

Internet allows people to sign up as campaign volunteers. Even just a few years ago, volunteers were drawn from a discrete group of individuals— friends and family of the candidate, party loyalists, or the persistent few who searched through directories to locate telephone numbers for campaign headquarters. Now campaigns draw on interested parties who submit their names through the candidate or party websites.

However, whether the Internet realizes its potential as a vehicle for reengaging an increasingly disassociated public in the democratic decisionmaking process depends partly on the laws created and adapted to govern it. So far, the law has had very little to say. In fact, the Internet remains largely exempted from regulation under the Bipartisan Campaign Reform Act of 2002 (BCRA) and subsequent Federal Election Commission (FEC) regulations.

This chapter discusses the evolution of election laws with regard to the Internet. First, it discusses the U.S. government's generally nonregulatory policy toward Internet communications and how it compares with the FEC's approach. Second, it explains the FEC's legal and regulatory approach to governing political activity over the Internet. Finally, it highlights non-election law issues relating to the political use of the Internet.[12]

General U.S. Policy toward Regulation of Internet Communications

To date, the U.S. government generally has allowed the Internet to develop with little or no intervention. Both the executive and legislative branches have promoted a strong national policy of fostering the continued growth of the Internet and refraining from unnecessary government regulation:

> It is the policy of the United States (1) to promote the continued development of the Internet and other interactive computer services and other interactive media; [and] (2) to preserve the vibrant and competitive free market that presently exists for the Internet and other interactive computer services, *unfettered by Federal or State regulation* [emphasis added].[13]

Specifically, Congress made the following findings:

(1) The rapidly developing array of Internet and other interactive computer services available to individual Americans represent an extraordinary advance in the availability of educational and informational resources to our citizens. . . .

(2) The Internet and other interactive computer services offer a forum for a true diversity of political discourse, unique opportunities for cultural development, and myriad avenues for intellectual activity. . . .

(3) The Internet and other interactive computer services have flourished, to the benefit of all Americans, *with a minimum of government regulation* [emphasis added].[14]

Most regulatory agencies have followed this statutory directive when considering regulations pertaining to the Internet. In its report on Broadband Internet access, the Federal Communications Commission (FCC) recommended that "[t]he Commission should forbear from imposing regulations and resist the urge to regulate prematurely."[15] The FCC concluded that "[t]he Internet, from its roots a quarter-century ago as a military and academic research tool, has become a global resource for millions of people. As it continues to grow, the Internet will generate tremendous benefits for the economy and society."[16] While minimal regulation of the Internet remains the predominant premise at the FCC, recent judicial opinions have put that position on increasingly shaky ground.[17] In response, the FCC has opened a series of rulemaking procedures addressing issues regarding Internet access and applications, though not necessarily Internet content.[18]

In contrast to other federal agencies, the Federal Election Commission initially took a more activist and inconsistent approach toward the applicability of existing laws and regulations to the Internet. Its inconsistency was largely a result of having to apply laws and regulations established in the 1970s to a technology that has only recently come of age.[19] The explosion of political activity over the Internet in the last two years portends a revolution in the way politics is conducted. In the 2004 election, every legitimate federal candidate had a website. Moreover, almost every politically active individual, group, political action committee (PAC), trade association, corporation, and union is becoming steadily more dependent on the Internet both to send and to receive everything from messages to money.

The questions regarding the applicability of federal election law to Internet activity are myriad. Most center, however, on whether a candidate or political party is receiving something of value and, if so, how it is to be valued, when it must be reported, and what responsibilities receipt imposes on the candidate or party. Federal election law sets limits on the amount that individuals and PACs may contribute to federal campaigns and determines whether the contributions or expenditures that they make must be reported to the FEC. It also prohibits contributions and expenditures "for the purpose of influencing a federal election" by corporations, foreign nationals, and government contractors. A "contribution" is defined as the provision of "anything of value" to a federal candidate or committee, while an "expenditure" is considered a payment made for the purpose of influencing a federal election. The difficulty, therefore, lies in determining how exactly those definitions apply to the use of the Internet.

The FEC held a public hearing on March 20, 2002, on issues raised by a notice of proposed rulemaking concerning the use of the Internet for campaign-related activity.[20] Testimony and questioning centered on the unique nature of web pages and the difficulties in determining their value. The commission indicated that the subject would require considerable additional work and research before rules could be promulgated. Accordingly, it concluded that for the time being it would not move forward on the issue until sufficient resources became available. Therefore, until rulemaking is completed and regulations are enacted, the role of the Internet continues to be governed primarily by a patchwork of ever-evolving advisory opinions issued periodically by the FEC.[21] From those opinions, some governing principles, discussed below, can be discerned.

Although the FEC has yet to adopt comprehensive regulations dealing with the use of the Internet for campaign-related activity, passage of BCRA in 2002 did require the FEC to adopt implementing regulations that touched on Internet usage. BCRA defines the term "public communication" to include broadcast, cable, satellite, and several forms of printed communication, but it does not mention the Internet. The statutory definition does, however, contain the catch-all phrase "or any other form of general public political advertising."[22] The FEC adopted a definition of the term "public communication" that is identical to the BCRA definition, but it added a sentence after the statutory language that reads: "The term public communication shall not include communications over the Internet."[23]

BCRA's congressional sponsors—unhappy with the FEC's regulatory definition of "public communication" because the exemption would have allowed state parties to spend unlimited corporate, labor, and other soft money on paid Internet ads as well as blast e-mail, list buys, web videos, and so forth—filed a lawsuit against the FEC in federal district court alleging that the FEC definition of "public communication" undermined the congressional purposes of BCRA. The district court ruled in September 2004 that the FEC's exclusion of the Internet from its definition of "public communication" undermines the FECA's purposes and ordered the FEC to rewrite the regulation.[24] The FEC opened a new rulemaking on this subject in 2005, but until a new regulation is promulgated by the FEC, the regulation excluding Internet communications remains in effect. The regulatory definition of "public communication" affects at least two areas of federal campaign finance law: regulating expenditures coordinated between candidates and noncandidates, which are considered in-kind contributions; and determining what constitutes federal election activity and, consequently, must be paid for with funds raised pursuant to federal law.

In other instances, the courts have agreed with the general U.S. policy of keeping "government interference in the medium to a minimum" in order to "maintain the robust nature of the Internet communications."[25] Thus the U.S. Supreme Court confirmed that Internet communications deserve a high level of First Amendment protection when it invalidated portions of the Communications Decency Act in *Reno* v. *ACLU*.[26] In determining that those provisions were unconstitutional, the Court held that the Internet deserved *more* First Amendment protection than television or radio communications. It stated that justifications for regulation of speech in broadcast media, including its "history of extensive government regulation," "scarcity," and "invasive" nature, "are not present in cyberspace." The Court also noted that "the vast democratic fora of the Internet" have not been subject to the type of government regulation that has attended the broadcast industry.[27]

Legal Overview of FEC Internet Regulation

As summarized above, federal election law operates on the presumption that communications to the general public about federal candidates cost money and that spending may be prohibited, limited, or required to be reported. The entire complicated structure of the federal regulation of political activity by individuals, corporations and labor unions, and political committees is based on accounting for the amount spent. Congress assumed in 1975 that without spending, political speech would consist merely of standing on a street corner and shouting, one of the few forms of public communication not regulated or reportable under the federal election laws.

The rise of the Internet as a medium of mass communication changes the fundamentals of political speech. It thereby presents a conundrum for the FEC, the agency charged with interpreting and enforcing the federal campaign finance laws. Individuals can reach hundreds of addresses through list serves and blast e-mails, and organizations can mobilize thousands of supporters through a posting on a website. Profit and nonprofit organizations have sprung up to convey political news on the Internet, complete with links to candidate and party websites, reprints of campaign materials, interviews and debates with candidates, and polling information.

One of the realities of the Internet is that usually there is no incremental cost to keystrokes, and thus none or little for e-mail, speech on websites, and hyperlinks. Now that some online service providers routinely make website creation software available to subscribers as part of their regular service package, entire web pages can be created without any identifiable incremental costs. With no cost of communication, current law has nothing to measure. Thus, the bans on corporate and labor spending for speech on behalf of federal candidates and the limits on in-kind contributions by individuals are difficult to interpret in the Internet context.

Moreover, the entire mechanism for disclosing political expenditures and requiring adequate information about the identity of the speaker is thrown into question. One difficulty is that much of the FEC's regulatory apparatus is ill suited to the Internet. For instance, the FEC traditionally has presumed that there are identifiable costs for the purchase of advertising to reach the general public and that contributions to presidential candidates are made only by check, signed in ink on paper, and so forth. A greater problem for the FEC is that political speakers prior to the Internet were largely parties, candidates, and well-organized groups of persons, all at least passingly familiar with the federal election laws and FEC reporting obligations. Internet political speakers, by contrast, tend to include large numbers of individuals who are completely unaware that federal election law may touch on their independent or volunteer activity. Internet speakers also increasingly include small newsletter publishers, news-based websites, private nonprofit entities, and government agencies, all of which assume that their activities should, by their very nonpartisan nature, be exempt from FEC requirements.

The FEC's initial reaction (which now has changed significantly) was to declare that speech on the Internet *does* have a cost and that it must be considered and quantified as "something of value" to a federal candidate. Logically, that led to the argument that the creation or use of websites and pages for disseminating federal election–related speech (including news, commentary, and candidate information) should be subject to regulation under the FECA. Likewise, providing a link to a federal candidate's website would be subject to the federal election laws.

More recently, the commissioners have taken a more accommodating and realistic view of political activity on the Internet. Commissioner Karl Sandstrom declared that "[i]n regulating the Internet, we should seek to unleash its promise. Only such regulation as is absolutely necessary to achieve the core purposes of the law is merited."[28]

More important, in advisory opinions issued to the Minnesota secretary of state, Democracy Net, and Election Zone, the commission concluded that nonpartisan activity on the web (loosely defined as providing campaign-related information and candidates' statements in a way that treats all candidates equally) is exempt from any FEC reporting requirements. In another advisory opinion, issued to the Bush campaign, the FEC found that Internet activity by campaign volunteers acting on their own did not have to be tracked and reported by the candidate's campaign committee. Those opinions reflect a growing consensus at the FEC that Internet activity should not be burdened by traditional campaign finance regulation unless it involves the expenditure of large sums of money for overtly partisan political speech. The cumulative effect of these and other advisory opinions is discussed in greater detail below.

Nonpartisan Political Websites

In separate advisory opinions issued to the Minnesota secretary of state, the Democracy Network (DNet, a nonprofit entity), and Election Zone (EZone, a for-profit entity), the FEC declared certain nonpartisan Internet activity to be neither an expenditure nor a contribution.[29] On the other hand, any website that on its own behalf expressly advocates[30] the election or defeat of a candidate or solicits contributions is subject to federal election laws and must, at a minimum, post a disclaimer that includes the site sponsor's full name and whether the site was authorized by a particular candidate.[31] In addition, if a website owner provides a free link to a campaign website, it is considered a contribution if the website owner normally charges a fee for such a link.[32]

The DNet advisory opinion confirmed that a website created and operated by a nonprofit organization that posted nonpartisan political information[33] was not considered to be making a contribution or an expenditure, but the commission declined to base its decision specifically on a combination of exemptions found in its regulations, such as the voter guide, press, or candidate debate exemptions.[34] Instead, basing its decision on the FECA, the commission concluded that the entire DNet website as designed was not an "expenditure in connection with a federal election" because it was "nonpartisan activity designed to encourage individuals to vote or to register to vote."[35]

Within weeks of the DNet opinion, the commission confirmed that the same nonpartisan exemption applicable to DNet's activity would apply equally to the same activity by a for-profit corporation that operated a commercial website.[36] In the EZone opinion, the FEC stated that it did not consider DNet's nonprofit status as a determining factor in advisory opinion 1999-25; it had instead focused on the fact that EZone "is not affiliated with any candidate, political party, PAC, or advocacy group" and that its candidate-related content followed the same nonpartisan, equal treatment approach as DNet's.[37]

In 2000, responding to an Advisory Opinion Request from a nonprofit group, the Third Millennium, the commission held that a nonprofit, nonpartisan corporation—whose purpose was to examine why young voters tend to be less involved in the political process—could study the effect of Internet political advertising on different groups of randomly selected viewers, even though the ads expressly advocated the election or defeat of specific presidential candidates.[38] The commissioners determined that its provision of free advertising did not constitute an illegal contribution to the candidates, but they could not agree on a rationale for their conclusion.

Republican FEC commissioners Wold, Mason, and Smith concluded that express advocacy of a candidate's election should be permitted on the Internet if it is clear from the stated intent and structure of the communication that its purpose is not to influence a federal election. Democratic commissioners McDonald and Thomas, on the other hand, found that the study at issue fell within the exemption for "nonpartisan get-out-the-vote activity."[39] The FEC has based several Internet advisory opinions (for example, Minnesota secretary of state, DNet, and EZone) on that exemption. Of greater significance to the Internet community is that the FEC commissioners were unwilling to let their lack of consensus on a legal rationale prevent their approval of the Third Millennium request, in an advisory opinion that reflects the FEC's continuing awareness of the dynamic and developing nature of the Internet and its desire not to hamper political activity on the Web (FEC Advisory Opinion 2000–16).

Political Websites Maintained by Individuals

An individual may participate in political activities over the Internet in countless ways but must be aware of the requirements and wary of the pitfalls associated with such activity. Individuals may spend an unlimited amount of money creating a website that discusses issues, legislation, and policy— and basically anything else provided that it does not expressly advocate the election or defeat of a federal candidate—without subjecting themselves to regulation by any federal election laws. On the other hand, they may spend an unlimited amount of money creating a website expressly advocating the election or defeat of a candidate, provided that they do not coordinate with a federal candidate or the candidate's campaign committee. In that case, however, the costs of creating and maintaining the website are considered "expenditures," which trigger reporting requirements to the FEC if they exceed $250.[40] Finally, individuals may create a website expressly advocating the election or defeat of a candidate in coordination with a federal campaign committee. Because they are coordinated with a campaign, however, the costs are considered "in-kind contributions" and count against their annual contribution limit of $2,100 per candidate per election.[41]

If an individual is working as a volunteer for a political campaign and the campaign does not control the volunteer's activity, then the personal costs incurred by the individual using the Internet for the activity are not considered a contribution to the campaign and are not counted against the individual's $2,100 contribution limit. A volunteer who is a corporate employee also may use corporate equipment to conduct campaign activity, provided that such use is occasional, isolated, and incidental. Otherwise, the campaign must reimburse the costs of the campaign activity to the corporation.[42] Finally, a volunteer who republishes speeches and issue papers by a candidate from the volunteer's home computer may do so without such republication being considered a contribution to the candidate's campaign.[43]

Corporate and Union Use of the Internet

Because federal election law prohibits contributions from corporations and labor unions, neither entity can donate Internet services that normally are provided for a fee.[44] Likewise, a corporation may not post its candidate endorsements on the website of its supporting PAC unless access to the endorsements is confined to members of the corporation's restricted class.[45] However, a corporation may post a general description of its corporate PAC and instructions on how to find additional information regarding the PAC on website locations for viewing by employees in or outside the restricted class provided that no PAC solicitations are posted.[46] A corporation also may send a newsletter containing a PAC solicitation by e-mail to secretaries of its executives, provided that a note accompanies the material informing the secretary that the material is intended for the executive.[47]

The publication of campaign material over the Internet by a corporation that is considered a news entity engaged in carrying out a legitimate press function is not considered a contribution and therefore would not be prohibited under federal election law.[48] This exemption does not apply to non–news entity corporations.[49] Corporations engaged in the business of assisting political campaigns and PACs in fundraising over the Internet may do so provided that certain safeguards, such as payment at the usual and ordinary rate, are met.[50]

Political Action Committees

Publicly available information on particular public officials may be posted on a PAC website without triggering expenditure requirements beyond those already associated with the operation of PACs. Further, PACs that are not connected to a corporation or union may solicit contributions from the general public through a website.[51] Nonconnected PACs may post political speeches that expressly advocate the election or defeat of a specific candidate and need only report the costs of doing so as overhead or operating expenses. Examples of such costs are expenses for registering and maintaining a domain name and website hosting and any expenses related to the purchase and use of computer hardware and software. Those expenses, however, must be reported as independent expenditures if they can be isolated and found to be directly attributable to a clearly identified candidate.[52]

Corporate PACs may engage in such general political speech as well, but they must pay for it out of contributed funds *only*. A PAC sending e-mail that expressly advocates the election or defeat of a clearly identified candidate is engaged in independent expenditure activities that must be reported if the costs exceed $200.[53] Likewise, if a PAC sends 100 or more e-mail messages containing express advocacy, the e-mail also must contain a disclaimer that includes the sponsor's full name and whether a particular candidate authorized the e-mail.[54]

PACs may receive contributions via electronic employee payroll deductions provided that their employees can electronically revoke or modify their deductions and the employer keeps records of the transactions.[55] A corporate or trade association PAC also may solicit its restricted class through a PAC website, but it must ensure (by use of a password or other security plan) that persons outside the restricted class do not have access to the solicitation.[56]

Internet Political Activity by Federal Candidates

Fundraising over the Internet

Individuals may contribute to political campaigns over the Internet by credit card or electronic check provided that the campaigns receiving the contributions have the appropriate safeguards in place.[57] For presidential campaigns, such contributions are eligible for federal matching funds.[58]

When soliciting contributions, federal candidate committees must include certain disclaimers (for example, "paid for by," "not tax-deductible," "no foreign contributions permitted"),[59] and they also are obligated to make their "best efforts" to obtain the name, address, occupation, and employer of each person who contributes more than $200 during a calendar year.[60] The FEC has determined that a committee making a solicitation "may substitute e-mail communications for written or oral communications as a means of exerting best efforts to obtain missing contributor information where the original contribution was received through the Internet, or where the Committee has otherwise obtained reliable information as to the donor's e-mail address."[61]

Disclosure of Sponsorship

Federal law requires campaign materials—whether printed or broadcast—that expressly advocate the election or defeat of a federal candidate to contain a disclosure statement that makes clear who paid for the material.[62] Most candidate-sponsored websites bear a similar disclosure statement so as to limit the potential for confusion.

Miscellaneous Internet Communications

In its X-PAC advisory opinion, the FEC requires a disclaimer on e-mail if it contains express advocacy and is sent to more than 100 e-mail addresses within a calendar year.[63] Text messages sent to cellular telephones, however, are exempt from the disclaimer requirement due to technological limitations. The FEC reasoned that text messages typically can contain a maximum of 160 characters; requiring a disclaimer would require using a significant percentage of the allowable characters, thus leaving little room for the actual content.[64] Although the FEC has not formally extended the X-PAC advisory opinion to entities other than PACs, groups are advised to adhere to the policy for PACs regarding e-mail communication.

Non-Election Law Issues Relating to the Political Use of the Internet

A range of other issues affect the political use of the Internet. These issues, such as cybersquatting, patent and trademark, and IRS rules, affect websites in general and are therefore of importance to political Internet users as well. Many of these issues are the responsibility of various other federal agencies, including the FCC, the IRS, and others.

Cybersquatting

"Cybersquatting" refers to the practice of registering Internet domain names containing trademarks or personal names by someone other than the owner of the trademark or the person with that name. A domain name—for example, "yahoo.com"—identifies a particular website.[65] Such names are issued on a "first come, first served" basis, and name registration requires only a modest investment of less than $100.[66] Realizing that desirable domain names are scarce, cybersquatters have hastened to acquire as many names as they can, including the names of political candidates.[67] Cybersquatters are motivated by different considerations. Some register a politician's name (or some variation thereof) hoping that it will increase the number of hits on their websites, many of which are parodies of the websites of actual candidates.[68] Others do so intending to hold the domain name hostage until the candidate agrees to pay a ransom in exchange for the name.[69] Regardless of their motives, cybersquatters create a great deal of confusion among those who want to learn more about the candidates and their positions on the issues by increasing the "search costs."

As search costs rise, so does the likelihood that citizens will quit their online searches before reaching reliable information provided by a particular candidate. Furthermore, a cybersquatter's control of a domain name that is similar to a candidate's will diminish the candidate's ability to spread his or her message because the cybersquatter's site will draw away Internet traffic that was intended for the candidate's official site. Also, the potential for abuse is significant. For example, on at least one occasion, an impostor website has taken campaign contributions intended for a particular presidential candidate.[70] Accordingly, "electronic democracy" will struggle as a truly transformative force in American political culture until the problems associated with cybersquatting are adequately resolved.

Adversarial proceedings under ICANN's Uniform Domain Name Dispute Resolution Policy[71] and the Anticybersquatting Consumer Protection Act (ACPA) do not appear to offer candidates much relief.[72] Several potential nonlitigation solutions to the cybersquatting problem have been suggested but not enacted, including having the FEC create a website that includes a registry of hypertext links to each federal candidate's web page; having the FEC establish a site that would serve as a common host for the official websites of all federal candidates; having Congress create a federal right of publicity for political candidates; and creating a new top-level domain (for example, ".pol") that could be used only by registered candidates.

In 1999, the Department of Commerce released a report to Congress[73] in response to section 3006 of the ACPA, which directed the secretary of commerce, in consultation with the Patent and Trademark Office and the FEC, to study and recommend to Congress "guidelines and procedures for resolving these disputes."[74] The report rejected the suggestion of using the FEC "to maintain an authoritative, centralized list of political candidates and campaigns and their Web sites," for several reasons. First, it noted that the FEC's general counsel had informed the Commerce Department that it had neither the resources nor the legislative mandate to act as the registry administrator. Second, even if the FEC had the resources and mandate, the FEC does not become involved with a candidate until his or her candidacy reaches a certain stage. Finally, the private sector has done an admirable job of creating candidates' site lists.[75]

Copyright and Trademark Law

Despite the fact that the U.S. government thus far has taken a hands-off approach to Internet regulation, operators of political websites must remain aware that principles of copyright and trademark law still apply online. In a recent case involving alleged copyright infringement by an Internet company, a federal judge stated that "some companies operating in the area of the Internet may have a misconception that, because their technology is somewhat novel, they are somehow immune from the ordinary applications of the laws of the United States, including copyright law. They need to understand that the law's domain knows no such limits."[76]

The copyright issues raised by the operation of a political website are similar to those raised by the publication of a newsletter. For instance, a publisher of a newsletter must receive permission before using copyrighted photographs; so must an operator of a website. Furthermore, both newsletters and websites must receive authorization before reprinting (in whole or in large part) the writings of others, especially if the reprinted material does not include any accompanying commentary. Newsletters and websites differ in one important respect, however; copyright infringement on the Internet can result in much higher damages than copyright infringement in a newsletter, primarily because the Internet allows for wider distribution of infringing copies than do older technologies.

Trademark issues also arise when a political website is created. Logos, graphics, and slogans used by a campaign are eligible for protection under trademark laws because they identify a particular source or provider of goods or services. Thus, if the operator of a political website were to copy graphics or logos from that website and then include them on his or her website, the operator could be liable for trademark infringement unless he or she first obtains permission.

IRS Regulation of Exempt Organizations Engaging in Political Activity on the Internet

In 2000, the IRS asked for comments on political activity and the Internet, but it has yet to issue any specific guidance on the subject. Until it takes further action, the same IRS rules governing other media apply to the Internet. The IRS defines political activity as any activity that is found, after review of all of the relevant facts and circumstances, to directly or indirectly support or oppose a particular candidate for elected public office. Under federal tax rules, section 501(c)(3) charitable organizations are prohibited from intervening in any campaign for elected public office; section 501(c)(4) (social welfare), 501(c)(5) (labor unions), and 501(c)(6) (trade associations and chambers of commerce) groups are allowed to intervene in campaigns if and only if their primary activity remains the furthering of their exempt purposes; section 527 groups (political organizations) may participate in political activity, but they must be organized and operated for the primary purpose of influencing the selection, including the election, of an individual for public office.[77]

The IRS has provided several examples of what constitutes political activity for tax purposes. Political activity includes endorsing a candidate, making a cash or in-kind contribution to a candidate's campaign (including coordinating activities with a campaign), raising funds for a candidate's campaign, distributing a "voter guide" or "candidate scorecard" that favors one candidate over another, and targeting individuals for voter registration or get-out-the-vote activities on the basis of their party affiliation or positions on candidates. The rules do, however, leave ample room for various nonpartisan activities. Examples of activity that does *not* constitute political activity under IRS rules include nonpartisan voter registration or get-out-the-vote drives (including activities targeting a particular demographic group if that group has historically been underrepresented), voter education on issues as opposed to candidates, nonpartisan candidate questionnaires, nonpartisan candidate forums or debates, participation by candidates in events for noncampaign reasons with no campaign activity permitted, and normal business transactions open to the public.[78]

FCC's Role in Regulating Internet Political Activity

The FCC has an enduring policy of promoting the development of the Internet by forbearing from regulation. Beginning in 1966 with *In the Matter of Regulatory and Policy Problems Presented by the Interdependence of Computer and Communications Services and Facilities* and continuing with *In the Matter of Federal-State Joint Board on Universal Service*, the FCC has refrained from issuing regulations governing the Internet.[79] Accordingly, it has not held the Internet community to the same requirements that it imposes on broadcast stations and cable systems.

Specifically, the Communications Act and the FCC's rules require, with several exceptions, broadcast stations, digital broadcasting service (DBS) systems, and cable systems to provide equal opportunities to opposing legally qualified candidates. The Communications Act and FCC rules also require that during the forty-five days before a primary election and sixty days before a general election, a station must offer time to political candidates at no more than the rate charged its most favored commercial advertiser for that amount of time and for that class.[80] The FCC has not attempted to apply those laws and regulations to the Internet.

Notes

1. Matea Gold, "Where Political Influence Is Only a Keyboard Away," *Los Angeles Times*, December 21, 2003, p. A41.

2. Ibid.

3. Institute for Politics, Democracy, and the Internet, *New Online Fundraising Primer Advises Candidates and Nonprofits on How to Use the Internet More Effectively to Raise Money*, press release, George Washington University, July 14, 2004.

4. Joseph Menn, "Internet Upstart Turns Insider," *Los Angeles Times*, May 30, 2004, p. A24.

5. Paula Festa, "Bush's Site Neck and Neck with Kerry's in Traffic Race," *CNET News*, May 18, 2004 (www.news.com.com [June 2005]).

6. Menn, "Internet Upstart Turns Insider," p. A24.

7. "75 Percent of Americans Boast Home Web Access," *Editor and Publisher* (www.editorandpublisher.com/eandp/departments/online/article_display.jsp?vnu_content_d=1000468326 [March 22, 2004]).

8. Aimee Picchi, "U.S. Users Show a Net Loss," *Australasian Business Intelligence*, November 14, 2000.

9. Nick Anderson, "Political Attack Ads Already Popping Up on the Web," *Los Angeles Times*, March 30, 2004, p. A13.

10. Senator Mitch McConnell, statement before the Senate Committee on Rules and Administration, *Hearings on Political Speech and the Internet*, 106 Cong. 2 sess., May 3, 2000.

11. Campaign Finance Institute, "CFI Analysis of the Presidential Candidates' Financial Reports Filed July 20, 2004," press release, July 23, 2004 (on file with author).

12. In addition, an online appendix to this chapter containing a description and analysis of FEC advisory opinions and other proceedings concerning the Internet is available at www.brookings.edu/gs/cf/newsourcebk.htm.

13. Telecommunications Act of 1996, Pub. L. 104-104, 110 Stat. 56, codified at 47 U.S.C. sec. 230(b); see also sec. 706 of the act, directing FCC to remove regulatory barriers that discourage the development of advanced telecommunications capability, including Internet access. See generally *Digital Tornado: The Internet and Telecommunications Policy*, OPP Working Paper Series (March 1997), p. ii: "In passing the 1996 Act, Congress expressed its intent to implement a 'pro-competitive deregulatory national communications policy.'"

14. 47 U.S.C. sec. 230(a).

15. Federal Communications Commission, *Broadband Today*, October 1999, p. 41.

16. *Digital Tornado*, p. i.

17. See *Brand X Internet Services* v. *F.C.C.*, 345 F.3d 1120 (9th Cir. 2003), holding that Internet service provided by cable companies would be considered exclusively as an interstate "information service." Despite FCC interpretations to the contrary, the court held that broadband cable service was not a "cable service" but instead part "information service" and part "telecommunications service."

18. See, for example, FCC Proposed Rule FCC 02-42, DA 02-485; 67 *Federal Register* 9232 (February 28, 2002).

19. Perhaps in reaction to the FEC's early actions in this area, Congressman Tom DeLay introduced an amendment to a bill that sought to exempt all Internet activity from regulation. See *Congressional Record* 145: H8255 (daily ed., September 14, 1999). The amendment was defeated by a 160-268 vote. Ibid., p. H8260. In opposition to the amendment, Congressman Tom Allen acknowledged the virtues of a hands-off policy but warned of taking that approach to an extreme:

"The Internet is growing at an exponential rate. Congress thus far has taken a hands-off policy to let the Internet grow and flourish. The DeLay amendment, however, could undermine the freedom of the Internet by making it the favored conduit for special interests to fund soft money and stealth issue ads into federal campaigns. Let us not poison the Internet and poison our democracy with this poison pill." Ibid., p. H8256.

20. "Notice of Proposed Rulemaking on the Use of the Internet in Federal Elections" (http://frwebgate.access.gpo.gov/cgi-bin/getdoc.cgi?dbname=2001_register&docid=01-24643-filed.pdf [October 3, 2001]). The NPRM was published in the *Federal Register* on October 3, 2001 and a total of twenty-four comments were received through the comment period ending December 3, 2001 (www.fec.gov/internet.html#comments).

21. See the online appendix for a description and analysis of FEC advisory opinions and other proceedings concerning the Internet.

22. 2 U.S.C. sec. 431(22). The full definition is as follows: "The term 'public communication' means a communication by means of any broadcast, cable, or satellite communication, newspaper, magazine, outdoor advertising facility, mass mailing, or telephone bank to the general public, or any other form of general public political advertising." Note that a "public communication" is distinct from the class of "electioneering communications" regulated by BCRA. The latter is limited unambiguously to certain broadcast,

cable, and satellite communications; Internet ads, e-mail, and websites are not subject to the electioneering communications provision. Accordingly, nonparty groups may run "issue" ads on the Internet throughout an election without being subject to the federal election laws.

23. 11 C.F.R. sec. 100.26.

24. *Shays* v. *FEC*, 337 F. Supp. 2d 28 (D.D.C. 2004). More precisely, the court considered the application of the FEC's definition of "public communication" in two different contexts. First, the court considered its application in the context of the FEC's regulation on coordinated communications and found that the exclusion of the Internet from the definition "severely undermines FECA's purposes"; id. at 70. Next, the court considered the incorporation of the definition into the regulation of generic campaign activity and found that the exclusion of the Internet in that context to be an "impermissible construction of the Act"; id. at 112.

25. *Zeran* v. *America Online, Inc.,* 129 F.3d 327, 330 (4th Cir. 1997).

26. *Reno* v. *ACLU,* 521 U.S. 844 (1997).

27. Id. at 868–69.

28. Karl Sandstrom, " . . . And the Internet," *Washington Post,* September 5, 1999, p. B7, available at 1999 WL 23301858 (hereafter Sandstrom). Likewise, in comments to the House Judiciary Committee's Constitution Subcommittee, FEC commissioner David M. Mason stated:

> The Internet presents First Amendment questions in a new and beneficial light, especially compared with broadcast communications.
>
> . . . .
>
> The combination of open access and relatively low cost threatens to undermine the rationale behind the campaign finance regime. Just as Internet stock valuations appear untethered to underlying finances, the value of political communications on the Internet is driven more by innovation and presentation—that is to say by ideas—than by placement and spending. When the political impact of a site appears to far exceed its dollar cost, or when marginal costs are extremely low, it is difficult to apply a regulatory regime founded upon limits on finances, intended, we must remember, only to prevent financial corruption.

David M. Mason, *Anonymity and the Internet: Constitutional Issues in Campaign Finance Regulation,* Practicing Law Institute, Corporate Law and Practice Course Handbook Series (New York: September 1999), p. 18.

29. FEC Advisory Opinion 1999-25 (Democracy Net); FEC Advisory Opinion 1999-24 (Election Zone); FEC Advisory Opinion 1999-7 (Minnesota Secretary of State).

30. Simply stated, if a communication "expressly advocates" the election or defeat of a clearly identified candidate, the communication may be regulated under federal law. "Express advocacy" is a political communication that includes specific language explicitly advocating election or defeat of a candidate by using specific phrases, so-called "magic words," such as "vote for," or "defeat." If a communication is not coordinated with a campaign and does not contain "express advocacy," it is not deemed to be "in connection with" a federal election and therefore is not regulated under federal law. Thus the sponsor may run an unlimited number of such "issue advocacy" communications and may pay for

the communication however it chooses, including from sources (such as corporations and unions) and in amounts otherwise prohibited by federal election laws.

31. FEC Advisory Opinion 1998-22 (1998) (Leo Smith); see also FEC Advisory Opinion 1999-17 (Bush for President Exploratory Committee).

32. FEC Advisory Opinion 1999-17; but see FEC Matter under Review 4340 (1998) (Tweezerman). See FEC Enforcement Query System at http://eqs.sdrdc.com/eqs/searcheqs.

33. DNet allows, *inter alia*, all federal, state, and local candidates in races it covers, on a nonpartisan basis and at no cost, to post their own unedited information on its site—including contact information, positions on issues, rebuttals to other candidates, biographical information, and endorsements.

34. FEC Advisory Opinion 1999-25. Several FEC commissioners have commented in various settings about the potential difficulties of applying the press exemption to the Internet. Nevertheless, the commission recently found that two Internet entities, iNEXTV and EXBTV, "both as to their purpose and function . . . are press entities for the purposes of the Act." FEC Advisory Opinion 2000-13 (iNEXTV).

35. Id. sec. 431(9)(B)(ii).

36. FEC Advisory Opinion 1999-24.

37. Id.

38. FEC Advisory Opinion 2000-16 (Third Millennium).

39. Id.

40. FEC Advisory Opinion 1998-22 (Smith).

41. Id.

42. FEC Advisory Opinion 1999-17.

43. Id.

44. FEC Advisory Opinion 1999-22 (Aristotle Publishing).

45. FEC Advisory Opinion 1997-16 (Oregon Natural Resources Council Action Federal PAC).

46. FEC Advisory Opinion 2000-7 (Alcatel); see also FEC Advisory Opinion 2000-10 (COMPAC).

47. FEC Advisory Opinion 1995-33 (Coastal Employee Action Fund).

48. FEC Advisory Opinion 1996-16 (Bloomberg); see also FEC Advisory Opinion 2000-13.

49. FEC Advisory Opinion 1996-2 (CompuServ).

50. FEC Advisory Opinion 1999-22.

51. FEC Advisory Opinion 1995-9 (NewtWatch).

52. FEC Advisory Opinion 1999-37 (X-PAC); see also FEC Advisory Opinion 1997-16 (ONRCAF PAC).

53. FEC Advisory Opinion 1999-37.

54. Id.

55. FEC Advisory Opinion 2001-4 (Morgan Stanley Dean Witter and Co.); FEC Advisory Opinion 1999-3 (Microsoft); see also FEC Advisory Opinion 2000-22 (the Associations), approving the use of an electronic signature by a corporate representative to authorize solicitations by a trade association for contributions to its PAC.

56. FEC Advisory Opinion 2000-10.

57. FEC Advisory Opinion 1999-9 (Bradley); FEC Advisory Opinion 1999-36 (Campaign Advantage).

58. 11 C.F.R. secs. 9034.2 and 9034.3; see FEC Advisory Opinion 1999-36.

59. 11 C.F.R. sec. 110.11(a).

60. 11 C.F.R. sec. 104.7(b).

61. FEC Advisory Opinion 1999-17.

62. 11 C.F.R. sec. 110.11(a)(1).

63. FEC Advisory Opinion 1999-37. The FEC stated that the disclaimers requirement is triggered by e-mail with "substantially similar content, in either the message text or in any attachments thereto" that is sent to more than 100 recipients.

64. FEC Advisory Opinion 2002-9 (Target Wireless).

65. Richard Lehv, "Cybersquatting in Focus: Are New Rules Needed or Will Existing Laws Suffice?" *New York Law Journal*, January 18, 2000, p. S4.

66. Richard J. Grabowski, "Strategies for Securing and Protecting Your Firm's Domain Name," *Legal Tech Newsletter*, February 2000, p. 7.

67. Ibid.

68. Robert D. Gilbert, "Squatters Beware: There Are Two New Ways to Get You," *New York Law Journal*, January 24, 2000, p. T5; see Phyllis Plitch, "Bounty Hunter, New Law Put Squeeze on Net Domain-Name Cybersquatters," *Wall Street Journal*, December 20, 1999, available in 1999 WL-WSJ 24926545. For example, George W. Bush's presidential campaign filed a complaint against Zack Exley, a graduate student who purchased sites such as www.gwbush.com and www.gbush.org and posted anti-Bush materials. Almost a year after the complaint was filed, the FEC determined that the Bush complaint did not warrant consideration and dismissed it without considering the merits. Exley was thus left free to continue his activities without fear of running afoul of federal election regulations. See Will Rodger, "Election Officials Weigh Legality of Net Campaigning," *Interactive Week from ZD Wire*, June 30, 2000. As a preemptive measure, Bush's campaign ultimately registered approximately 260 Bush-related domain names, including negative addresses such as www.bushblows.com. Mark K. Anderson, "Bush-Whacker," *New Haven Advocate* (www.newhavenadvocate.com/articles/gwbush4.html [April 25, 2002]).

69. Ibid.

70. Brian Blomquist and Daniel Jeffreys, "FBI Crashes Campaign Web-$cam Site," *New York Post*, February 20, 2000, p. 26.

71. See "Uniform Domain-Name Dispute-Resolution Policy" (www.icann.org/udrp/udrp.htm [April 25, 2002]).

72. The Anticybersquatting Consumer Protection Act (ACPA) is based on the premise that a commercial and political presence on the Internet is dependent on having a memorable domain name. The core of the act (section 3002(a), 113 Stat. 1501, 1501A-545 to -546) provides that:

> [a] person shall be liable in a civil action by the owner of a mark, including a personal name which is protected as a mark under this section, if, without regard to the goods or services of the parties, that person—
>> (i) has a bad faith intent to profit from that mark, including a personal name which is protected as a mark under this section
>> (ii) registers, traffics in, or uses a domain name that—

(I) in the case of a mark that is distinctive at the time of registration of the domain name, is identical or confusingly similar to that mark; [or]

(II) in the case of a famous mark that is famous at the time of registration of the domain name, is identical or confusingly similar to or dilutive of that mark.

Thus the ACPA ultimately requires the aggrieved party to prove "bad-faith intent *to profit*" (emphasis added) on the part of the cybersquatter. Once a court determines that a bad-faith intent to profit exists, a domain name pirate may be held liable for a variety of activities, from mere registration, to actual use, to resale of the Internet address. Damages available under the bill consist of the traditional trademark remedies, including injunctive relief and damages (statutory damages are available in an amount not less than $1,000 and not more than $100,000 per domain name); section 3003(b), 113 Stat. at 1501A-549. For candidates, however, it typically is not helpful because the candidate's name is not a "mark" or because the cyberpirate does not intend to profit from it but rather to harass or parody the candidate. Moreover, the proceedings could easily take longer than the election cycle to resolve the dispute.

73. Department of Commerce, *Report to Congress: The Anticybersquatting Consumer Protection Act of 1999, Section 3006 Concerning the Abusive Registration of Domain Names* (www.uspto.gov).

74. Anticybersquatting Consumer Protection Act, Pub. L. 106-113, sec. 3006, 113 Stat. 1501, 1501A-550 (1999).

75. The report listed Voter.com (www.voter.com), Common Cause (www.commoncause.org), the League of Women Voters (www.lwv.org), and SmartVoter (www.smartvoter.org).

76. *UMG Recordings, Inc.*, v. *MP3.com, Inc.*, no. 00-472, 2000 WL 1262528, at *6 (S.D.N.Y., September 6, 2000).

77. See American Bar Association, Exempt Organizations Committee, "Comments of the Individual Members of the Exempt Organizations Committee's Task Force on Section 501(c)(4) and Politics," May 25, 2004, pp. 17–19 (www.abanet.org/tax/pubpolicy/2004/040525exo.pdf [June 22, 2004]).

78. See Internal Revenue Service, *Tax Guide for Churches and Religious Organizations*, IRS Pub. 1828 (www.irs.gov/pub/irs-pdf/p1828.pdf [June 30, 2005]); see also 11 C.F.R. sec. 100.

79. *In the Matter of Regulatory and Policy Problems Presented by the Interdependence of Computer and Communications Services and Facilities*, 7 FCC 2d 11(1966). "In the Matter of Federal-State Joint Board on Universal Service," Report to Congress, *FCC Record* 13: 8776 (1998). As noted previously, in light of the Ninth Circuit court ruling in Brand X, the FCC may be forced to issue a more detailed set of rules governing the Internet (see note 16 above).

80. For example, if a station normally charges $100 for a particular advertisement but sells it for $90 to a commercial advertiser that purchases 100 ads, the candidate also is charged $90, even if he or she purchases only one ad. To receive the lowest unit charge, the advertising must contain either the candidate's voice or photo likeness and the candidate's appearance must be in connection with his campaign. The lowest unit charge is available only to the candidate or his representative. During times outside of the forty-five- and sixty-day periods, stations must charge political candidates rates that are comparable to those charged to commercial advertisers.

10

Reform Agenda

Thomas E. Mann

After Congress passed a major restructuring of federal campaign finance regulation in 1974, the Supreme Court in *Buckley* v. *Valeo* found significant parts of the new law unconstitutional.[1] Important components of the law—contribution limits, public financing of presidential elections, and disclosure—remained in force, and Congress moved quickly to resurrect the FEC's legal status and broad responsibilities after the Court struck down part of the agency's appointment process. However, nothing was done to compensate for the Court's deletion of other major elements of the regulatory system crafted by Congress. By failing to legislate an alternative definition of express advocacy and to seek new ways of balancing supply and demand for political funds in congressional elections, Congress set the stage for the subsequent collapse of the system.

The passage of the Bipartisan Campaign Reform Act of 2002 (BCRA) culminated years of effort at the national level to rewrite federal election law and address the campaign finance system's shortcomings. By upholding the constitutionality of the two major elements of the 2002 law—the prohibition of soft money and the regulation of electioneering communications that fell short of the then-current test of express advocacy—the Supreme Court in *McConnell* v. *FEC* spared Congress the need for a wholesale repair of BCRA.[2]

Now the attention of reformers has naturally shifted to issues surrounding the law's implementation and the next stage of the reform agenda.

An extraordinary confluence of problems, events, proposals, and advocacy was necessary for BCRA to pass. While it is difficult to imagine history repeating itself anytime soon, a number of developments in the last election cycle will force campaign finance issues back onto the agenda. As documented in chapter 6, the public system for financing presidential elections has suffered severe strains in recent election cycles. BCRA exacerbated some of those strains, and congressional action is now needed to salvage the system. The much-criticized Federal Election Commission (FEC) has been given important new rulemaking and enforcement responsibilities by the act. Many believe, as discussed in chapter 8, that the FEC is ill-structured to carry out its new responsibilities. Indeed, initial rounds of rulemaking on the new law have been very contentious, and some FEC rules have been thrown out by the courts. Proposals to replace or restructure the FEC will be high on the reform agenda. The rise of section 527 organizations, which were formed to influence the 2004 presidential election and operate largely beyond the reach of federal campaign finance law, has prompted calls for legislation to tighten the definition of "political committee" and to establish more reasonable allocation rules for the use of federal and nonfederal funds to finance their activities. In addition, the elimination of party soft money and the dramatic increase in party independent expenditures in presidential and congressional elections have placed the elimination of caps on party coordinated spending on behalf of federal candidates back on the reform agenda.

The new law was relatively modest in its ambitions, designed to repair tears in the regulatory fabric that had developed over the preceding decade or so. It aims to prevent the corruption or the appearance of corruption created by the huge soft money contributions solicited by federal officeholders and candidates. It also seeks to prevent the use of issue advocacy as a vehicle for circumventing contribution limits and disclosure requirements. Thus BCRA seeks to combat corruption rather than to increase competitiveness and participation. In that sense it is less an end in itself than a prerequisite for additional improvements in the campaign finance system, particularly ones designed to encourage a broader base of contributors and to increase the level of electoral competition. The most prominent ideas include tax credits for small donors, various forms of direct and indirect public subsidies, free or reduced-cost broadcast time for candidates and parties, and increased public affairs programming on television and radio. Advocates will be pushing those proposals in the months and years ahead.

A reform agenda prompted only by the need or desire to respond to or supplement the new law by no means exhausts the possibilities. An alternative is to replace the entire regulatory regime. Some critics of the current system argue for a repeal of all limits on contributions, effectively deregulating money in politics and relying exclusively on public disclosure. At the other end of the spectrum, champions of full public financing seek to banish all but nominal qualifying private contributions from election campaigns. That approach—labeled Clean Money, Clean Elections—is similar to the full public financing program currently in place for presidential general elections. Both of these approaches have been adopted or proposed in some of the states. A rich variety of state and local experience with these and other campaign finance innovations offers lessons for federal policymakers.

A final item on the reform agenda flows from the digital revolution and the rise of the Internet. Chapter 9 summarizes the current state of federal law as it relates to political fundraising and campaigning on the Internet. Radical changes in modes of communication and forms of political campaigning lie not too distant on the horizon. They may well render obsolete much of the regulatory approach embedded in federal election law and force major rethinking on how best to manage money in politics and the problems associated with it.

Adjustments to the Present System

Initial experience under BCRA during the 2004 election cycle already has prompted a number of legislative initiatives to revise federal election law. While members of the reform community highlighted the need to shore up the public financing system for presidential elections and to regulate 527 organizations more fully, the majority on the Committee on House Administration moved in the opposite direction. They reported a bill—named for its cosponsors, Mike Pence (R-Ind.) and Albert Wynn (D-Md.)—that would repeal aggregate limits on individual contributions, allow political parties to solicit large donations once again, and remove caps on party coordinated spending.

Repairing the Public Funding System for Presidential Elections

Public funding has been a centerpiece of presidential elections since 1976, but its role in future elections is very much in doubt. In 2000, George W. Bush was the first successful candidate to decline matching public funds in the presidential nominating process. In 2004, both President Bush and

Democratic presidential nominee Senator John Kerry opted out of the public funding system during the primaries, thereby avoiding the associated spending limits. Both enjoyed extraordinary fundraising success. Their exception could well become the rule, in the general election as well as the nominating process, if changes are not made in the system.

Both the matching funds program in the nomination phase and the full public grant in the general election are threatened by a severe shortfall of funds, which are raised through the personal income tax form check-off, and by spending limits, which are adjusted only for inflation, not for rising campaign costs. The increase in contribution limits from $1,000 to $2,000 (indexed for inflation) without a corresponding rise in the maximum amount of a private contribution that is matched with public funds ($250) reduces the value of the public subsidy, especially when weighed against a tight spending limit, and makes it relatively easier for candidates to finance their campaigns privately. Banning party soft money and reining in party issue ads imperils even more the position of publicly financed candidates who have effectively won their party's nomination but run out of spending room months before the national convention.

A major effort is required to salvage the showcase of public financing in U.S. elections. Replenishing the check-off fund—by increasing the amount ($3) that can be designated for public financing on individual tax returns, changing the default position (from "no" to "yes") on the check-off used by tax preparers and in tax software programs, launching public education initiatives, or directly appropriating funds—is essential. Eliminating state spending limits, raising the overall limit, and increasing the value of the public match would make the program more attractive to candidates. So too would raising the spending limit for participating candidates who face an opponent opting out of the public funding system. Others ideas include linking the availability of the public grant in the general election to participation in the public matching program in the primaries, raising or eliminating any limit on the amount of hard money parties can spend in coordination with their candidates, and providing free or reduced-rate broadcast time for candidates and parties.

The Campaign Finance Institute Task Force on Presidential Nomination Financing grappled with the potential collapse of the public finance program and recommended reforms to salvage it.[3] FEC commissioners Scott Thomas and Michael Toner have offered their own ideas for saving the public financing system, and legislation has been introduced in Congress to achieve that objective.[4]

Strengthening Enforcement

The absence of effective enforcement machinery has long plagued campaign finance law. Congress finally agreed to establish an enforcement agency in 1974, but it took special care—through the bipartisan structure of the Federal Election Commission, the appointment of commissioners, tight budgetary control, complex and time-consuming procedural requirements, and the prohibition on random audits—to ensure that the agency had little independent authority.

Alternative enforcement models—ones featuring less partisan agencies with more independent authority—are available within the United States (for example, in New York City) and in other countries (for example, the United Kingdom). Ideas for restructuring or replacing the FEC are discussed in chapter 8. They include replacing the current six-member commission with either a single prominent administrator or an odd number of commissioners recruited in part or whole from nonpartisan settings. Reforms also seek to provide sufficient authority and resources for the commission to act in a timely manner and to impose appropriate penalties. Senator McCain and his colleagues have introduced legislation proposing one such plan.[5]

Some analysts, including law professor and FEC commissioner Bradley Smith, believe that toughened enforcement of campaign finance law will do more harm than good, encouraging a further criminalization of the political process. From that perspective, it is best to repeal all limitations on contributions and rely on public disclosure to discipline the role of money in politics. Criminal prosecution would be limited to bribery, extortion, misuse of public facilities for fundraising, and illegal contributions from abroad.

Regulating Section 527 Organizations

One controversy roiling the 2004 election arose with the formation of a small number of new political organizations—widely viewed as shadow committees of the political parties—explicitly designed to influence federal elections but not registered as federal political action committees (PACs). The most prominent of these groups—America Coming Together and the Media Fund on the Democratic side and Progress for America and Swift Boat Veterans and POWs for Truth on the Republican side—raised a major share of their funds in large individual contributions, sometimes measured in the millions of dollars. Some sponsored broadcast ads attacking or supporting federal candidates but falling short of express advocacy. Others organized massive get-out-the-vote (GOTV) activities in presidential battleground states. Critics argued that the groups should be required to register with the FEC as political action committees and operate under the contribution limits prescribed by federal law. In responding to complaints, the FEC decided not to compel registration in the 2004 election cycle but approved several modest rule changes for the 2006 elections—most important, those setting the mix of hard and soft dollars required to finance GOTV activities.

Legislation has been introduced to bring 527 organizations engaged in federal election activity under the purview of federal election law.[6] That entails redefining what constitutes a federal political committee and determining what share, if any, of committee activities may be financed with nonfederal funds. Reformers also seek to improve the timeliness of disclosure by section 527 organizations, since many of the groups are required to report their financial activities on only a quarterly basis. One important legal question not yet fully resolved is whether limits can be imposed on individual contributions to political committees that make independent expenditures exclusively. Another concern is whether reform will reduce the efficacy of current disclosure laws, since more stringent regulation of 527 organizations may encourage some groups to try to circumvent the law by shifting their political activity to other tax-exempt entities, such as section 501(c)4 organizations, that are not subject to full public disclosure.

Reducing Restrictions on Party Expenditures

In the wake of BCRA, the national political party committees are restricted to hard money funds—that is, none from corporate and union treasuries—and there are limits on the size of contributions that national political party committees can receive from individuals and PACs. But there are no effective limits on what parties can spend on their candidates' behalf. In its *Colorado I* decision, the Court affirmed the right of parties to engage in unlimited independent spending, a decision reinforced in *McConnell* when the Court threw out the provision in BCRA requiring a party to make a choice at the time of a candidate's nomination as to whether to support that candidate with coordinated or independent expenditures, but not both.[7] Chapter 5 chronicles how parties in the 2004 elections shifted from soft money–financed issue ads to ads financed by independent and hybrid expenditures (a form of generic advertising coordinated and financed jointly by presidential candidates and parties) while continuing to make coordinated expenditures. In highly contested elections, particularly the presidential race, the parties spent money both in coordination with and independent of their candidates.

Many scholars and practitioners consider party independent expenditures an oxymoron at best, a perversion of the whole purpose of political parties at worst. Parties are now required to set up entirely independent operations and avoid any contact or coordination with the candidates whom they intend to help by making independent expenditures in order to spend money independently on those candidates' behalf. It is not obvious what public purpose is served by these awkward and inefficient requirements. The only impact of current limits on party coordinated spending is to restrict how much the parties can speak with their candidates, not how much they can spend. As initially proposed in 1996 in *Five Ideas for Practical Campaign Reform*, one reform is to eliminate the caps on party coordinated spending, thereby eliminating the incentive to engage in independent spending.[8] The *Colorado II* decision affirmed the constitutionality of those caps, but not their wisdom or efficacy.[9] Congress clearly has the authority to legislate their elimination.

Proposals to Enhance Competition and Participation

None of these adjustments to BCRA and the FECA would do much to counter the trend toward declining competition in congressional elections. In response to this problem and to the desire to broaden the base of financial contributors, reformers have suggested a number of steps that might be taken.

Tax Credits for Small Donors

Only a fraction—less than 10 percent at most—of adult citizens contribute to federal candidates, parties, and political committees. Moreover, the number and total contributions of small donors (those giving $200 or less) fell before the enactment of BCRA.[10] Most fundraising activity was devoted to courting large soft money donors and those who were able and willing to contribute up to the maximum hard money limit. As part of the new law banning party soft money, limits on individual contributions to candidates were increased from $1,000 to $2,000 (indexed for inflation) per election, and the aggregate amount any individual can contribute in federal elections to candidates, parties, and PACs was increased from $50,000 to $95,000 (with adjustments for inflation) during a two-year election cycle. Those upward adjustments, which compensate only partially for the effects of inflation since 1974, would appear to reinforce the recent trend toward a decline in the importance of small donors in federal elections. Nonetheless, the 2004 election cycle witnessed an explosion of small donor fundraising, much of it through the Internet, beginning with Howard Dean but extending to George

Bush, John Kerry, and both political parties. Millions of new donors were added to party and candidate rolls.

The question now arises of how best to build on that explosion of small-donor fundraising. Interest in proposals to increase the incentives for the solicitation and contribution of small donations appears to be growing, reviving discussions of the benefits of tax incentives for small donors. Federal tax credits for political contributions were initiated in 1972 but then repealed as part of the Tax Reform Act of 1986. Three states—Oregon, Minnesota, and Ohio—have considerable experience with tax credits. Three other states—Arkansas, Arizona, and Virginia—recently approved tax credit programs. In addition, legislation has been introduced to reestablish a federal tax credit for political donations.

Experience at the federal and state levels suggests that tax credits do encourage more active participation in the political process by average citizens, but the effects are modest. Participation averaged just under 5 percent of eligible households in the federal program, generally less in the state programs. And not all of the credits went to new contributors or small donors; credits also were claimed by old donors, some of whom made a larger contribution than was eligible for the credit. The structure of a tax credit program clearly shapes the level and composition of participation. Is the credit set at 100 percent or some fraction of the contribution? Is it refundable? What is the maximum donation to which the credit applies? Does it apply to contributions to candidates, parties, and political action committees? Does it cover state and local as well as federal candidates? Is it limited to households earning below a certain income? Is it combined with other incentives for candidates and parties to seek small donations (for example, qualifying for public matches or free air time)?

Concerns about the inefficiency of tax credits and their limited impact have led some reformers to propose a more ambitious voucher program, as a supplement to private contributions or as a self-contained substitute for the present system of campaign finance.[11] Registered voters would be given a publicly financed voucher that they could contribute in whole or in part to candidates and political organizations. The strengths of this idea are its universality and egalitarianism. The weaknesses lie with its costs and practical problems of administration.

Public Subsidies

Proposals to extend public funding at the federal level from presidential to congressional elections have always faltered in Congress, even as a number of states have moved to provide public matching funds tied to voluntary spending limits or full public grants to qualifying candidates. The problems of the presidential election public funding system make it even less likely that Congress will consider a major public funding initiative in Senate and House elections anytime soon. Yet the attraction of public subsidies—to increase the number of competitive races, reduce the dominance of large contributors, diminish conflicts of interest, and slow the money chase—ensures that some variant will remain on the reform agenda. Tax credits are, of course, an indirect public subsidy. Vouchers are a direct public subsidy of campaigns, although delivered through a market-based process that is very different from most public funding schemes. Other forms of public subsidy include free or reduced-cost mailings, voter brochures, and free broadcast time.

Free Air Time

Perhaps the most intriguing and most visible proposal to reduce the barriers to entry for challengers, expand the competitive terrain of congressional elections, and lower the demand for political money is to provide free broadcast time for political ads. The cost of political advertising on television has sky-rocketed in recent election cycles, as parties and groups running "issue ads" have competed with candidates for prime time on local stations. While the efficiency of television advertising varies greatly across House districts, on average such ads now account for half of the expenditures in competitive congressional elections and substantially more in some tight Senate races.

The Alliance for Better Campaigns, as part of its Our Democracy, Our Airways campaign, has developed a plan to finance a system of broadcast vouchers with a small spectrum usage fee on the broadcast industry.[12] Instead of purchasing the air time with taxpayer dollars, this proposal would levy a charge on broadcasters for their use of the spectrum, which is indisputably a public asset. Candidates would qualify for the vouchers by raising a threshold amount from small contributions, after which they would receive a two-for-one match of small donations up to a specific limit set separately for House and Senate candidates. They could spend the vouchers on their local television and radio stations or, if their media markets make such advertising prohibitively expensive, trade the vouchers to finance more efficient modes of political communication. The plan is designed to provide a floor of resources for politically viable candidates in House and Senate elections in order to reduce the barriers to entry for potential candidates and to ensure a minimal campaign presence in congressional districts and states across the country. Parties could use their vouchers to support state and local candidates, to boost candidates in competitive federal races, and to create a secondary market for vouchers that promotes their more efficient use.

While free political air time is a commonplace in democracies around the world, its adoption in the United States faces formidable opposition from the broadcast industry and a number of constitutional and legal challenges. The latter address First Amendment considerations as well as the Takings Clause of the Fifth Amendment.

Public Affairs Programming on Television and Radio

Television and radio stations are licensed to use the broadcast spectrum (they are given exclusive rights to an assigned frequency within a defined geographic area) in return for agreeing to serve "the public interest, convenience and necessity." How effectively stations meet their public interest obligation is a matter of some dispute. What is not in dispute is the declining coverage of election campaigns by the national television networks and by local stations. In response to the shrinking of substantive campaign coverage, the Alliance for Better Campaigns has advanced a second proposal: all television and radio stations should be required to air at least two hours a week (half in prime time or drive time) of candidate issue discussion in the month preceding the election.[13] The stations would choose their preferred format— debates, interviews, town hall meetings, or something else—as well as the contests covered, length of segments, and time of airing.

While that proposal does not directly affect the financing of campaigns for federal office, it has the potential to reduce modestly the demand for political money, especially among challengers, and convey to a much larger slice of the citizenry at least the semblance of a contested election.

Alternatives to the Present System

Frustrated by the Court's embrace in *Buckley* of a clear distinction in the constitutional protection accorded political contributions and expenditures and by the unanticipated and sometimes perverse consequences of campaign finance laws, some reformers have urged a more radical restructuring or replacement of the present regulatory regime. Three very different alternatives have been championed: full public financing, deregulation, and a new constitutional basis for spending limits.

Full Public Financing

Six states have adopted voluntary full public financing systems for state office, three by initiative (Maine, Arizona, and Massachusetts) and three by state legislative action (Vermont, North Carolina, and New Mexico). Only two— Maine and Arizona—have laws that come close to the plans envisioned by the architects of Clean Money, Clean Elections. The Massachusetts law was repealed by the state legislature before it had any significant impact on campaign finance practices. Full public financing applies to a limited set of offices in the three remaining states: governor and lieutenant governor in Vermont, high-level judicial candidates in North Carolina, and public regulation commission members in New Mexico.

The Arizona and Maine full public financing programs provide public grants to candidates in primary and general elections who meet a low qualifying threshold in small contributions from their district or state. The public grant, which constitutes a ceiling on permissible expenditures and varies depending on the type of election being funded, is based on average expenditures in comparable races in the previous two elections. The idea is to substitute "clean money," as labeled by its advocates, for private contributions, thereby producing "clean elections." Maine and Arizona permit modest private fundraising for seed money in order to allow a candidate to maintain his or her campaign until it is certified for the public grant. They also provide additional public funds to candidates facing a privately funded, high-spending opponent or independent expenditures.

Maine and Arizona have conducted three rounds of elections—in 2000, 2002, and 2004—under the new public financing system. Assessments of their impact on competitiveness have varied. Advocates are heartened by the experience in both states.[14] They report that a substantial number of candidates for state legislative races participated in the public financing program and that the competitiveness of the elections increased, while the spending gap between incumbents and challengers declined. The U.S. General Accounting Office, in a study (mandated by BCRA) of the Maine and Arizona full public financing programs, was more cautious.[15] Its analysis found that it was too early to draw conclusions about the impact of the systems. The most recent study, by Kenneth Mayer and his associates at the University of Wisconsin-Madison, is less ebullient than the advocates but more upbeat than the GAO.[16] The Mayer report concludes that full public funding increased the pool of candidates willing and able to run for state legislative office and increased the likelihood that an incumbent would have a competitive race.

Whether that bodes well for the continuation and spread of full public financing systems among the states is doubtful. Public Campaign is leading a grassroots campaign in other states to support this approach to campaign finance reform, but the movement suffered a setback in 2000 when two states, Missouri and Oregon, handily defeated Clean Election ballot initiatives. No other state victories are clearly on the horizon. Skeptics argue that citizen support for full public financing may prove evanescent, especially as Clean Election systems try to gain a foothold in more populous states that feature expensive media-based campaigns. Eliminating all private money in politics, they argue, is neither possible nor desirable; moreover, the ability to raise money is one measure of a candidate's political support and of the intensity of the electorate's preferences. Contributing money to campaigns is one important channel for organized political action, an essential element of representative democracy.

Public Campaign continues to work with activists around the country to press for full public financing in state and local elections. If any headway is made, it will almost certainly be at those levels. Congress shows no sign of seriously entertaining such reform in House or Senate elections, especially while a similar system for presidential elections is teetering on the brink of collapse.

Deregulation

While Clean Election advocates want to banish private money in politics, deregulation champions want to remove all restrictions on its flow. Deregulation has the virtue of simplicity and clarity. Its adherents, ranging from Kathleen Sullivan, the former dean of Stanford Law School, and the American Civil Liberties Union (ACLU) on the left to FEC commissioner Bradley Smith and the National Right to Life Committee on the right, embrace one central argument: the *Buckley* distinction between contributions (which can be regulated) and expenditures (which cannot) is deeply flawed. In their minds, all contribution restrictions, including source prohibitions (from corporate and union treasuries) and limits on amounts, are unconstitutional, unworkable, and unwise.

Most champions of deregulation offer mandatory disclosure of contributions and expenditures as a tool for preventing abusive finance practices, but many opposed the disclosure requirement in BCRA relating to the fastest-growing component of campaign finance—electioneering communications that do not meet the Court's current test of express advocacy. Deregulation advocates disagree on the virtue of public subsidies of election campaigns. Those on the right would repeal existing law regarding public financing of presidential elections. Sullivan and the ACLU would extend public subsidies to congressional elections but avoid any link to voluntary spending limits or other mechanisms designed to restrict private donations.

The major "deregulate and disclose" bill in the last Congress, sponsored by Representative John Doolittle (R-Calif.), would remove all restrictions on the sources and size of contributions to candidates and parties, end all public financing, and mandate electronic filing and timely disclosure on the Internet of reports on contributions to candidates for federal office. Doolittle offers an intellectually disarming and emotionally compelling vision of a political marketplace disciplined not by arcane rules and zealous regulators but by rational citizens exercising their franchise.

Skeptics of deregulation question whether any such marketplace is feasible. Voters would find it difficult to use the ballot to discipline extravagant candidates, particularly when large economic interests invest heavily in both parties or contribute to winning candidates after the election and when each party or candidate attracts campaign contributions from different, but equally offensive, sources. In any case, voters would be unlikely to disregard factors such as party identification, political ideology, peace and prosperity, or the candidate's character and instead focus exclusively and quixotically on the struggle to contain the harmful effects of money in politics.

As a practical matter, deregulation is unlikely to be embraced in the near term by the Supreme Court or Congress. In the Court's most recent decisions on campaign finance—*Shrink Missouri, Colorado II, Beaumont,* and *McConnell*—only Justices Thomas and Scalia were willing to repudiate the *Buckley* framework and initiate a judicially imposed march to a deregulated campaign finance system.[17] That minority sentiment is unlikely to gain a majority during George W. Bush's presidency. And the Doolittle bill showed little sign of life in Congress. At the peak of its popularity, the bill garnered only 71 House cosponsors and 131 votes on the floor. Given the history of past efforts to limit the direct involvement of corporations and unions in federal election financing and the widespread populist view in the country that political money buys special influence, relatively few politicians feel comfortable publicly defending a repeal of all limits on political donations.

Toppling Buckley

Deregulators would like to see the fall of *Buckley*'s defense of the constitutionality of the regulation of political contributions. Another group of reformers also hopes *Buckley* topples—but in the opposite direction. They would like to persuade the Supreme Court to overrule the parts of the decision that prevent legislatures from enacting reasonable limits on campaign spending.[18] Adherents of the latter approach concede that campaign spending deserves full First

Amendment protection, but they argue that "judges should uphold carefully tailored regulations of such spending that are supported by compelling governmental interests." In addition to preventing corruption or the appearance of corruption, such interests might include expanding the pool of candidates, slowing the money chase, restoring public confidence in the democratic process, equalizing the voices of citizens, reducing the disproportionate influence of concentrated wealth, and promoting the constitutional rights to vote and to petition.

While several members of the Supreme Court, including Justices Breyer and Stevens, have expressed some sympathy with those arguments, prospects on the Court are no brighter for such an alternative to *Buckley* than for the one advanced by deregulators. An alternative route to a similar outcome—a constitutional amendment giving Congress and the states authority to set reasonable limits on funds expended to influence the outcome of elections—has garnered relatively little support on Capitol Hill.

Campaign Finance and the Internet

Congress and the FEC have begun to grapple with the challenges of applying the current regulatory framework for campaign finance to a radically different and rapidly changing mode of communication. Many of these issues are elucidated in chapter 9. The economics of political communication on the Internet is already forcing some reconsideration of the appropriateness of disclosure and contribution regulations for digital communications. Congress did not make explicit mention of the Internet in BCRA, leaving to the FEC the task of determining how campaign finance law should apply to the medium. Since the new law's passage, the FEC generally has attempted to minimize regulation of political communication on the Internet, a clear break from its earlier attempts to apply legislation from the 1970s to Internet communications.

Beyond such immediate regulatory issues, however, lies a more exciting and potentially liberating reform agenda. Internet-based fundraising, reinforced by tax credits, may lead to a dominant role for small donors, thereby easing concerns about the role of big, interested money in elections. And if technology-based transformations in election campaigning dramatically reduce the cost of political communications, demands on campaign finance regulation could well lessen. The regulatory challenges that currently drive reform efforts could recede in tandem with television's status as the principal medium for political advertising.

The problems associated with money in politics will never be definitively solved and the challenges of campaign finance regulation will continue to confront reformers. The *McConnell* Court acknowledged as much when it concluded its majority opinion with these words: "We are under no illusion that BCRA will be the last congressional statement on the matter. Money, like water, will always find an outlet. What problems arise, and how Congress will respond, are concerns for another day."

Notes

1. *Buckley* v. *Valeo*, 424 U.S. 1 (1976).

2. *McConnell* v. *FEC*, 124 S. Ct. 169 (2003).

3. The Campaign Finance Institute Task Force on Presidential Nomination Financing, *Participation, Competition, Engagement: How to Revive and Improve Public Funding for Presidential Nomination Politics* (Washington: Campaign Finance Institute, 2003).

4. See S. 1913, a bill introduced in the 108th Congress as the Presidential Funding Act of 2003 by Senators John McCain and Russell Feingold.

5. In the 108th Congress, Senator McCain introduced the Senate version of the bill, S. 1388, which was entitled Federal Election Administration Act of 2003.

6. A number of senators and representatives cosponsored a bill to that effect in the 108th Congress. The legislation, S. 2828 in the Senate, was entitled 527 Reform Act of 2004.

7. *Colorado Republican Federal Campaign Committee* v. *FEC*, 518 U.S. 604 (1996).

8. Norman J. Ornstein and others, *Five Ideas for Practical Campaign Reform* (Washington: League of Women Voters Education Fund, 1997).

9. *FEC* v. *Colorado Republican Federal Campaign Committee*, 533 U.S. 431 (2001).

10. David Rosenberg, *Broadening the Base: The Case for a New Federal Tax Credit for Political Contributions* (Washington: American Enterprise Institute, 2002).

11. Bruce A. Ackerman and Ian Ayres, *Voting with Dollars: A New Paradigm for Campaign Finance* (Yale University Press, 2002); and Richard L. Hasen, "Clipping Coupons for Democracy: An Egalitarian/Public Choice Defense of Campaign Finance Vouchers," *California Law Review* 84 (January 1996): 1–59.

12. Alliance for Better Campaigns, "Our Democracy, Our Airwaves Campaign" (www.bettercampaigns.org/docs/index.php?DocID=11 [January 2005]).

13. Ibid.

14. Marc Breslow, Janet Groat, and Paul Saba, *Revitalizing Democracy: Clean Election Reform Shows the Way Forward* (2002) (www.followthemoney.org/press/Reports/200201011.pdf [January 2005]).

15. U.S. General Accounting Office, *Campaign Finance Reform: Early Experiences of Two States That Offer Full Public Funding for Political Candidates*, GAO-03-453 (May 2003).

16. Kenneth R. Mayer, Timothy Werner, and Amanda Williams, "Do Public Funding Programs Enhance Electoral Competition?" paper prepared for "Laboratories of Democracy: Public Policy in the American States," Fourth Annual Conference on State Politics and Policy, Kent State University, April 30–May 1, 2004.

17. *FEC* v. *Beaumont*, 539 U.S. 146 (2003); *Nixon* v. *Shrink Missouri Government PAC*, 528 U.S. 377 (2000).

18. E. Joshua Rosenkranz and the Twentieth Century Fund Working Group on Campaign Finance Litigation, *Buckley Stops Here: Loosening the Judicial Stranglehold on Campaign Finance Reform* (New York: Century Foundation Press, 1998).

Index